Parachuting
The Skydiver's Handbook

Dan Poynter
Mike Turoff

Ninth Revised Edition

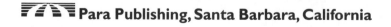
Para Publishing, Santa Barbara, California

Parachuting
The Skydiver's Handbook

Dan Poynter
Mike Turoff

Published by

Para Publishing
Post Office Box 8206
Santa Barbara, CA 93118-8206, USA
Orders@ParaPublishing.com
http://www.ParaPublishing.com

Copyright © 1978, 1983, 1989, 1992, 1998, 2000, 2004
Dan Poynter and Mike Turoff
First edition 1978
Eighth edition 2000, revised
Ninth edition 2004, completely revised

Printed in the United States of America

Library of Congress Cataloging-In-Publication Data
Poynter, Dan
Parachuting: The Skydiver's Handbook/Dan Poynter. —9th rev ed
p. cm. Includes bibliographical references (p.   ) and index.
ISBN 1-56860-087-9
1. Skydiving. 2. Skydiving—Handbooks, manuals, etc. I. Title.
GV 770.P69 1997 797.5'6—DC21   2003107510
                                                                    CIP

What others are saying:

This is the only up-to-date basic sport parachuting handbook and it is highly recommended.

— *The Next Whole Earth Catalog*

Poynter's latest fills the bill of educating while entertaining. He says it well.

— *Parachutist* magazine

For a lesson or just some vicarious thrills, read *Parachuting: The Skydiver's Handbook.*

— *New York Post*

A valuable collection of information and a good first look at the sport.

— *Library Journal*

Dan's strength as a writer lies in his technical descriptions of equipment; these are faultless.

— British *Sport Parachutist* magazine

This handy volume falls into the "Everything you need to know about . . ." category and is required reading for everyone who wants to jump out of and aeroplane.

— *Flight International*

All aspects are covered in a clear and authoritative fashion.

— *Air International*

Chapters cover an overview of the sport, detailed discussion of each facet of the first jump, the history of parachuting, and an in-depth study of parachuting emergencies. Other sections discuss specialized jumping and equipment.
Appendix contains a glossary and a list of drop zones, books, magazines and films.

— *Sporting Goods Business*

Well-written, this volume is profusely illustrated with photos and drawings. A useful addition to the public library collection.

— *Choice*

Dan Poynter has done it again.

— *Spotter NewsMagazine*

Contents

About the Authors

Dan Poynter is past president of the Parachute Industry Association, past chairman of the Board of the U.S. Parachute Association, an expert parachutist with all the highest licenses and ratings, a pilot and a master parachute rigger who has written more books on parachutes and skydiving than any other author. He has made more than 1,200 jumps since 1962.

Dan made the North Pole jump in 1994 and directed the International Parachute Symposium in 1997 and 1999.

Dan is one of sport parachuting's most energetic, experienced and respected leaders.

Mike Turoff is a USPA D-licensed expert parachutist and an Instructor Examiner in all four USPA training methods. Mike is also an FAA certificated commercially licensed, instrument rated pilot and has performed worked as a Jump Pilot at several dropzones. Mike's real-world career job is that of an analytical chemist, but during his weekends of jumping, he is a dedicated instructor and he has made over 3,300 jumps since 1977.

Mike has contributed to the sport in many ways. He has authored numerous articles dealing with safety and training practices which have appeared in both Parachutist and Skydiving magazines. Mike serves as an advisor to the USPA's Safety and Training Committee. He has participated as an evaluator at AFF Training Camps and Certification Courses, and has been rated to perform Tandem instruction using Relative Workshop, Strong Enterprises, and Stunts Equipment tandem parachute systems. Mike serves as a Tandem Examiner for The Relative Workshop.

Few instructors have given as much thought to working with students, explaining how things happen and applying safety to skydiving as Mike.

Introduction

This book is written around the newer equipment that is making our sport even more exciting: faster square ram-air canopies and advanced piggyback container systems. Student equipment and training techniques vary from skydiving school to skydiving school so the descriptions here may not be precisely what you will see at your nearest drop zone. Ask your instructor for an explanation or clarification. See the Glossary in the back of this book for words that are not familiar to you.

Check the Appendix of this book for the drop zone, club, school, commercial center and/or equipment dealer nearest you. Then call or visit for more local information.

Acknowledgment

This book is a group effort. Many thanks for the advice received from Jeff Jones, Steve Mack, pilot Bob Jones, Tony Dell, Grayson Hoffman, John Brasher, Don Balch, Mike Smith, Linda Piatchek, and Dan Tarasievich. Drawings came from Para-Flite, Inc., Performance Designs, Bernard Parker and George Galloway of Precision Aerodynamics. Peer reviewers who checked chapters in which they have a special expertise were Kevin Gibson, Mike Johnston, Paul Sitter, Doc Maglaughlin, Rob Laidlaw, Jan Meyer, Bill Dause, Paul Fayard, Jim Mowrey, Bill Gargano, Don Balch, Al Gramando, Danny Page and Sandy Reid. Photographs were supplied by Robert Tomany, Tom Sanders, Bill Lamping, Richard "Jake" Jacobson, Murray Stevens, Douglas Feick, Mike McGowan, Michael Williams and Norman Kent. And many thanks to Gail Kearns for her copy editing, Chris Nolt for her design, typesetting and layout, Karen Stedman for fact checking and to Paul Fraser for his illustrations,

I sincerely thank all these fine people and I know they are proud of the part they have played in the development of the parachute, the training and the sport, as well as of their contribution to this work.

Cover photo by Art Ingrao

Warning Disclaimer

Whenever a person leaves the ground, he or she risks injury or even death. Whether to accept or reject this risk and its accompanying challenge must be a personal decision; one must weigh the risk and the reward. This book is designed to promote safety through education.

This is not a do-it-yourself text. The information contained here is intended as an introduction to the sport and as a source of reference. After reading this book, visit one or more of the firms listed herein for further information and instruction.

This book is designed to provide accurate and authoritative information in regard to the subject matter covered. It is not the purpose of this manual to reprint all the information that is otherwise available, but to complement, amplify and supplement other courses and texts. For more information, see the many references in the Appendix.

The purpose of this manual is to educate and entertain. Every effort has been made to make this book as complete and as accurate as possible. However, there may be mistakes both typographical and in content. Therefore, this text should be used only as a general guide and not as the ultimate source of skydiving information. Furthermore, this manual contains information only up to the printing date.

Para Publishing warrants this book to be free of defects in materials and workmanship. This warranty shall be in lieu of any other warranty, express or implied.

The authors and Para Publishing shall have neither liability for, nor responsibility to, any person or entity with respect to any loss or damage caused or alleged to be caused directly or indirectly by the information contained in this book. If you do not agree with the above, you may return this book to the publisher for a full refund.

Your parachuting instructor will be happy to explain any area of this book that is not clear to you.

Chapter One

Jump? Out of an Airplane?

Jumping is fun! Skydiving is not just falling, it is flying—the closest we have been able to come to free, unencumbered, non-mechanical individual flight. Nearly everyone flies in his or her dreams; the young idolize Superman while the old admire the birds. Anyone who has sprung from the three meter board, jumped from the hayloft into a haystack, or even stood on a hill in a high wind with arms outstretched has experienced a form of non-mechanical flight. Skydiving, individual and group human flight, is what this book is all about.

See the equipment chapter and the Glossary in the back of this book for any words that are new to you.

Since skydiving began to catch on as a sport in the late fifties, it has become a well-organized, widely recognized form of aviation activity and is now an established recreational pursuit. Just as airline travel has changed dramatically since its beginnings back in the early 1900s, advances in techniques and equipment have made the sport of skydiving relatively safe and thoroughly fun.

Equipment. Sport jumpers wear a highly maneuverable *main* parachute that, when controlled properly, lets them down so softly that they can easily stand up on landing. They usually wear protective clothing: a helmet, a jumpsuit, and

---

If riding in an airplane is *flying*, then riding in a boat is *swimming*. If you want to experience the element, get out of the vehicle.

perhaps goggles and gloves. They wear an extra *reserve* parachute for the same reason you use a seat belt in your car—for protection in that rare case when something goes wrong.

Going up. After you suit up, you climb aboard the aircraft with fellow parachutists for a ride to thousands of feet above the ground. The higher you go, the longer your freefall can be. A common freefall time is 60 seconds, starting from 12,500 feet (approximately 3,800 meters) above the ground (also written as AGL or *Above Ground Level*). Once the aircraft reaches the planned jump altitude, the jumpmaster directs the pilot to fly the plane over the proper point (the *spot*) on the ground so that even with some wind, you can land on target. Then out you go!

Skydiving. After leaving a perfectly good airplane, you will accelerate for twelve seconds until you reach about 120 mph downward, which is nominal *terminal velocity*, that speed at which the pull of gravity (force on your body) equals your wind resistance. You will continue to fall at this same speed unless you alter your body position. We will explain why later.

Does it feel as if you are falling? No—it's more like laying on a very noisy, partially deflated air mattress. Although you reach 120 miles per hour in a belly-to-earth "stable" (arched) position (or even 200 miles per hour in a head-down dive), you merely feel the pressure of the air against your body. It is a simple matter to use that air pressure to perform loops and rolls and even to

What goes up must come down.

track (move horizontally) across the ground. Experienced

Only skydivers know why the birds sing.

jumpers frequently exit the airplane with fellow jumpers, then by maneuvering their bodies, join in countless formations, and they still have time to move away from each other to open their parachutes in an uncrowded sky.

After checking your altimeter, you end your freefall by deploying your parachute at 3,500 feet (approximately 1,066) AGL. A rustle of nylon and a tug at the shoulders — and then there is the rapid flutter of your slider as you hang it beneath a multi-colored nylon wing for the two to three minute flight to the landing area.

The canopy ride. When you deploy your parachute, you suddenly increase the ten square feet of air resistance of your body to approximately 250 square feet of drag provided by a nylon canopy measuring some 11 x 23 feet. This wing-like soft nylon structure descends at 16 feet per second and may be flared like an airplane for a soft, tiptoe landing. The ground below is a panorama of color. The air smells fresh and there is a constant wind in your face due to the forward and downward flight of the canopy.

Landings may be like hopping off a cable car or, if you are not from San Francisco, like jumping off the rear bumper of a truck moving slowly at 3 to 5 mph. It is not hard, but tricky because of the horizontal movement produced by the wind and the forward motion of the canopy. As you gain experience, your landings will become softer and more precise. By flaring your canopy at just the right moment, you will land just like a bird on a branch. Skydiving isn't as rough and tumble as its Army Airborne heritage would lead you to believe.

It must be remembered that the combat-scarred airborne trooper jumping into battle is using the parachute only as transportation; for him it is the fastest, safest and simplest way down. His physical conditioning prepares him for the mission, which begins after the jump. Sport parachuting is considerably easier; anyone in reasonably good physical condition may participate.

Gravity: It's not just a good idea, it's the law!

⚠ WARNING ⚠

Parachuting is a high risk activity which may cause or result in serious injury or death.

The dangers. Without adequate initial training, proper equipment, and safe jumping procedures, the sport could be dangerous. During its early phases, skydiving was dangerous. But just as flying has been made safer, new and modern equipment, improved techniques and close supervision have minimized every major cause of danger to the sport parachutist.

In a recent year, 302,250 people made 3,250,000 civilian jumps in the United States, with very few serious injuries. Thirty thousand active skydivers are making 100 to 125 jumps apiece each year while some 100,000 students are graduating from their *First Jump Course* (FJC). Like other action sports, skydiving is not without its *routine* minor injuries. However, the majority of injuries among skydivers are incurred when deviating from accepted safe jumping practices. Injuries, both fatal and non-fatal, do occur and this is why we have devoted a complete chapter in this book to the subject of parachuting emergencies.

Safety and Training Advisors. There are over 300 parachute centers across North America and jumping everywhere is under the guidance of nearly 300 Safety and Training Advisors appointed by the national organizations. Skydiving coaches and instructors are rated by the U.S. Parachute Association in the United States and the Canadian Sport Parachuting Association in Canada, after undergoing rigorous training and testing sessions. Some private organizations, such as Skydive University, also issue coach ratings.

I suspected skydiving was dangerous when they asked me to sign a waiver. They confirmed my suspicions when they asked me to pay in advance.

Parachute riggers. Main parachutes to be used by others and all reserve parachutes must be packed only by federally-certificated parachute riggers. Experienced parachutists may pack their own main parachutes. Eventually, you will pack your own main, under supervision of a rigger, until you learn how.

Competition. Parachutists have been competing for more than eighty years — in fact, since the Cleveland Air Races in the 1920s. Today, competitions range in size and scope from local fun meets, or *boogies*, to regional meets, and from the National Parachuting Championships to the World Parachuting Championships with over thirty participating countries. The sport is also popular at the collegiate level, for which the National Collegiate Parachuting Committee, an affiliate of the USPA, sanctions local meets and conducts an annual championship meet that draws competitors from over twenty-five colleges and universities across the nation.

Not everyone competes. As in other sports, many participants enjoy the sport without the pressures of competition.

Who skydives? You are probably not much different from the thousands of other newcomers to the sport who find skydiving a terrific new adventure and a lot of fun! Today's weekend sport parachuting enthusiasts come from almost every station in life. According to USPA figures, 17.9% of the skydivers are in top or middle management, 7.5% have supervisory positions, 19.5% are professionals, 13.3% are in the military, 16.5% are skilled labor, 6.6% are students and 18.7% fall into the miscellaneous column. Since skydiving is not inexpensive, it tends to attract those who can afford it. While 66% of all Americans have a high school diploma, over 90% of the sport parachutists do. Similarly,

---

"If you can pack all those damn parachutes, you can fold your own shirts and make up your own bed!" [What Mom told me when I was still living at home at age 23, absolutely obsessed with skydiving!] circa 1972   —*George Galloway*

while 16% of the U.S. population has finished college, 40% of the skydivers have. In fact, over 20% of all jumpers have attended graduate school.

The median age for skydivers in the U.S. is thirty-one years while for the total population it is thirty. But while 60% of the eligible U.S. population is married, only 39% of all skydivers are.

They all come out on the weekend to share a great common experience. There is no single classification, not even in physical condition. There are jumpers with one leg and some with no legs, with one eye and, yes, even blind or deaf. They start at sixteen years, the minimum age, and go through to their eighties. Some have prior military jump experience and more than 20% are female, and this percentage is growing.

Since sport parachuting began to grow fifty years ago, skydivers have racked up a lot of experience and some interesting statistics. In the U.S. almost 6,300 have been awarded their Gold Wings for completing 1,000 jumps, more than 2,300 have over 2,000 jumps and nearly 600 have crossed the 4,000-jump mark. Almost 26,000 have qualified for the USPA Class D, Master Parachutist License. Jumpers also record their seconds of freefall time. So far, over 4,700 have been awarded the 12-Hour Freefall Badge, 2,100 have crossed 24 hours and 650 have even managed 48 hours, for two whole days of skydiving!

But there is more to do besides just collecting jumps. Ten percent of the skydivers in the U.S. are hard core competitors in one or more of the individual or team events. While some of the rest instruct students, engage in formation flying Canopy Relative Work (CRW), or fall with a camera, most pursue relative work — formation skydiving with large or small teams.

Where? Sport parachutists often band together into small clubs for both economic and operational reasons. Also, because of the rapid expansion of the sport, many permanent commercial skydiving centers, similar to ski centers,

---

Skydivers are people who enjoy falling down.
—Allen Roulston

Michael Williams reviews equipment with students waiting to make a Tandem jump.

have been established to cater to the public's skydiving needs. Most of these 300 groups may be found at small airports around North America.

To contact your nearest sport parachuting operation, consult the *Yellow Pages* under *parachutes* or *skydiving instruction* and/or call the nearest Federal Aviation Administration facility. Look under *U.S. Government, Transportation, Department of.* Or you may contact your national organization for a directory (see the Appendix). You may also get a current list of jump schools from the Parachute Industry Association's web site and other web sites. See the Appendix. If you live in a large metropolitan area, there are probably a couple of jump operations within easy driving distance. They won't be in the middle of town because there isn't any room to land an airplane there.

Signing up. Upon arriving at the jump center, you will register with the school. The registration form will ask for your name, address, age, weight, occupation, and the name, address, telephone number of someone to contact in case of

---

Parachuting is an adventure . . . A rousing adventure which is as thrilling and challenging and rewarding as any sport yet known to any age.   *—Russ Gunby*

Signing up

emergency. You will also be asked to sign a *waiver* or legal release and you must be of legal age to sign a contract. The release verifies that you understand there is an element of risk in skydiving and that you freely agree to accept that risk for yourself. There was a time when judges looked skeptically at recreation-facility waivers. They questioned whether people really understood they were signing away their right to sue, or even thought about the hazards. Today, there is a trend toward accepting signed legal releases. These cases never even reach the trial stage.

Age. To participate in skydiving activities, you must have reached the age of legal majority which is eighteen in forty-seven states, higher in only three others (this is strictly a state law item). Some dropzones may allow you to jump if you are at least sixteen years old and have notarized parental or guardian consent, however in today's legal climate, this is becoming more of a rarity rather than a rule. To make Tandem jumps, you must be eighteen. If you are under eighteen, check with the dropzone to see if they will allow you to jump and ask if they have a standard form for you to have filled out and notarized prior to your arrival at the DZ. Be sure to bring proof of age with you to the dropzone.

Now judges are coming to believe that individuals generally should be bound by what they sign. —*The Wall Street Journal*

There is no upper age limit. Former president George Bush made his second jump at the age of seventy-three. People who are in their eighties and nineties do jump.

Medical. The forms also include a medical statement to alert you to the importance of being in good physical condition and not on any medication. The form will ask if you have been treated for, or diagnosed as having, any cardiac or pulmonary conditions or diseases, diabetes, fainting spells or convulsions, nervous disorders, kidney or related diseases, high or low blood pressure, or any disability which might affect your ability to participate in skydiving. These and other problems will not necessarily eliminate you from parachuting; some conditions can be properly managed if the instructor knows about them. If you are over fifty years of age, you must show an adequate level of strength and agility. Skydiving is not a strenuous activity but poor physical shape or being overweight can increase the potential for injury. You should avoid skydiving or flying for at least twenty-four hours after scuba diving to avoid the possibility of getting "the bends."

Training. Static Line (S/L), Instructor Assisted Deployment (IAD) and Accelerated FreeFall (AFF) stu-

Classroom training

FIRST JUMP COURSE
1. Lecture
2. Exit Class
3. Static Line, IAD or AFF Procedures
4. Emergency Procedures
5. Equipment Issue
6. The Jump
7. Critique and Certificate

Course overview

Exit training

Horizontal trainer

Apparently man has a need to have that hollow elevator feeling in his stomach when he straps on a helmet. —*Mike Truffer*

Canopy steering   Breakaway training

Parachute landing falls from a one meter platform

dents undergo a thorough half-day training session to acquaint them with the equipment, the exit procedure, jump procedures, canopy steering, landings, and emergency procedures. Some of the training is indoors in a classroom, and some is outside with various pieces of training equipment. The instruction, equipment rental (which includes its packing), airplane ride, instructor fees, etc., are all included in the price of the first jump course. Tandem jumps require less training; we will cover Tandem instruction later on in this chapter.

Initial jumps. Today you have a choice as to how you wish to progress in parachuting. Each choice will provide you with certain basic skills.

Static line jump

Static line. The traditional system of first jump instruction is the static line method, it accounts for 24% of first jumps. This is a solo jump from 3,500 feet AGL where the static line, which is attached to the aircraft, opens the main container as you fall away from the aircraft. It aids the deployment of your main parachute. Once your canopy opens, you fly it to the landing area. The first jump course is typically

---

Skydivers don't stop to ask for directions. —*Jerry Kromberg*

three to five hours but this may vary depending on the size of the class, type of equipment, and your learning rate.

IAD. Some drop zones use a variation called *Instructor Assisted Deployment*. With the IAD system, the instructor holds the pilot chute in the airstream as the student exits. While the static line is eliminated, the principle is the same. Therefore, we will refer to static line deployment throughout this text with the understanding that IAD procedures are the same once the pilot chute is launched into the airstream.

The first five jumps (minimum) are with a static line which activates the main parachute automatically. From there you go to short freefalls, then you progress to longer ones from higher and higher altitudes. After a *clear and pull* from 4,000 feet, you will make two 10-second freefalls from 5,000 feet, two 15-second skydives from 6,000 feet, two 30-second freefalls from 9,500 feet, and three 45-second jumps from 11,000 feet.

The first jump will cost $150 - $200. Your second static line jump will run $75 - $100. You may make it the same day as your first jump, weather and daylight permitting — many students do! Many drop zones also offer a block of jumps in a package at an attractive price. Once you have about 15 jumps, do not require an instructor or coach and purchase your own gear, jumps may cost $15 - $20 each.

Accelerated Freefall. AFF jumps start at 9,000 feet AGL or higher for a freefall of at least 30 seconds. Two AFF rated instructors, one holding on each side, are with you during exit and freefall. By 4,500 feet AGL, you deploy your main canopy and your instructors fall away, leaving you to fly your canopy to the landing area. Accelerated Freefall requires additional exit, freefall, and deployment-procedure training, an automatic release on the reserve parachute, and two AFF-rated instructors during the jump. AFF is called *Progressive Freefall* in Canada. Some 19% of first jumps are AFF.

Accelerated freefall training gets the student into the action sooner. This elimination of the static line and low altitude jumps allows the student to progress much faster and to begin enjoying the freedoms of freefall flight much earlier. AFF is considered a faster and perhaps safer method of learning skydiving because control of the student does not stop at the exit (as in S/L or IAD jumps), and in the air learning and body position correction can occur from the influence of the instructors. Indeed, the instructors function as both shock absorbers and "training wheels" or "outriggers" for the student by stabilizing, monitoring, and guiding the student's freefall experience.

AFF jump

The cost for the first AFF jump is typically $250 - $350. AFF jumps in the USPA's Integrated Student Program Categories A through C (see chapter 5 for a complete discussion of this program) with two instructors, run $150 - $200. Once you proceed to where you only need one AFF instructor (the later portion of category C through category E), the price may be around $100 - $125. Then, the price drops to $60 - $80 for categories F through H. It is in these later categories that you can jump with a freefall coach and

---

. . . And once you have tasted flight, you will walk the earth with your eyes turned skyward, for there you have been, and there you long to return. . .

improve the basic skills you learned in your earlier jumps. Finally, after you are signed off of student status by your instructor (meaning that you no longer need formal supervision) and you own your own equipment, your jumps may decrease in cost from $15 - $20.

Tandem jump exit

Tandem jumps require only a brief checkout before you are attached to the front of a rated instructor with oversized parachutes. You are carried as a passenger throughout the jump from exit at 7,500 feet or higher, into freefall, and under the canopy for about four minutes, flying time to landing. Your freefall may even include some altitude-awareness exercises and your instructor may let you pull the ripcord. After opening by 4,500 feet, your instructor will probably let you steer the canopy. More than 57% of first jumps are tandem.

Tandem equipment is highly specialized. The main canopy is much larger than a typical student canopy. A drogue chute is used in freefall to slow the descent to normal freefall speeds and assure stability, and the student's harness is designed to snap onto the instructor's at four places. Tandem jumps are also used as part of AFF, static line, and IAD orientation courses to introduce students to canopy fly-

Tandem jump under the canopy

ing. Tandem training may be substituted for some early jumps in all other training programs if you attend a comprehensive first jump course. There is even a hybrid program called Tandem/Instructor Assisted Freefall, which combines a Tandem jump with AFF jumps and coursework (ground school). The cost for a Tandem jump is $150 – $250.

The choice. Each of the methods of training offer you the opportunity to exit the aircraft, feel the parachute open and fly the canopy to the landing area. Since Tandem training may be a substitute for early jumps in other programs, let's compare the static line instruction with the AFF method.

A basic static line or IAD course conducted according to the USPA's ISP will require about 24 jumps to complete. At this point, you will have spent about $2,000 to accomplish all of the basic freefall maneuvers, be qualified to make unsupervised 60-second delay freefall jumps and you will have amassed almost ten minutes of freefall time. You will also be participating in small group relative work. Of course, prices may vary from school to school.

The AFF training program course and the Tandem to AFF transition course conducted according to the USPA's ISP will require about 20 jumps. The cost in these programs is approximately $2,000 - $2,150 therefore they are similar to or just slightly higher than that of the S/L IAD program. However you will have amassed about thirteen minutes of freefall time and have more relative work flying because the instructors and coaches will have been in the air with you from your very first jump.

In any of these programs, if you have not met the "Performance Objectives" (POs) of the category of the training as outlined in the USPA's ISP, you will have to repeat some jumps and this will cause the costs to be slightly higher. So, pay attention to your instructors to keep your costs down! (Performance objectives may also be referred to as Targeted Learning Objectives…"TLOs".)

Some dropzones may offer you a discount on pre-purchased training packages that can save you a couple of hundred dollars when you pay "up front." The prices in any of these programs will be lower once you purchase your own parachutes. The true difference in the programs is in the amount of individualized attention you get from your instructors. Having them in the air with you on the early jumps increases the speed at which you can learn those tasks by providing "in the air" feedback and control as necessary. This is something to think about when deciding just what type of training you wish to participate in. (Read chapter 5 for details on the training programs.)

If you want the experience of freefall and canopy flying without lengthy training, choose Tandem jumping. If you want to make just one parachute jump by yourself, choose static line or IAD training. If you plan to stay in the sport, AFF is the easiest, fastest and (ultimately) least expensive way to learn. Some commercial centers will offer combinations of jumps in packages. For example, you might make three Tandem jumps and then continue with AFF.

For clarity, the rest of this chapter will assume you are in the static line course. Once off *the rope* (the static line), most experiences and principles are the same.

Training verification. After completing the first jump course, you will be required to pass oral, written and practical tests before making your first jump. The practical tests will allow you to actually demonstrate the reactions and skills you have learned. They will provide both you and your instructor with the confidence that you have learned enough to make a safe parachute jump.

Students are required to explain and demonstrate their skills prior to each jump. This training verification is especially important if the student has not jumped regularly. Layoffs of 30 days or more require refresher training. Experienced jumpers qualify for licenses (Classes A, B, C, and D) which demonstrate their qualifications. Log books document a jumper's and currency.

Instructors are rated by the United States Parachute Association and the Canadian Sport Parachuting Association as being properly trained for each type of instruction. All instructors are not necessarily checked out on all four training methods: static line, IAD, AFF and Tandem. Ask to see the credentials of your instructor to verify that he or she is appropriately rated for the type of training being offered. Tandem equipment manufacturers certify Tandem Examiners that rate Tandem Instructors for use of their equipment. A manufacturer-specific rating and USPA currency are required to exercise the privilege of that rating.

Insurance. The insurance covers personal liability and property damage in case you descend into the spectator area or damage a fruit tree. USPA provides this insurance coverage as part of their membership; this is one of the major benefits in joining. Students can purchase medical insurance for their jumps through USPA.

Regulations. The Federal Aviation Administration (FAA) has a number of air traffic regulations affecting pilots of jump aircraft. In addition, there are a few for the individual skydiver: You must not be under the influence of alcohol or drugs and you should know that the reduction in air pressure at higher altitudes often magnifies their effect. You must have two parachutes; a main and a reserve. The main parachute must be packed by the person using it or a certificated parachute rigger within 120 days of use, while the reserve must be inspected and packed by a certificated parachute rigger within 120 days of being worn. Skydivers making night jumps must carry a light visible for three miles. Seat belts must be worn when the aircraft is taxing, taking off and landing.

A few states and some local communities have regulations affecting parachuting activities. Most restate some of the Federal Aviation Regulations (FARs) or USPA's *Basic Safety Requirements* (BSRs).

The United States Parachute Association (USPA) *Basic Safety Requirements* (BSRs) require (among other things) that students use ram-air (square) canopies, piggyback containers, automatic activation devices (AADs), rigid helmets and flotation gear (when jumping in close proximity to water). The BSRs have evolved over many years and reflect commonly accepted standards for safe skydiving. See the BSRs in Chapter Four.

Each drop zone will have its own local rules. Many of them will reference local hazards such as roads, power lines, bodies of water and the occasional unfriendly neighbor.

Automatic activation devices. USPA *Basic Safety Requirements* require students to use an automatic activation device. The AAD is usually placed on the reserve parachute system, but may be placed on the main.

AADs are mechanical or electro-mechanical devices designed to release the parachute container flaps when the skydiver is below normal opening altitude *and* is exceeding a certain speed. For example, it should not activate when you descend through 1,000 feet under a properly flying canopy but it should release the reserve canopy if you descend past 1,000 feet in freefall. AADs are intended to be back-up devices only and should not be relied upon. Being

Think of your equipment as life insurance. The first time you use your parachute, it pays for itself. All future jumps are with free insurance; ensuring your continued enjoyment of the sport.

—*Mike Turoff*

man-made devices, they are subject to failure. See the Equipment Chapter for more information on AADs and remember: **There is no substitute for proper and timely action on the part of the skydiver.**

Packing. You will probably begin learning to pack the main parachute after your first jump. Learning may take 10 to 15 packjobs and jumps. Once you are signed off to pack your own main, you will save the packing charge which can be as much as ten dollars. Your reserve parachute will be serviced by a federally-certificated parachute rigger at least every 120 days. Riggers usually charge about $45 to air, inspect and repack a reserve parachute.

Spotting. In the USPA's ISP (see Chapter Five), you are introduced to spotting (selecting the exit point) in category D and by the time you reach category F, you will be either participating in the spotting process or be spotting for yourself. There will be more technical information presented on spotting in Chapter Six. You will do this task under the supervision of either a Coach or an Instructor.

Equipment. After you decide to become a long-term participant in this sport, you will undoubtedly purchase your gear to avoid the rental fees. Like skiing, parachuting is cheaper when you own your equipment. Experienced jumpers pay $15 to $20 per jump depending upon the altitude they want. They will spend from $1,000 to over $4,500 for equipment depending upon whether it is new or used, plain or fancy, and whether or not it has an AAD. See the buying discussion in the Equipment Chapter.

Flying. For some skydiving students, their first jump is also their first airplane ride, and it is for this reason that some instructors may encourage them to take an observation ride first. As an observer, you will wear a parachute and be strapped in with a seat belt right next to the door so that you can see the jumpers leave. In fact, they may have to crawl over you to get out the door.

Practice Deployment Sequences. When making your static line or IAD jumps, usually beginning with the third, you will be making a Practice RipCord Pull (PRCP) or Practice Pilot Chute Throw (PPCT). As you make your exit and go through your count, you will extract a practice handle or simulated pilot chute from the equipment as you are trained to. Instead of them being connected to your main container's closing loop, they have a brightly colored flag so that the instructor can see it as you fall away from the jump plane. If you make a good PRCP on three successive jumps, you will move on to freefall on jump number six. Your instructor will try to schedule your training so that your last PRCP static line and your first freefall jumps are on the same day. If your instructor is assisting the deployment of your pilot chute, where they use "Instructor Assisted Deployment" procedures instead of using a static line, your PRCT will be called a *Practice Pilot Chute Toss*.

All jumps are recorded in your log book

Log book. During your entire student career, you will be under the direct supervision of a rated instructor. You will keep a logbook, and your instructor will help you to write in all the particulars from each jump. For you, the log will be a great source of pride, something you will keep and cherish forever. For the instructor, it will be a reference so that he can refresh his memory and monitor your progress. It is also a means of communication between instructors as to your progress and demonstrated abilities. This is particularly important at centers where you may not get the same instructor for each of your jumps.

Advancement. Once you begin your skydiving training, only your initiative and wallet (including credit-card companies) will limit your progress. Whether you start with static line, IAD, AFF, Tandem or a combination, there is a lot to learn in the first 20 jumps. For the quickest progress, make two or three jumps per day; don't take any weekends off, and even take some time off from work if you can. Many jumpers head for the DZ after work. Gaps in training require retraining, and retraining means lost time and greater expense. It is highly recommended that you read and understand this manual prior to the first jump course. It will place you far ahead of your classmates.

Measurements. You will note as you read that measurements are given interchangeably in English, metric and navigational figures and you will encounter the same situation on the drop zone. Altitude is usually given in feet, wind speed in knots, landing measurements in meters, descent speed in feet per second, climb rate in feet per minute, etc. Because of international competition, the sport of parachuting converted some measurements to metric some time ago. In this text, many measurements are provided in two sets of figures and many of the conversions are approximate. For further help, consult the conversion chart in Chapter Two.

Progress. The sport of skydiving is undergoing revolutionary changes. While round canopies, chest-mounted reserves and static line training were yesterday's standards, times have changed. Today, ram-air wings provide reliable openings, more interesting rides and softer landings. Piggyback containers offer greater comfort and freedom of movement. Training methods such as AFF and Tandem/Instructor Assisted Freefall (Tandem Transistion Programs) have replaced static line instruction. This book tries to reflect these changes.

This manual is designed as a basic handbook, a training text to be used in conjunction with your first jump course. If there is anything here you do not understand, ask your instructors. That's what they are there for.

John Brasher uses the equipment to answer a question.

You already know skydiving is fun. Don't worry about it; think about it. Don't guess about it; find out about it. Don't fumble around; practice. And hang around that drop zone. You don't learn about skydiving by talking (or bragging) to your whuffo friends.
                                                                              —George Wright

Chapter Two

Your First Jump and Your Second and Your Third...

For the first part of this chapter, we will assume that you will be making a static line (S/L) or Instructor-Assisted Deployment (IAD) jump. After those procedures have been discussed, we will cover the major differences associated with an AFF jump. If you are making a Tandem jump, and some 70% of first jumpers do, much of the static line and AFF discussion will apply to you too.

The next step is the big one. Now that you have completed both your classroom and outdoor ground training, you are ready for that long, lonely leap. In some ways it is probably unfortunate that the jump won't be as great a thrill as you expected it to be. After reading this chapter and taking the first jump course, it will all seem so simple, more like your second jump than your first — as though you have been here before. This familiarity reflects your understanding and mastery of the basics of sport parachuting which are essential ingredients for safe, enjoyable jumps. It is the purpose of your ground training to simulate, as closely as possible, what you will find in the air. Yes, *the best surprise is no surprise*, particularly in skydiving.

Equipment issue. Now that you have completed all the necessary preliminaries, you will be issued your parachutes. There are two of them in that pack; a *main* on the bottom and a *reserve* on the top. If you were not wearing a jumpsuit and helmet for the first jump course, or if this instruction took place on another day, you will get them now. Your jump instructor, who may or may not also be your classroom instructor, will help you into the 30 - 35 lbs. of well-engineered equipment. Most of the weight hangs heavily on the back and tugs at the shoulders as it grips you tightly. It makes you somewhat clumsy as you move about and reminds you what life would be like if you were grossly overweight.

Equipment check. No doubt, you and your classmates have been signed up or *manifested* for a separate student flight, so your instructor will be the only experienced jumper on

Jumpsuit issue

Don Balch performs the equipment check prior to boarding the aircraft

board the small airplane. Later in your jump career, you will share the *lift* with other skydivers of varying experience levels. Your instructor will line you up on the *flight line* for the equipment check. This is where jumping begins to seem sort of military and, indeed, many of sport parachuting's training and jump techniques have been adapted from the armed services. The *equipment check*, or *gear check* as it is commonly called, is the final visual and physical inspection made by the instructor on all parachutists prior to boarding the aircraft. It may be referred to as the JPI (Jumper Personnel Inspection) or it may even be called a *pin check*, but many things are checked besides the pins. The equipment check is a systematic inspection of the entire parachutist both front and rear, from top to bottom. If for any reason the flight is delayed, the check will be made again. The instructor will present himself for a check by another experienced jumper. The equipment check is so important that there is a complete discussion of it in the equipment chapter.

Teamwork. The pilot and instructor work as a team with the pilot being primarily responsible for the aircraft and the instructor taking charge of the contents. While technically, even legally, the pilot is *captain* of the ship, these two must and do work together. Misunderstandings are most easily

Your jump ship may be large or small

avoided when the pilot communicates with the instructor, and the instructor directs the rest of the jumpers. Student lifts are pretty routine, so the planning is not complex.

Aircraft. Jumps can and have been made from just about every type of aircraft and airplane, but some are much more suitable than others. Since the object of the plane ride is to get up in order to come down, a high-wing model will offer greater visibility in the direction that interests skydivers most. Low-wing airplanes not only have limited downward visibility, they also do not offer exit aids such as a wing strut to grip and a wheel or step to stand on. Most skydiving operations use high-winged Cessnas carrying three to four jumpers and a pilot. You may jump from a low-winged monoplane such as a Piper Cherokee 6 or even a helicopter if you are in a military sport parachute club. For larger team jumps, you may leap from a Twin Otter, a Caravan, a Casa, a Sky Van, a King Air, a Twin Bonanza, a DC3, or some other large and possibly even vintage aircraft. Some of the larger aircraft may even be equipped with bench seats to maximize the ease of loading and unloading as well as improve the comfort of the jumpers during the ride to altitude.

The single-engine monoplane will have all seats but the pilot's removed and will be otherwise stripped out for jumping. Upholstery provides comfort you won't be needing as you are well padded and making a short flight. Jump gear tears upholstery quickly anyway. Like extra instruments and even fuel, upholstery contributes to the weight of the overall flying machine, and it is just not economical to carry it up to altitude on a short flight only to bring it back down. The aircraft will be prepared for jumping by taping over any sharp objects and removing protrusions (such as handles) which could snag your gear, especially near the door. The door will either be removed or refitted with a model with hinges on the top or tracks so it can slide up, to permit opening and closing in flight.

Jump pilots have an open door policy.

Boarding. When the airplane arrives, follow the commands of your instructor. Always approach airplanes from the rear and helicopters from the front. If you are suddenly reminded that you need something from your car, walk away from the prop or tail rotor. Spinning propellers are difficult to see, particularly in all this excitement, and they are very efficient meat slicers. Incidentally, if you really love your dog and your rug rats, leave them home; an airport is a dangerous place to romp and play. Even if the skydiving center does have facilities to accommodate children, remember that it is your responsibility to ensure that they are properly supervised and stay out of harm's way. Smoking isn't allowed around fuel-laden aircraft or the fuel pumps.

Boarding the aircraft

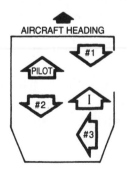

Typical Cessna seating arrangement. The jumpmaster dispatches the students in the order shown.

You will board the aircraft in the reverse order of exit; the last one in will be the first one out. Boarding may be in a random manner or the instructor may place the heaviest students forward to improve the takeoff and flight characteristics of the plane. Some instructors like to put the female students out first on the theory that their male classmates won't balk once the woman has jumped. Actually, very few students refuse to jump once aloft, but you have a right to do so. There is nothing wrong with changing your mind and riding down with the aircraft. The instructor will be boarding last.

Never walk around the front of an airplane or the tail of a helicopter

If your first jump is with a static line and this is a large aircraft, your static line may not be hooked up until the plane has climbed past 1,000 feet or until just before your jump. Most instructors prefer to hook up their students, especially the first one to exit, before cramming them into a small jump ship. In either case, it is your responsibility to confirm that your static line is hooked up. Tug on it after it is snapped closed and again on jump run.

Guarding and routing the static line. The instructor will help you into your seating area. The parachutes are heavy and tend to pull you backwards when you sit down. You are inclined to lay back and relax as best you can, but you

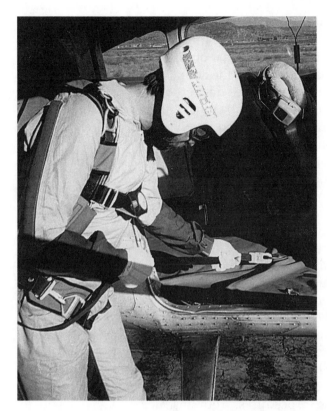

For your own peace of mind, yank on the static line to confirm its security.

Cover and guard the ripcords and canopy release handle

Skydiving: The highest speed reached by an individual in a non-mechanical sport. —*The Guinness Book of World Records*

should be sitting upright. Lounging takes up more precious floor space and may bring your main locking pin in contact with the seat runners or other objects on the floor. This could cause the main to open in the aircraft, which is troublesome, expensive, and sometimes dangerous (See page 120). Other good reasons for sitting up straight are that you may be able to see out the windows, and it will be easier to get up when the time comes.

Your static line will be routed over the shoulder farthest from the door, S-folded to take up the slack, and it may be placed in your hand or in your chest strap. Your other hand and arm should cover your breakaway, main and reserve handles. Until you are completely out the door, your two most important responsibilities are to guard your static line and your handles. You can also monitor your lift mates (others in the aircraft) to make sure they don't have any problems that require the instructor's immediate attention. If you are equipped with an instructor-assisted deployment system rather than a static line rig, guard the pilot chute in its pouch.

Seat belts. The Federal Aviation Administration requires that seat belts be provided for all passengers for use whenever the aircraft is moving on the ground, and in take-off and landing procedures. Your instructor may tell you to release the seat belt right after take-off or at a designated altitude (which is determined by local drop zone policy and the pilot's discretion). Belts are secured across the lap, where you have bulky clothing and a lot of other straps so the buckle could be very difficult to locate in an emergency. In a crash, you might trap those in the rear while you are trying to find the buckle. On the other hand, if you are sitting by an open door, you will feel more secure with, and should wear, the fastened seat belt.

Door. If the plane has an in-flight, swing-up door and it is winter, the pilot will close it as soon as all are aboard. If the

---

It's usually the student we are worried about. He doesn't realize how dangerous that ripcord handle can be when he gets near the door.   *—John Garrity*

weather is hot, he will wait until just before takeoff to swing it shut. All of you are pretty close by now; it's tighter than a phone booth jamming contest.

Your aircraft taking off

Takeoff. The pilot starts the engine and taxies out to the end of the runway. Turning the plane away from the runway, he locks the wheels and gives the engine some fuel, making it roar. The plane vibrates all over as the engine and prop strain against the brakes and you get the unmistakable airplane smell of wind and exhaust. He glances over the many instruments and revs up the engine to check the engine and propeller systems. Then he checks the sky for other aircraft, turns the plane around to the *active* runway and rams the throttle home. In most planes, it helps if everyone leans forward. There is so much dense cargo that just a small bit of forward-shifted weight makes a big difference. After takeoff when the pilot raises the flaps, reduces power and trims out for climb, sit back and relax — if you can.

> You swallow hard, thinking to yourself, it must be all right, thousands of people have done it before. Then . . . but this time it's me—that's the difference. —*Charles Shea-Simonds*

Climb up to jump altitude. Your instructor will probably try to add to your education and, at the same time, occupy your otherwise nervous mind by bringing a number of interesting things to your attention. If you are like many first-jump students, this may be your first ride in a small plane or even any aircraft. For you, this is a never-before-seen sight and it is particularly exciting. Look for the altimeter in the instrument panel and at the one you are wearing. At 200 feet, take a look outside at the ground so you will recognize how the ground will look at that altitude during your parachute descent (when you should be faced into the wind [on *final approach*] for landing). Locate the target and any hazardous areas you were told to avoid in class. Some DZs have a *hostile farmer or neighbor* who keeps the gear brought on to his property by trespassers. Find the pond, the power lines, and the road; get oriented. Now which way is the wind blowing? Look at the windsock.

Keep your movement in the plane to a minimum or you will wear out the pilot. The aircraft must be balanced or the pilot has to correct the trim with the controls. Imagine driving your car with a soft front tire, first on one side and then the other. The tires would pull to one side and you would have to apply constant pressure to the steering wheel to keep the car straight. But the pilot has an adjustable trim tab to relieve this pressure and he will readjust the trim every time you move. Relax and enjoy the view. Your ride up to 3,000 feet AGL will take around six to eight minutes.

The seat belts come off when the instructor or pilot tells you it is okay to unbuckle them. Unfasten yours and stow the belts away. Slide the hardware to the end of the strap and lay it on the floor as far from the door as possible. A metal-tipped seat belt trailing out the door may chip the paint or make a dent in the fuselage. Seat belts should never be fastened together except when worn. Loose, fastened belts can catch legs as skydivers scramble during an exit.

Wind determination. Unless this flight followed the previous lift by just a few minutes, the instructor may be preparing to drop a wind drift indicator. A WDI is a piece of weighted crepe paper measuring 10" x 20' which is designed to descend at the same rate as a jumper under an open canopy. The instructor will use the WDI to determine the exit point. Wind varies in speed and direction at various levels. It may be calm on the ground and blowing briskly at jump altitude. With accurate wind information (which way and how much), he will be able to select the best place for your exit so that you can drift into the target area. There will be a detailed explanation of *spotting* in a later chapter but here is what you may experience the first time. At about 2,000 feet AGL, the pilot will turn approximately into the wind (according to his best guess), fly across the drop zone (DZ), and open the door. The instructor will look out and down, relaying corrections, if needed, to the pilot (to go the right or left) and then he will throw the wind drift indicator out as the aircraft passes over the target. Banking slightly to the right, the pilot will continue to guide the aircraft in its climbing turn while the instructor keeps the WDI in sight. During the next two minutes the WDI will become smaller and harder to see as it descends to nature's camouflaged terrain. Noting the distance and direction it travels from the landing area, your instructor will select an exit point upwind of the target.

Some clubs teach their students to *spot*, or select the exit point, right from the first jump. This early training keeps their mind occupied, off the worries of the jump, and gives them more confidence and a feeling of being useful. Some other operations start spotting practice on the second jump and many wait until the tenth jump or so.

Jump run. As you near 3,500 feet on *base leg* (90 degrees to the wind line) and are about to turn onto *jump run*, your instructor will relieve you of your handful of static line and point out three important things: the *target*, the *exit point* and the *wind line* which runs through them. If you are rigged for Instructor Assisted Deployment, he will remove your pilot chute from the container and hold it in his free hand.

Never in my life can I remember such a feeling of accomplishment.
—*Michèle Gratton*

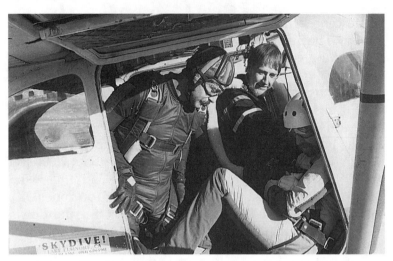

Jump run. The pilot and jumpmaster are busy with last minute details such as giving you a good spot.

After turning on jump run, the pilot (or instructor with the pilot's permission) will reach over and unlatch the swing-up door. The wind will pull the door open, holding it snugly up against the underside of the wing. The instructor will stick his head out as the jump ship flies upwind, crossing the target and heading for the exit point. He may give the pilot some slight course corrections either verbally or with hand signals. You will notice the buffeting, cool wind, the noise and smell of the engine, and it will be hard to hear. At this point, your instructor may give you a little pep talk and review of the essentials: *Protect your handles and your static line as you move about the aircraft. Take your time — I'll do the rest. Remember as you climb out: left foot, left hand, right foot, right hand. When I give you the GO command, GO. I want to see you exit with a hard arch. Look up and keep your eyes on me and your position will be good. We will be listening for your count but you will have to shout as loud as you can. Don't be afraid to pull the reserve if you think it may be necessary. Don't forget to face into the wind on landing; today that means toward the gas pumps.*

Skydivers know where they're going.

Think and make it a good one. See you on the ground. Or, his last minute advice may consist of just a few words. It is largely a matter of individual style.

Just before you cross the target (about fifteen to twenty seconds before you let go of the aircraft), your instructor will give you the first exit command: *PUT YOUR FEET OUT (or perhaps SIT IN THE DOOR).* Swing your legs out while continuing to guard your ripcords and canopy release handle and visually monitor the routing of your static line. If it snakes under your arm, you will get a rude awakening when you reach the end of it. Also stay clear of your instructor's ripcord handles; don't knock them out. Leave some room in the doorway so your instructor can peer over your shoulder at the exit point.

In the door. The wind will probably try to blow your feet away from the step.

Exiting the aircraft. About five seconds prior to your climbing out of the aircraft, the instructor will yell *cut* (asking the pilot to reduce the engine's power). The pilot will throttle back the engine to make it easier for you to climb out of the aircraft. The noise will fade and the plane will slow down slightly. Just how much the pilot slows the airplane will depend on you and your size because — and here's the tradeoff — if you exit at 85 mph, the higher speed will provide you with more body control, and parachute deployment will be cleaner. However, all this wind makes climbing out and holding on more difficult, so for smaller, weaker students, the pilot may throttle back to 75 mph.

Once your feet are clear of the door and on the step, you may discontinue guarding the handles. Grasp the wing strut with your left hand and the right side of the door frame with your right. It will be very windy in the prop blast. Do not, at any time, grab the hand strap that may be over the door; they pinch fingers. It will be harder than you think to place your feet on the step because of the wind blast.

Poised exit. The traditional method.

CLIMB OUT, STAY LOW (or perhaps GET ON THE STEP) your instructor will shout as the second exit command. Put your left hand on the strut about one-and-a-half feet out from the door, your left elbow onto the strut, and reach across vigorously with the right hand to grasp the strut about one foot further out from your left hand, hooking your

On unstable exits, students get a glance at the airplane only about once on each revolution. *—Don Grant*

fingers around the leading edge of it. Look forward to the strut and your body and feet will turn toward it. Now pull yourself onto your feet on the step. If you have short arms, you may have to proceed one grip at a time, and you may require some help from your instructor. (Your instructor will probably assist you by lifting your backpack off of the door-sill and pushing it forward while keeping your backpack low, away from the door handles.) Do not try to reach out too far or you could lose your grip or balance.

Exit. You may be taught to make either a *poised exit, hanging exit* or a *sitting exit*.

—Poised exit. Standing on the step with your left leg, let your right leg hang in the breeze. Or your instructor may teach you to place both feet together out on the end of the step. Support your weight with your leg(s); your handholds are only for keeping you oriented and balanced.

Hanging exit

—Hanging exit. An alternative is the hanging exit, where you go out past the step, sliding your hands along the strut while maintaining your grip until you are hanging from the strut by your hands. With your legs blowing back in the slipstream, you are in a perfect arched position and a clean, stable exit is almost assured.

—**Sitting exit.** Poised and hanging are the two most common exit techniques. However, you may find yourself jumping from a Cessna 206 where you have to sit on the floor in the door and scoot out into the prop blast. Whatever aircraft and techniques you encounter, your instructor will train you for the necessary exit.

Now that you are set, get your head up and turn to look your instructor in the eyes.

GO!

The instructor will emphasize the third and final command; GO!—often with a sharp slap across your thigh so you will know he is yelling at you. If you feel anything besides a slap on the thigh, don't jump. You may be past the spot, or for some other reason he may want you to re-enter the plane for a go-around. (This can be extremely hazardous.) On GO, simply step off to the side (or just let go in a hanging exit), then arch your back, spreading your arms and legs. Stretch those muscles. Your body will follow your head that is led by the eyes. If you are looking down, you will probably bend over forward and do a front loop. Look up at your instructor and the result should be a good arch.

Pointing your toes also helps. The best body position on exit is perpendicular to the relative (on-coming) wind, about 45 degrees to the ground. If the angle is much more or less than this, a slight rotation of your body may result. At this point in your jump career, your exit position is more important than your body form since you don't have enough airspeed to correct for a poor exit. The goal is to make a stable exit. Simultaneously with your exit, you will shout your count, beginning with *Arch thousand*. The arch and count may be practiced in class or at home using a table or wall. The sessions should be practiced until they become smooth and automatic.

It is very unlikely that you will hit the tail of the airplane as you exit. Because you are going the same speed as the aircraft, you will continue traveling forward on exit, appearing to drop almost straight down from the door.

As you fall away, the instructor carefully monitors your body attitude and allows the looped static line to pay out of his hand. He will allow you to fall to the end of the eight to fifteen foot static line unless you begin to roll. In this case, he may choke off the S-folds in his hand and *short line* you, initiating an earlier deployment, reducing chances of entanglement. He is also making a mental record of your air work that he will discuss with you in the post-jump critique.

EXITING THE AIRCRAFT. Attaining and maintaining the proper body position. Illustrations are for C-180 aircraft. Instructions will be altered by your jumpmaster for other aircraft. The exit and count should be practiced until they become smooth and automatic. Your exit position is more important than your body form; you don't have the airspeed or time required to correct for a poor exit. Your jumpmaster will give you these commands.

A. IN THE DOOR. Swing legs out into the wind and grasp the wing strut with the left hand. Protect ripcord handles and canopy release until clear of the door.

B. ON THE STEP. Pull yourself out on to the step and face forward grasping the wing strut firmly with both hands. Keep your head up and look at the instructor.

C. GO! Side-step off to the right.

NOTE: Your DZ may teach the hanging exit.

1. ARCH-THOUSAND! Arch your back. Keep the head up and look at the jumpmaster. Start the count sequence out loud:

A capsulized review of the poised exit from a Cessna 180 aircraft

Stability. You want your canopy to deploy while you are in a stable fall, face-to-earth, shoulders-level position so that it may deploy freely, directly away from the body. A good arch will provide you with the best body position for a clean parachute deployment and an easier opening. A hard arch places your center of gravity at your belly and maintains you in a position like the shuttlecock, belly-to-earth.

The spread stable position

HIGH CENTER OF GRAVITY   LOW CENTER OF GRAVITY
      (unstable)   (stable)

The body compared with a shuttlecock

Stability may be practiced in your living room. Lie face down on the floor with your arms and legs extended. Then, on the word *GO*, force a hard arch by lifting the arms, legs and head as high off the floor as possible. Hold this position for five to six seconds and then rest. Keep practicing it over and over. It will help you to make a better jump and it's great for the stomach muscles. During the actual jump, this position will be easier to maintain because the relative wind helps

Skydiving is easy. Anyone can fall.

blow the arms and legs into position and gravity doesn't pull them down below your belly. Lying face down on a partially deflated air mattress is the best ground level simulation of the actual forces on your body in the belly-to-earth position.

Once the static line or pilot chute has unlocked the container and pulled out the canopy, you are on your own; your instructor can do nothing now — but watch. If you weren't the first student to jump on this lift, you saw him reel in the previous jumper's static line, unhook it and stow it either beneath the pilot's seat or in the rear of the cabin. Meanwhile the pilot was making a one-to-two minute orbit back to jump run for the next student's exit. Watching the first student's approach to the landing area allows the instructor to correct the exit spot (if necessary) if the student on the first jump missed the target area (for reasons other than canopy control).

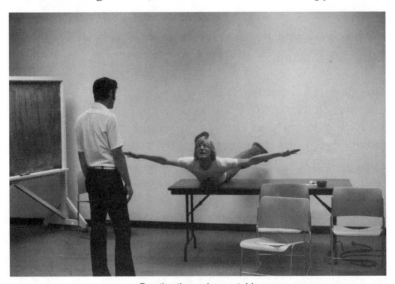

Practice the arch on a table

Well, so much for all the interesting peripheral discussion. We left you back in freefall, arching and shouting.

Counting helps you to keep track of time. The count and emergency procedures should be practiced prior to each jump. You should also go through the entire sequence in a suspended harness every 30 days. While the count sequence varies slightly with changes in parachute equipment, this is the usual order.

Normal Procedure for the Static Line Program with a Practice RipCord

1. ARCH-THOUSAND. Exit aircraft, hard arch, arms and legs spread. head back.

2. LOOK-THOUSAND. Maintaining arch, tuck in chin and look at the main ripcord handle.

3. REACH-THOUSAND. Maintain arch, bend arms at elbows and grasp ripcord handle.

4. PULL-THOUSAND. Maintain arch, pull vigorously going back out into the spread position, head back.

5. CHECK-THOUSAND. Check the canopy (look back over the shoulder for pilot chute hesitation, malfunction, etc). Body may roll slightly.

(The canopy normally opens between REACH-THOUSAND and PULL-THOUSAND (3-4 seconds) but you must continue the count through CHECK-THOUSAND (5) and pull the practice ripcord handle. Practice the entire count of nine.)

The exit count

PRCP or PPCT. Some jump operations start their students off making *Practice RipCord Pulls* (or *dummy ripcord pulls*) or *Practice Pilot Chute Throws* on their first static line jump while others teach the spread position initially and then switch to the PRCP motions on jumps two or three. For a PRCP, you must perform your count and the indicated movements until the canopy opens, bringing you upright. The canopy will normally open between *reach thousand* and *pull thousand,* but you must ignore the upward pull and continue the count until you have pulled the practice ripcord. In the S/L or IAD program, you won't advance to freefall until you have five jumps and have demonstrated to your instructor your ability to successfully pull your ripcord or toss your practice pilot chute on three successive jumps. So, start practicing now.

The purpose of the Practice RipCord Pull is to create a behavior pattern in your mind so that you may safely pull your own ripcord.
—*Chuck Ryan*

As you practice your exit-count from the table and your arch on the floor, go through the entire eight-step count. Practice and practice until the count and motions become automatic.

6. LOOK AND
REACH THOUSAND.
Let go of the main ripcord;
Locate and grasp the reserve
ripcord with both hands, Peel
it out of its poacket or velcro.

7. PULL THOUSAND.
Pull the reserve ripcord and
all attached cables all the
way out of the housings.

8. ARCH THOUSAND.
Spread your hands to clear
the cables from the housings
if they are not already clear
of them. Let go of the handle.

Emergency procedure count for a total malfunction

Malfunctions. Total malfunctions are rare but if they didn't occur now and then, we wouldn't bother counting past *pull thousand* on the PRCP. If you reach the count of five (check thousand) and aren't being jerked upright by your filling canopy, look over your left shoulder and bring your right hand to the reserve ripcord area. If there is nothing deploying where you're looking, don't hesitate — pull the reserve ripcord.

Of course, there are many other types of malfunctions and remedies, but only a total malfunction normally occurs in this part of the jump sequence. Other parachute malfunctions and some interesting airport dangers are covered later in the *Skydiving Emergencies* chapter.

Opening sequence. When the static line or ripcord is pulled, the main container is unlocked allowing the *pilot chute* to get into the airstream. Acting like an anchor, the pilot chute draws the bagged canopy out of the container as you fall away. The suspension lines unstow from their rubber bands with the last two to four stows unlocking the *bag*.

The canopy pulls out of the bag but the *slider* (which is under the lower surface of the canopy) keeps the canopy from spreading too rapidly. You are pulled upright as the cells of the canopy inflate and spread apart. As the canopy spreads, the slider moves down the lines. Lastly, the bag and pilot chute fall on top of the canopy or trail behind it.

Deployment. As your blossoming canopy pulls you upright, you experience an overwhelming exhilaration. You look up to see your new nylon friend, the one who plucked you from freefall, and find the canopy to be larger than you imag-

Deployment bag lifting
out of main container

ined. You are at about 3,500 feet AGL and it's both beautiful and strangely quiet. The air is brisk and clean. But this is no time for sightseeing; time's a wasting and there is work to be done.

Your canopy descent has three distinct phases: the canopy check, steering for the target and preparing to land. *Look up* and check the canopy. It should be rectangular, flying straight, the slider should be down with no twists in the lines, and the end cells should be fully inflated. If the canopy is anything but perfect, you will follow the instructions as outlined in the chapter on emergency procedures. Make a *traffic check*: are there any other jumpers flying in front of you? Stow your practice ripcord handle if you have one. You may slip it down the front of your jumpsuit. Don't lose it. Dropped from half a mile up, it could injure someone on the ground and, besides, most clubs have penalties for lost ripcords, usually beginning with a case of beer. Release the

Slider slowing the spread of the main canopy

deployment brakes by reaching up and grasping the steering lines by their loops on the risers and pulling them out of their locking loops. Push the steering toggles down to your pelvis for a count of two, then bring them back up to their keepers (arms all the way up). This action, which simulates a landing flare that will be explained later, is part of a *"controllability check"* of the canopy. If the slider does not come all the way down, push the toggles down again. Continue the *controllability check*: turn right 360 degrees, turn left 360 degrees, then bring the toggles down to half brakes. If the canopy responds correctly to your control inputs and doesn't do anything radical, you may conclude that it is a "good" canopy. *Look down* at the ground and get yourself oriented. Find the target and windsock. Determine the wind line and head toward the target. Check your altimeter.

Communications. Listen or watch for ground instructions as you have been taught. Your DZ may be using radios, a bullhorn, P.A. system, arrow or ground panels to guide you down. But equipment fails, drop zone personnel may be off helping the student ahead of you and, of course, it always helps to understand why you are doing what you are doing. So, read on. Fly to the *landing area entry point* (sometimes called the staging area).

Find the windsock. It will not only show you the direction of the wind, but with practice you will be able to judge wind speed by the sock's angle to the ground. Later you will use other wind indicators such as smoke from factory chimneys, ripples on ponds, flapping flags, etc. Winds vary in direction and intensity at different altitudes; wind determination will become even more important when you reach long freefalls.

Your ride from opening to landing will be influenced by four major factors: gravity, wind (speed and direction), canopy forward speed and atmospheric conditions such as temperature and humidity. While you can't expect to make precision landings right from the start, and should not try, an understanding of certain basics will enable you to avoid obstacles by steering around them.

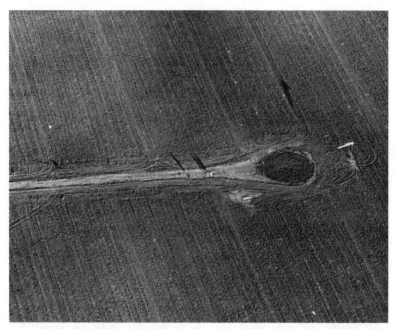

The small end of the windsock points in the direction the wind is going

Gravity, the first factor affecting your flight, depends on your *exit weight* — *the* total weight of you and all your parachute gear. If you weigh 170 lbs. and have 30 lbs. of gear including parachutes, helmet, etc., you can expect to descend at about 12 to 16 feet per second. This means you will have about three-and-a-half minutes from the time you open at 3,500 feet AGL until you touch down. If you weigh more, you will come down faster. In fact, if you weigh much more, you will be issued a larger canopy so that your descent rate will be about the same as that just described.

Your canopy is a collapsible, deployable flying wing held open by internal ram-air pressurization. As the wing moves forward, air enters the openings in the *leading edge* to inflate and pressurize the wing. Now if you weigh 170 lbs. you can expect a canopy speed of about 20 mph and a glide angle of 72 degrees.

Full flight. The canopy is designed to run at its maximum forward speed when the steering lines are all the way up.

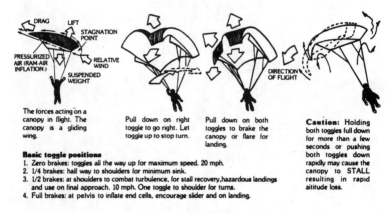

The forces acting on a canopy in flight. The canopy is a gliding wing.

Pull down on right toggle to go right. Let toggle up to stop turn.

Pull down on both toggles to brake the canopy or flare for landing.

Caution: Holding both toggles full down for more than a few seconds or pushing both toggles down rapidly may cause the canopy to STALL resulting in rapid altitude loss.

Basic toggle positions
1. Zero brakes: toggles all the way up for maximum speed. 20 mph.
2. 1/4 brakes: half way to shoulders for minimum sink.
3. 1/2 brakes: at shoulders to combat turbulence, for stall recovery, hazardous landings and use on final approach. 10 mph. One toggle to shoulder for turns.
4. Full brakes: at pelvis to inflate end cells, encourage slider and on landing.

Flying the ram-air "square" canopy

The turning of the canopy is accomplished by pulling down on the steering line on the side to which you wish to turn. The faster and further you pull down the line, the quicker the canopy will turn. Fast turns also make you swing out from under the canopy in a wide arc and increase the rate of descent considerably. Because of this swinging and increased descent rate, major turns (such as a fast 180 degrees or more) should not be made below 1,000 feet AGL (the AAD may even activate due to the increased descent rate), and especially not near the ground. It is best to make all turns gently. Steering lines should be pulled down in front of you where you can see your hands in relation to the turn being produced.

Braking. Pulling down on both steering lines evenly will cause the canopy to *brake* or slow its forward speed.

Upper winds. There probably isn't any such thing as a *no wind day* because there is usually some movement up there. In fact, if there is some wind on the ground, there is almost always more movement up higher. While the wind may be blowing 5 mph on the ground where it can be easily measured, it may be blowing 15 mph at 1,000 feet. This is

You have nowhere to go but down.

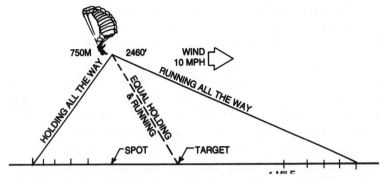

Which way is the wind blowing? Are you drifting toward or away from the target?

because there is more frictional drag near the ground. It is just like a stream where the water moves faster in the center than at the sides. If the ground winds are 15 mph and your canopy has a forward speed of 20, it sounds fine until you find the upper winds are 25 and you are backing up. In these conditions, once you venture downwind of the target, you may never get back and will have to select an alternative landing area.

> You at 20 mph ➜⬅ wind at 10 mph = a ground speed of 10
> You at 20 mph ➜➜ wind at 10 mph = a ground speed of 30

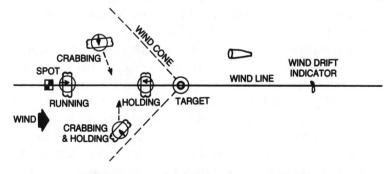

The wind cone is that maneuvering area to either side of the wind line which will still allow you to land on the target. The cone will be narrower if canopy performance is lower or the wind is higher.

Did you open over the desired opening point? If you are very far upwind (*long*), you will be *running* with the wind a lot, while if you opened closer to the target than you planned, you will spend most of your canopy ride *holding* against the wind. If you find yourself left or right of the opening point, you are off the wind line and will be *crabbing* across the wind line to get back to it. If the opening point was correct and if you opened over it, you will require an equal amount of running and holding to hit the target. You will use extra running and holding only to compensate for changes in the wind speed. You will use crabbing to make up for wind direction changes. Since holding provides you the slowest drift across the ground, you should make your landings into the wind.

Reserve canopies. Your reserve will probably be a ram-air canopy and just as maneuverable as your main, or it may be a less maneuverable and slower round canopy. The wind cone for a round canopy is much narrower than for a square. Your instructor will explain the steering of your round or square reserve canopy.

Wind line verification. After opening, turn and face the target. If you are on the wind line, the target will appear to be moving toward you, remaining stationary or moving away from you. If it is moving toward you, turn and hold so as not to overshoot it. While holding, make slight turns so you can watch the target and its movement. If it moves away from you, turn and run toward it. If the target appears to be moving to one side, you are off the wind line and must crab back to it.

Penetration check. Check the strength of the upper winds by facing into the wind (the direction that gives you the slowest speed across the ground) and pulling your toggles to 1/4, 1/2 and 3/4 brakes while looking between your feet at an object on the ground. Try each brake position for several seconds to settle into a steady flying state. Note the brake setting at which you do not make progress over the ground. If you find you are moving at an angle during your penetration check, you have selected the wrong wind line. Make a corrective turn and try again.

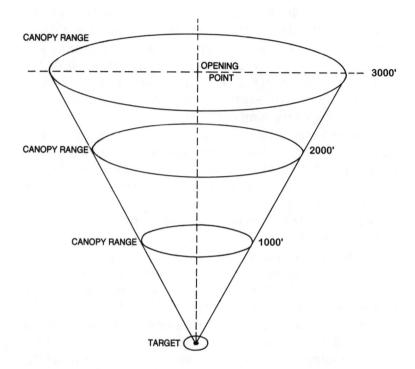

Three-dimensional diagram showing wind cone under no-wind conditions (side view)

The closer you get to the target, both horizontally and vertically, the less room you have to maneuver laterally. Note that the wind cone becomes smaller as you descend. If you stay within it, you will have the ability to hit the target. But if, for example, you venture just five meters outside it, there is no way you can land any closer than five meters from the target. When you are in the center of the cone, all headings are equally correct. But as you move nearer to the side of the cone your options decrease, and when you reach the edge of the cone, your directional choices are reduced to one.

> If the good Lord had wanted people to stay on the ground, he would have given us roots.

The principle is simply that if you are *long*, you must use the wind to assist you to cover more ground by running (going with the wind), and if you are *short*, you must counteract the wind by holding (going against the wind). The ideal spot will permit you to make gentle S-turns astride the wind line. If the target begins to move closer or farther away, you will adjust your S-turns accordingly, and you may add some holding or running time too.

Right-of-way. The lower person has the right-of-way, both in freefall and under the canopy. The higher person (with the better view) should always yield to anyone below. Everyone has a responsibility to avoid collisions and this basic right-of-way rule sorts out the duties. Right-of-way is discussed in detail in "Skydiving Rules of the Air" at the end of Chapter Four.

Atmospheric conditions. There are also certain atmospheric conditions that will affect your spotting and canopy ride. At higher elevations such as Denver, your descent rate will be faster since the air is rarer, or less dense. Similarly, descent rates increase when the barometric pressure drops or when the air is humid and/or on hot days. So, as atmospheric conditions change, your canopy will react differently.

Changes in descent on a single jump may be felt as you cross certain areas such as a forest to a highway. Some areas absorb or give off more of the sun's heat than others. Runways and tin roofs may produce *thermals*, boiling bubbles of warmed air which rise quickly. If you pass through one of these invisible lift machines, your descent will slow and you may even ascend a bit, thus your canopy ride may be extended by several minutes.

Your canopy is an aircraft, a glider. It is not powered and cannot go back up on command. While it does not have the shallow glide angle and low sink rate of a Blanik sailplane, it is much smaller, weighs a lot less and is much less expensive. So, there is a trade-off but both are gliders and your parachute canopy is superior in many ways.

Because you are flying a glider, you have one chance at landing — you can't go around for another attempt. Every landing has to be good — preferably perfect.

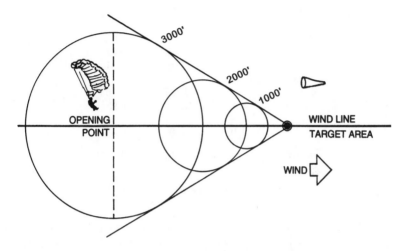

The wind cone with wind added (top view)

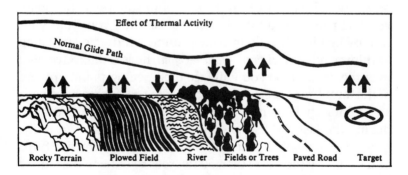

The effect of convection currents on canopy flight

METERS PER SECOND	MPH	KM per Hour	Knots
0.45	1	1.61	0.87
0.89	2	3.22	1.74
1.34	3	4.83	2.61
1.78	4	6.44	3.47
2.23	5	8.05	4.34
2.68	6	9.66	5.21
3.12	7	11.27	6.88
3.57	8	12.87	6.95
4.02	9	14.48	7.82
4.47	10	16.09	8.68

For higher speeds, add the applicable figures.

Speed Conversion Table

Flying the landing approach. Your approach to the target area is quite similar to an airplane's approach to a runway, with a *crosswind leg*, *a downwind leg*, a *base leg* and a *final approach*.

These are the basics of flying the pattern. For more details and tips on very accurate landings, see Chapter Six.

Preparing to land. You are about to enter the third and final phase of the canopy ride; the preparation for the *parachute landing fall*, or PLF. In steering your canopy at this point, you want to concentrate on two areas. First, you want your canopy headed directly into the ground wind when you land to minimize your *ground speed* — *your* horizontal movement over the ground. So you will face the opening point, upwind of the target, and check the windsock to see if there have been any minor changes in the lower or *ground* winds. Secondly, during the last 200 feet and 10+ seconds travel down to the ground, you want to avoid all but very minor corrective turns to the canopy (no more than 30 degrees to either side) since a large turn will only increase your horizontal travel by swing-

The best time to prepare for a landing is before you get into the plane. Observe ground wind speed and direction, and whether it is steady or variable. —*Eric Roberts*

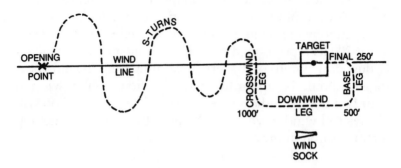

Flying the pattern

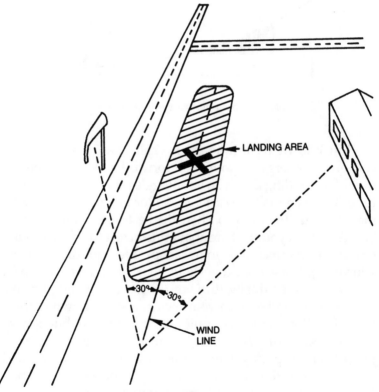

The landing approach

ing you out from under the canopy. Let's not forget that a canopy's descent rate increases during turns. So, land with a stable canopy and land as slowly as possible. Now here you are at 200 feet, positioned over the landing area in the vicinity (just downwind) of the target and preparing to land. Your toggles should be up for full glide. Caution: Feeling wind in your face doesn't indicate you are *faced into the wind*. You will always feel wind in your face because the canopy is moving forward through the air.

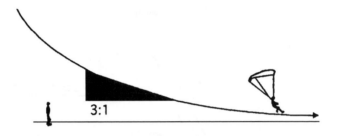

Bleed off speed and turn it into temporary lift

Touchdown technique. Your challenge in landing is to convert the energy of your high forward speed into temporary lift by pulling down on your toggles at precisely the right time. The secret is the *smooth flare*. Normally, this is done by making your final approach with the toggles full up (zero brakes). When your feet are about fifteen feet from the ground (when the ground and your canopy are equi-distant from your eyes), bring both toggles to your shoulders, then your breast bone, then finally, turn your wrists down and push the toggles down in between your legs in a smooth two to three second motion (sometimes called out on a radio or bullhorn as *Flare Thousand, Two thousand, Three Thousand*). As you progress jump after jump, this flare will become more automatic and you may even find yourself starting it a bit lower and performing it faster to achieve a more dramatic stop.

You will find that in higher winds it takes less time and altitude to flare. In the maximum winds allowed for student jumps (14 mph for a square reserve), you might fly the canopy at one-quarter brakes to combat turbulence and flare it at three to five feet. If the winds are moderate, say seven to ten mph, flare it at eight to ten feet. These figures are approximate and depend on your *exit weight* and type of canopy being used. If you have difficulty judging just what to do, you can start your flare at a reasonable height (such as when your canopy and the ground are an equal distance from your eyes) and flare just enough to stop all forward movement, no further. This will allow you to descend gently to the ground through the last few feet. NEVER flare the canopy so much that it will start moving backwards or stall. Stalls can lead to compression injuries, fractures, or worse. Going slightly backwards on landing may not be so bad, but it can be unsettling to you. If you find yourself having flared just a bit too much and too early, you can always raise the toggles up a few inches — just enough to allow the canopy to start forward progress across the ground again. Then, if necessary, continue the flare to its final conclusion — ground contact.

Parachute Landing Fall. A PLF is a method of falling down on landing which tranmits the vertical energy (which can smart), into a rotational energy (which shouldn't hurt), without placing any breakable bony part of your torso on the ground until the process is successfully completed. In some landings, there is a lot of energy that must be absorbed, so spread it around while protecting the body areas subject to breaking. The drawings show a forward-left PLF, one of the most common. Your drift may dictate that it be to the back or to the side but the principle is the same: to distribute the landing force over as much of the fleshy and muscular parts of the body as possible instead of the joints.

If the wind is low-to-moderate and you are faced directly into it when you flare the canopy at the correct moment, you will land so softly that you may not fall over. *Stand-up landings* avoid bruises, keep your jumpsuit clean and make you look great to spectators.

It is a good idea to know how to make good PLFs for those jumps when you land in higher or lower winds, are off

PARACHUTE LANDING FALLS

You might not fall down when landing under a main canopy. However, PLF's should be practiced for reserve landings. Use this outline to refresh your memory as you practice from a 4' height. Remember, there is some horizontal flight in addition to the vertical descent. Practice falls to the front, side and rear until they become automatic.

A. PREPARE TO LAND (at about 200' over clear ground): Check for obstacles. Face into the wind to minimize horizontal drift. Hands on steering toggles making slight corrections. Remember, all points of contact should be along the wind (fall) line.

Approach at full flight, toggles up. Press feet & knees together, knees bent slightly, toes extended downward, leg muscles tensed, elbows in, look down.

Flare at 15', push both toggles down to pelvis.

B. GROUND CONTACT
Feet. Leg muscles tensed and prepared to absorb ninety percent of the impact force.

Rotate your body in the direction of fall allowing the knees to move in the direction of force. Head down.

Calf. Elbows and hands forward in front of chest and face.

C. FOLLOW THROUGH
Stand up and run around the canopy to dump its air and deflate it. If you are being dragged and cannot get up, roll over on your back and pull down all the way on one toggle.

Thigh. Keep the elbows in.

Butt. Continue roll in one long smooth continuous motion.

Shoulder. First one . . . and then on through to the other.

Feet over. contacting with the line of fall (wind line.)

The Parachute Landing Fall

the drop zone, find yourself under a round reserve or blow the timing on the landing flare. Practice PLFs to the front, each side and to the rear from a four-foot height until they become automatic.

All landings should be made facing into the wind unless it is necessary to take evasive action to avoid obstacles. Of course, avoiding obstacles should have been accomplished through proper canopy control well in advance to landing. That's why we have steerable canopies: — so we can select and guide ourselves to a wide open, obstacle-free landing area.

Ground guidance is merely advisory in nature. It is the jumper's responsibility to continually estimate the probable landing point and make appropriate adjustments to land properly in a clear area.

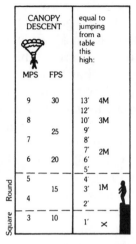

CANOPY DESCENT		equal to jumping from a table this high:		Note Relationships:
MPS	FPS			feet/meters per second and height.
				Descent varies with weight.
9	30	13′ 4M		Square canopies may be flared to reduce both forward and vertical speed.
		12′		
8		10′ 3M		
	25	9′		
7		8′		
		7′ 2M		
6	20	6′		
		5′		
5		4′		
	15	3′ 1M		
4		2′		
3	10	1′ ✕		

Round / Square

Canopy descent table

One second is about all it takes to make the parachute landing fall; not much time to think about or change your landing plans. The impact is about what you would encounter from jumping off a four-foot platform. But there is some horizontal movement so it is more like jumping off the bumper of a truck doing four mph. Actually, PLFs are easier with some drift than when coming straight down. On ground contact, you will execute your PLF in the direction of drift, and it may be in any direction: forward, backward, to one side or the other. You will practice landings from a low platform.

Think about parachute landing falls in three parts: the vertical force absorption, the horizontal force absorption, and getting back on your feet. The points of contact are:

1. The balls of the feet

2. The side of the calf

3. The side of the thigh

4. The side of the buttock

5. The side of the back

Just prior to touchdown, your toes are pointed down, your knees are slightly bent (unlocked), and your leg muscles are tensed to absorb perhaps 90% of the vertical force. Your feet and knees are pressed firmly together so that you will be able to roll. You are looking down at 45 degrees, not away from the ground and not directly at it. At this angle, you can better judge your altitude. Your hands are on the toggles, so now you bring your elbows down, shoulder-width apart, in front of your face and prepare to flare the canopy. Tuck your head forward and down to avoid whiplash in the case of a backward landing. Watch the ground at 45 degrees in order to anticipate it and begin your roll, noting the direction of drift so that you will roll with it.

Your knees are bent but tensioned to accept the vertical force. You are protecting your breakable wrists by bringing them together in front of you. You touch the ground absorbing most of the shock in your leg muscles. Limp leg muscles and spread-apart feet are probably the primary cause of injuries on landing. If you have good leg muscle tension, with your legs firmly together and knees unlocked, you are unlikely to be hurt on landing. Practice and discipline yourself. If your legs are limp, you will wind up with a bruised hip and will find walking difficult until just before it is time to return on the weekend for your next jump. You may even manage to remain standing if there is little horizontal drift, but it isn't likely with your feet and knees pressed tightly together. Even if you feel you can remain on your feet, it is a good idea to continue through with the PLF both for the practice and because your instructor may require it.

There is some drift today so it is time to take care of it. As you are absorbing the vertical force, shift the pressed knees and rotate your shoulders and trunk toward the *fall line*. Keep the elbows, hands and head in; let yourself go. You will roll like a ball. Continue on through and spring back up on your feet. Try practicing the vertical and horizontal parts of the landing separately and then use a platform to go through the whole PLF. Jump, absorb forces in the legs, roll and stand up.

There is a lot to remember and it will be difficult to select and execute the proper PLF for each line of drift, and to decide which way to shift and rotate. You will also find that

PLFs use previously ignored muscles so do not be surprised if you have trouble getting out of bed the next day.

Knowing some of the common mistakes may help you to avoid them. Some students anticipate the ground and begin their landing roll before they reach it by retracting their legs; the butt usually absorbs the vertical forces. Some put their legs out in front of them, and some go entirely limp. All three produce bruises and occasionally a break. Backing-up landings sometimes result in feet-butt-head ground contact that is to be avoided. If you find yourself backing up in strong winds, turn the canopy as much as 20-30 degrees from the wind line so you will be able to make a good sideways PLF. Similarly, if the wind is very light and you are moving forward on touchdown because you failed to flare the canopy enough, you will want to turn slightly again. This will permit you to do a PLF rather than a FHF (Feet, Hands, Face).

Warning: Don't try to stop the fall with your hands. Such an action may lead to a broken wrist or worse. Some canopies have slight built-in turns, and all canopies suffer occasionally from turns when the bag and pilot chute hang up on a suspension line. Keep the toggles in your hands. If your knees are not firmly pressed together, you will tend to sit down on touchdown, absorbing the force in the wrong area. That may be your last sitting for a while.

Landing hazards. Some landings can be potentially extremely hazardous, such as descending into water, power lines or trees. If any of these dangers exist in the area of your drop zone, your instructor will make special reference to them and will outline a particular corrective action. We will cover these hazards and others in detail in the chapter on emergency procedures.

Dragging. Your PLF should lead into an immediate stand-up recovery in order for you to avoid being dragged by the wind or covered by the deflating canopy. You will want to get right back up on your feet for another reason:

Never land in a turn. A low turn is much more harmful than a downwind landing.

You want to show the staff that you are OK. Some students are so overcome by their recent jumping accomplishment that they just want to lie on the ground, relax and think about it. That is one sure way to draw a concerned crowd.

How is this quick recovery accomplished? Perhaps like this: You have just flared for the landing. Now as soon as your toes touch the ground, keep one toggle depressed and let go of the other one. If your landing was a stand-up, pivot (up to) 180 degrees to the side of the depressed toggle. If you made a PLF, get up. The canopy should rotate and dive into the ground. Now run around the canopy. Think about these landing techniques and practice them on the ground. Plan to use these landing techniques on every jump. If you happen to have a no-wind day, the canopy will deflate without your assistance but it may fall all around you in a tangled mess. If you are quick in following through on your PLF and get up on your feet, you will be able to run out from under it, keeping the lines tensioned and straight. If you are in the target area, you should pull the canopy off to one side to uncover the disc for the next jumper.

There are five basic ways to spill the air from an inflated canopy:

1. Get up and run around either side of it to turn the canopy out of the wind.
2. Pull down all the way on a steering line to rotate the canopy and drive it into the ground.
3. Have a buddy grab an edge and pull the canopy around, upwind of you.
4. Grab the riser and then the lines closest to the ground and pull them toward you hand over hand.

Or,

5. In a harm-threatening situation, jettison the canopy by pulling the breakaway handle.

Normally, you will simply follow through with your PLF by rolling, recovering and running around your canopy. If you find yourself being dragged into harm's way and unable to stand up, pulling all the way down on one toggle should take care of the canopy. Choice number five is a last ditch method and it is doubtful that you will experience winds strong enough to need it while adhering to student wind limits. Jettisoning a canopy will make a tangled mess of it, and in high winds, the risers will take off like a shot from a sling; so don't attempt it in a crowded DZ area unless it is an absolute life-saving necessity. With most student parachute systems, jettisoning the main canopy also opens the reserve container. However, the reserve will probably not come out of its deployment device; it will merely fall in an expensive pile onto the ground.

Skydiving is a worldwide fraternity

The most important thing to remember in your recovery is to act quickly. A gentle dragging across the DZ can begin as an entertaining ride and quickly turn into a high speed, dangerous situation where you are not in complete control.

Camaraderie. After you land, other jumpers will probably come over, pump your hand and welcome you to the great worldwide fraternity of skydiving. They know your excitement and they want to encourage it and join you in your moment of glory.

Sling the canopy over your shoulder

Field packing. Now comes the field care of your parachute, or preparing it for transport back to the packing area. Stick the toggles to their Velcro strips on the risers, then work the slider up as you coil the lines and grasp them firmly in one hand. Grab the canopy by the lines adjacent to the canopy and sling the canopy over your shoulder. If you are short, or have a large canopy, pick it up in your arms like a bundle of loose laundry. Do not let the canopy drag on the ground. Experienced jumpers who land a great distance from the drop zone often pack their main on the spot before hiking back.

Debrief. Next it is time for the jump debriefing or *after-jump critique* from your instructor, who has only recently

A lie fed to a receptive mind is the most powerful truth of all. So keep the tall tales about skydiving down to a believable level, eh?
—*Ted Dentay*

arrived on the target. If you are to learn from your experience and improve upon the last jump, you must solicit an objective observation of your performance. The instructor will check with the ground crew on your canopy work, and he may debrief all the students at one time. This is to your advantage, as you will learn from the experiences of others. First, he will probably ask you what you did. This helps you to remember; he wants to know what you think and how you interpret your own performance. Then he will tell you what he and the ground crew saw so you can confirm or re-evaluate your impressions with this new information. He may prescribe some corrective ground practice and will tell you what to concentrate on during the next jump.

The First Jump Certificate

Log book. The jump will be recorded in your log book, criticisms and all, in order to maintain a continuing record of your skydiving progress. This is for your reference, the instructor's benefit, and a communication tool for any other instructors you may have on future jumps. This log will be with you forever so learn how to fill it out (keep it neat) before you take pen in hand.

Packing. If you are jumping with a club, you will probably venture to the packing area next to repack your parachute. If this is a commercial center, they may do it for you and you are free to sign up for jump number two if daylight, aircraft and staffing allow.

The next jump. Some students make two jumps the first day. Incidentally, Richard Bach, the author of *Jonathan Livingston Seagull*, made seven jumps, including two freefalls, his first day out. But jumping, especially all the preparation, is tiring and you will probably be limited to three jumps per day initially. If you hustle and you have the financial resources to do it, you can be on freefall by next weekend!

AFF Jump Procedures.

All of the procedures described above with the exception of the climb to altitude, the exit, and the use of the static line to deploy the main parachute are the same in both types of programs. The big differences are as follows:

Climb up to altitude. As stated in chapter one, the minimum exit altitude for a routine AFF jump is 9,000 feet AGL, with 12,000 plus being the more common altitude for DZs with large aircraft. In a Cessna 182, two instructors and you (and usually a videographer) are seated in the aircraft for the twenty to thirty-plus-minute ride to altitude. In a larger aircraft with a faster climb rate, this climb time is considerably shorter. During this climb, your instructors will review various aspects of the jump with you and familiarize you with what the ground looks like at different altitudes. If it is possible, they'll make sure you get to look at the airport during the climb. Sometime during the climb up, they will make an extra gear check to ensure that everything is ready for your jump.

Moving into exit position. Just like the S/L jump, the aircraft has to be directed over the exit point. At the proper time and place, the pilot will receive the request to "cut" (slow down) the engine, and you will be asked those memorable words: "Are you ready to SKYDIVE?" to which you are expected to answer a hearty and hail "YES!" There are many different types of large aircraft exit protocol, and the discussion of them, as well as videographer exit procedures, will be left to your DZ personnel. Here is a typical C-182 exit protocol for you and your two instructors.

A videographer may climb out first or may follow your group out.

The right side (main/primary ripcord) instructor tells you, "PUT YOUR FEET OUT AFTER ME." The instructor climbs out into his position on the step and holds onto the strut with his right hand. Your job is to position yourself sitting in the doorway, feet out on the step; your left hand is placed about one to two feet out the door, holding onto the strut; your right hand may be down on the door sill or on the right side of the doorway. The wind may try to blow your feet off the step before you have them firmly planted there, so concentrate on what you are supposed to be doing. The left (reserve/secondary ripcord) side instructor, still in the aircraft, will help you. Look in at the instructor in the aircraft for further instructions. When the instructor who climbed out is ready to receive you on the step, he will nod an "OK" to the instructor still in the aircraft. That inside instructor will then tell you, "CLIMB OUT, STAY LOW." The reminder to stay low is important because you don't want to drag the parachute container across the door latch mechanism, possibly opening it prematurely. Place your right hand next to your left hand on the strut, then pivot forward on your feet and pull yourself off the floor towards the strut. Climb out slowly and deliberately, positioning yourself close to the right-side instructor with your arms a little bit wider than shoulder width apart. Put your right foot in a trailing position behind you, arching your back, lifting your right knee and thigh up towards the wing, and point your toe into the space behind you. In the meantime, your left-side instructor has also climbed into his exit position. At this point, control of the exit is in your hands and mind. Your instructors are waiting for you to signal that you're ready to go. Do this in the pre-exit check.

Pre-exit check. Here you are, standing outside of an aircraft with two instructors holding onto you and the aircraft, all ready to go somewhere fast. To let them know you're ready, you do what is commonly referred to as a "HOTEL CHECK." You look to your left, to the inside of the aircraft, looking directly at that instructor's eyes and shout "CHECK IN" (or "CHECK LEFT"). Your left-side instructor will let you know that he is ready for your exit by answering "OK." You then look to your right, to the outside of the aircraft, looking directly at that instructor's eyes and shout "CHECK OUT" (or "CHECK RIGHT"). Your right-side instructor will let you know that he is ready for your exit by answering "OK." Now your job is to do a good exit and arch.

The exit: You are now the team leader of the skydive. Lift your head up and look at the propeller (this arches your back a bit), and shout and move through the exit command sequence:

PROP: Look up at the propeller and arch your neck and back.

UP: Move slightly up towards the wing. The instructor will feel this movement and hopefully hear your shout. They consider this equivalent to the word "READY."

DOWN: Move slightly down towards the step. The instructors will feel this movement and hopefully hear your shout. They consider this equivalent to the word "SET."

ARCH: Take your hands off the strut while moving your body up and off of the step, a bit to the right, spreading your whole body into the arch position that you have been trained to do. Arching is the most important thing you do as you leave the aircraft. A good arch sets the stage for a good jump. Congratulations, you just let go of the aircraft and are on your way to a terminal-velocity freefall.

Sensory overload. As you let go of the aircraft, your instructors are holding onto you with both of their arms to stabilize you through what is called sub-terminal freefall. They are acting like training wheels on a bicycle or outriggers on a canoe. Hopefully, your eyes are open and you are taking stock of your senses. Quite often, your brain gets so flooded with information that everything seems to slow down. You mentally take a step back and ask yourself "Did I really just do this?" Of course, the answer is yes. When you realize that you are okay, you should let your instructors know that you are alert and ready to do your job by performing a "circle of awareness."

First circle of awareness. This action allows you to let your instructors know you are alert and ready to do your job. It also provides them with a means to give you some in-the-air guidance and body position correction signals so that your freefall is smoother and more enjoyable. Those signals may involve repositioning your legs, arms, improving your arch, or relaxing a bit. Specific signals and their meanings will be covered in your first jump course and will be reviewed by your instructors prior to your jump. The elements of the "circle of awareness" are given a variety of acronyms. Two common ones are GASP (Ground, Altimeter, Secondary I, Primary I) and HALR (Horizon, Altimeter, Left I, Right I).

Ground or Horizon. Look out on the horizon and pick up a ground reference to remember for your debriefing. Locating something out there will let you know if you are turning or holding a heading.

Altimeter. Whether you're wearing a wrist or chest altimeter, look at it briefly like you would look at a clock or a speedometer. Get an idea of what the altimeter reading is to the nearest 500 feet. (If you have a digital altimeter, you can read the hundred feet increments easily.)

Secondary or Left I. Look towards the left-side instructor, preferably right at his eyes. Shout the altitude you read to him. Shouting it will help you remember it during your debriefing. He may even hear it and remember it himself. If you are given a body position correction signal, do what you think the instructor is telling you to do, then look back at him for an "OK" or for another signal. Once you get an okay, proceed to the next step. If you received several correction signals while looking at the I, it might be wise to briefly check your altitude again.

Primary or Right I. Repeat the actions you just did for the left-side I to the right-side I. Once you have received an okay, it is time to move onto the next step.

Three PRCPs or PPCTs. Practice RipCord Pulls or Practice Pilot Chute Throws. You will do three of these using coordinated arm movements, placing your left hand just above your head and your right hand on the deployment device which is either a ripcord or the bottom of the container if it has a hand deployed pilot chute. The reason for the left hand's position is to prevent a tendency to roll like a weather vane in a high wind or drop your head low like a dive-bomber. (Ask your instructor.) A practice deployment is done using the following steps.

For ripcord handle equipped gear, LOOK down the right side of your body towards the ripcord.

Maintain the body's arch (Note: If this is a hand-deployed system, you don't do this action.)

REACH for the ripcord on a ripcord equipped rig or for the pilot chute's top on a hand-deployed system using a coordinated motion (described by your instructor and above). Remember, for ripcord equipped rigs, you can use your eyes to guide your right hand to the ripcord. (If you have a hand-deployed system, there is no need to use your eyes for this action.) Your left hand should move to just above your head as your right hand goes to the ripcord. Maintain the body's arch.

TOUCH the ripcord or pilot chute's top with your right hand (called the Practice Touch). Maintain the body's arch.

ARCH: Return to the normal arched position for stable freefall.

Second circle of awareness. This is an exact repeat of the first circle of awareness, but by now, you're quite a bit lower. What you're looking for is a sense of how long it took you to do the tasks above, and how long you have until it is "PULL TIME" (about 4,500 feet AGL).

Fun and awareness time. For the remainder of the freefall portion of this skydive, you are encouraged to look around and enjoy what is happening. About every four to six seconds, briefly check your altimeter. If you like, you can glance towards either or both Is too. These checks are called short circles of awareness because they do not require eye to eye contact and an OK from your Instructors for you to continue on in the skydive.

Five-five Waveoff. When you're about 5,500 feet AGL, it is important to let your Is know that you are altitude aware and that you're getting ready to do the most important part of the skydive — deploying the parachute to save your life. Your waveoff signal to them is done by waving your hands over the front of your head. This tells your instructors that you are aware of your altitude and that you are about to deploy your parachute system.

The real pull. Now that you have signaled them that you're about to deploy your parachute system, take a real deep breath, savoring the last few seconds of clean air and freefall. Then, in a smooth and deliberate action, execute THE REAL PULL: ARCH, LOOK (only for ripcord equipped rigs), REACH, PULL (and for hand deployed systems, add the action THROW the pilot chute). Just like you did the practice pulls, except this time, you pull for real. Remember, if you have a ripcord equipped rig, you will want to hold onto the ripcord so that you don't have to pay a ripcord replacement fee. If you have a hand-deployed system, you must throw/release the pilot chute into the slipstream of air beside you in order to effect the deployment of your parachute system.

Pull Thousand. As you deploy your parachute system, you follow your right hand with your eyes back to the arch position, ensuring that you still have the ripcord or have released the pilot chute. As you initiate the pull action, your right-side instructor lets go of you and clears the area to reduce the turbulent airflow over your back so your pilot chute will get a better bite of air.

Two Thousand. Use your eyes to check over your right shoulder for the start of the parachute's deployment.

Three Thousand. By now, you should feel the first stages of opening shock. Continue the count for another two seconds to "Five Thousand" or until you feel the opening shock. Once your lines stretch out and your canopy starts deploying, the reserve-side I can no longer stay up with you. He lets go of you so as to not interfere with the deployment of your parachute and he clears the area in preparation to deploying his parachute.

Four Thousand
Five Thousand

Check. If you haven't had the opening shock by now, you should take your right hand and move it over to the left side of your ribcage, where your reserve ripcord is located. Of course, this will be discussed more thoroughly in the *Skydiving Emergencies* chapter, so we will assume that everything worked fine this time.

Check canopy: Is it rectangular? You bet. (It's a good parachute.)

Check ahead: Make sure that you're not going to run into anyone else in the air.

Controllability check: Does it flare properly? Does it turn properly. Follow the 3S rule or the RST rule. Is it square, stable, and steerable or is it rectangular, stable, and turnable.

Stow your ripcord (if you have one) inside your jumpsuit so that you don't lose it and have to pay the lost-ripcord fee. Do not slip the ripcord handle over your wrist. If you go through power lines, the metal might conduct electricity to your arm.

Steering for the landing area/canopy descent.

At this point, the procedures are the same as for the AFF, static line or IAD jumps described earlier. However, the instructors will probably beat you down to the ground and be in the landing area waiting for your triumphant return to earth. You will have a real desire to ask them how you performed, but they are trained to ask you about the dive first to get your impressions during the "walk and talk" debrief before telling you their (and perhaps the video camera's) perceptions of how the skydive went.

FREEFALL HAND SIGNALS

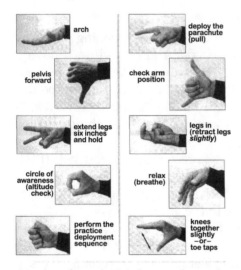

USPA Hand Signals
(courtesy USPA)

You've done it! It's been a long day and you have accomplished and learned so much. You have a greater appreciation for the air, aviation, weather and especially yourself. You notice the wind, its direction and velocity. Weather no longer provides *nice days* and *lousy days*, now they are *jumpable* or *terrible*. You begin to look up and you notice many things you have never seen before. Canopy nylon has a great aroma all its own. And you have a warm feeling of newfound confidence. After all, anyone can jump (falling comes naturally), but few people will. You did it and you are proud. You have conquered another fear, that of falling. It's just like when you learned to swim, only better.

Your instruction does not end with your first jump. You will be carefully supervised until you acquire your first license. Then the challenges change but the learning continues as you work on your skydiving proficiency. Always remember to ask your instructor about any techniques that are not clear to you.

> You know it is Spring when the four feet of snow, which covered the runway making it impossible to jump, have melted to one foot of mud, making it impossible to jump. *—The Spotter Newsmagazine*

Chapter Three

Parachuting Down Through the Ages
A Brief History

During the last ten centuries, parachutes and skydiving have passed through three basic developmental stages. The earliest occurred before the balloon and other aircraft, before there was an actual need. The second took place during the last three centuries when there was a requirement to be able to escape damaged balloons, airplanes and spacecraft. The last stage has been taking place from the late 1950s to the present within the sport of skydiving. The sport requires significantly different equipment, and since 1960 there have been more improvements to the parachute than in all previously recorded history.

1100s. There is evidence the Chinese amused themselves by jumping from high places with rigid umbrella-like structures. Early accounts are impossible to verify due to the lack of recorded data and it should be noted that most parachutes were one of a kind; there was no standardization until World War I. Further, after careful study, one suspects that many of these early pioneers con-

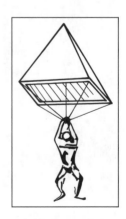

da Vinci's parachute

fused vertical descent with horizontal flight. They probably wished to emulate the birds, not the down of a thistle.

1495. Leonardo da Vinci's parachute was pyramid-shaped and was held open by four wooden poles. There is no evidence that he constructed any working models; he left only a sketch.

1595. Fausto Veranzio's parachute consisted of a square wooden frame covered with canvas and it is claimed he jumped from a tower in Venice in either 1595 or 1617.

1687. One of the earliest written accounts of parachuting comes from Siam. According to the French envoy, one of the king's tumblers would jump from high

Veranzio's parachute

places with two large umbrellas. The launch point must have been quite high as the wind sometimes carried him into trees, roof tops and occasionally the river.

1783. Sebastian Lenormand jumped from a tower with a 14-foot diameter parachute hoping to perfect a way to escape burning buildings. The Montgolfier brothers made their first balloon flight. Later, the Montgolfier brothers tested various parachute designs. In one experiment, a sheep was safely lowered on a seven-foot canopy.

Lenormand jumps from a rooftop in Montpellier, France

1785. J. P. Blanchard devised the collapsible silk parachute. Prior to this all canopies had been held open by a rigid framework. There is some evidence that he jumped from a balloon in 1793, and he did break a leg about this time.

1797. Andre Jacques Garnerin gets credit for being the first real parachutist because he made so many jumps, beginning with one from 2,000 feet (600m) over Paris. In 1802 he made a jump from 8,000 feet over London with a silk canopy some 23 feet in diameter. It oscillated terribly, making him airsick.

1804. A Frenchman named Bourget jumped with a collapsible canopy. Lelandes, a French astronomer, added a vent to his canopy to reduce the oscillations and it worked.

Garnerin descends over London in 1802

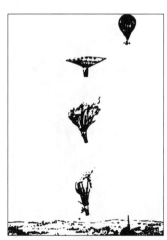

Robert Cocking, the first parachuting fatality

1808. A Polish balloonist named Jodaki Kuparento made the first emergency jump when his balloon caught fire over Warsaw.

Early 1800s. Sir George Cayley, an English aviation pioneer, was the first to propose an inverted cone canopy. His was very unstable. This design is being investigated again today. Lorenz Hengler, a German, made several jumps from a balloon at 30 to 120 meters.

1837. Robert Cocking released his inverted cone

parachute over Lea Green in England and fell to his death when it collapsed. It was 107 feet in circumference and weighed over 200 lbs. The release was on the balloon, not the canopy, and it is supposed that he may have wrapped the release line around his wrist to obtain a better grip. This would have jerked him upward into the cone, breaking it.

1838. John Wise twice permitted his balloon to explode at 13,000 feet over the U.S. Each time, the underside of the envelope inverted assuming a parachute shape and lowering him safely.

1887. Captain Tom Baldwin invented the harness in the U.S. He would ride up in the balloon, sitting on a trapeze bar. The apex of the silk canopy was tied to the trapeze. When ready to jump, he would simply slip off. He dispensed with the basket entirely.

1890. Paul Letteman and Kathe Paulus are credited with being the first to use the *remote automatic sack type* parachute; the design is still used for cargo drops today. The apex of the canopy is tied to the inside of the canvas bag with breakcord. The canopy and lines are then folded into the bag and

Kathe Paulus was the first German professional parachutist. The folded exhibition attached type was used by many of the early jumpers. Here the suspension lines were attached to a concentration ring made of wood with a tennis racket-like mesh. The lines were coiled on the mesh and the canopy was accordion-folded on the lines. Two perpendicular tie ropes secured the canopy to the ring. A ring knife was used to release the canopy and there was a breakcord from the apex of the canopy to the balloon.

Mike Blodgett models a variation of the pack on the aircraft type parachute. The container is fitted with a Ford steering wheel and is laced together with string. Two thin leather leg straps are missing from the model. Newspaper is packed between the folds of the canopy and loops of line.

The Broadwick Coatpack

the mouth is tied closed with breakcord. The risers lead out to the load and the bag is affixed to the balloon or airplane.

1901. Charles Broadwick designed the *pack on the aviator* type parachute. His *coatpack* was laced together with break-cord. A static line broke the lacing and pulled out the canopy.

1903. The Wright brothers made the first powered flight and parachute development picked up speed.

1908. A. Leo Stevens invents the ripcord in New York. Georgia Thompson (Tiny) Broadwick begins her 1,100-jump career by parachuting from a balloon over Raleigh, North Carolina. She used the parachutes designed by her foster father, Charles Broadwick.

1911. An Italian named Joseph Pino gets credit for design-ing the pilot chute. He mounted it on an aviator's cap and it was held open by a small framework. When he jumped, the pilot chute was supposed to remove the helmet and pull the canopy from the *knapsack* on his back. Grant Morton didn't use any pack at all when he jumped from a Wright Model B aircraft over Venice, California. He simply rolled and folded the canopy in his arms. When he jumped, he just threw it into the air. While this was the first non-static line jump, it may not be the first freefall jump; there is a question of interpreta-tion. S. L. Van Meter of Lexington, Kentucky, filed for a patent on a *soaring type parachute*. A pilot in distress could pull a rip-cord releasing the canopy into the air and it would pull him free of the aircraft. G. E. Kotelnikov had his parachute designs rejected by the Russian government; they felt that the presence of a parachute would tempt pilots to jump rather than attempt to save the aircraft.

1912. When Captain Albert Berry made his jump from an aircraft over Jefferson Barracks, Missouri, his parachute was packed in a metal cylinder attached to the underside of the plane over the axle. He just climbed down to the axle, slipped into the harness and jumped. As he fell away, his weight pulled the canopy from the container. About this same time, M. Hervieu was making dummy drops from the Eiffel Tower. M. Bonnet successfully lowered an airplane fuselage with a dummy from a balloon over France. Frederick Law made a jump from the Statue of Liberty.

1913. M. Adolphe Pegoud successfully tested a soaring type parachute over Chateaufort, France. Captain M. Douade designed a canopy for lowering entire aircraft but World War I canceled his development plans.

Tiny Broadwick became the first woman to jump from an *airplane* when Glenn Martin took her aloft over Los Angeles. Later that year she became the first woman to make a water jump when she parachuted from a hydroplane into Lake Michigan.

1914. Tiny Broadwick was demonstrating the parachute to the Army in San Diego when, on her fourth jump, the static line caught briefly on the tail section

Tiny Broadwick is credited with many parachuting firsts

of the Martin Trainer. Fearful it might happen again, she cut the line. On the last demonstration jump, she pulled it herself and made history: the first jump on a *manually operated* parachute.

1917. Most nations adopted parachutes for use in balloons (there was no time to evaluate the situation once the hydrogen-filled balloon was hit by enemy fire) and airplanes, as the aerial portion of World War I heated up. All parachutes, operated on the static line principle, were too heavy and much too weak. Juseke Fuji of Stanton, New Mexico, filed a patent on a manually-operated parachute. And late in the year, J. Floyd Smith wore a manually operated parachute of his own design while flying.

1918. Floyd Smith filed for a patent on his manually operated parachute.

1919. Leslie Irvin developed a static line-operated parachute and filed for a patent.

The Army set up a parachute design center at McCook Field in Dayton and staffed it with Floyd Smith and Major E. L.

The Smith Aerial Life Pack was the first of the modern manually operated parachutes

Hoffman. On April 28th, Leslie Irvin made a freefall jump to test the product as Floyd Smith piloted the plane. The manually operated parachute was basically the same one that Smith had designed earlier. Irvin immediately formed *Irving Air Chutes* and built the first 300 units for the Army. A rushed typist mistakenly added the "g" to Irvin and the company kept it for some 50 years. The McCook Field team consisted of Hoffman, Smith, Irvin, Guy M. Ball, "Jimmy" M. Russell, J. J. Higgins, and M/Sgt. Ralph W. Bottreill. Most remained in the parachute field and were responsible for virtually all of the parachute development over the next 30 years.

1922. Lt. Harold R. Harris became the first to make an emergency freefall jump from a disabled airplane. He had difficulty locating the ripcord handle and freefell some 2,000 feet. It is interesting to contrast this jump with all those made in World War I; they were all static lined. One month later, the Caterpillar Club was established. Those who were saved by parachute were awarded a small gold (silk spinning) caterpillar pin.

1924. The parachute rigging school was opened at the Naval Air Station at Lakehurst, New Jersey.

1925. Steven Budreau, an Army instructor, made a jump from 7,000 feet and freefell to 3,500 feet over Selfridge Field, Michigan. He proved that the body could fall in a stable position and not go out of control.

1926. Charles Lindbergh makes his fourth emergency jump. Later that same year, James Clark made the first camera jump.

1927. Charles Lindbergh made the first transatlantic solo flight. This was also the year that Security Parachute Co. was established as Johnny's Parachute Loft at the Oakland Airport, and the Switlik Company began making parachutes in Trenton, New Jersey.

1928. General Billy Mitchell had six military men jump from a Martin bomber at Kelly Field, Texas, and set up a machine gun. This was the first demonstration of the usefulness of paratroops.

1929. E. L. Hoffman filed for a patent on his triangular shaped canopy. The quick release box was patented in Great Britain thus making a single point release harness possible.

1930. The Russians stage the first parachute meet at the Sports Festival. Amateurs competed to see who could land nearest a specified target.

1932. Forty parachutists competed at the National Air Races at Roosevelt Field, New York. The organizational work is credited to Joe Crane who persuaded the National Aeronautic Association to formally sanction sport parachuting competitions. Later he formed the National Parachute Jumpers Association, a predecessor of the USPA.

1933. The Russians unified all sport parachute clubs into a national organization. Later they staged the first

From the infield of the racetrack of the fairgrounds at Rochester, NH, Charles Dame goes aloft for a triple parachute jump. The three parachute packs are visible just above his head. (September 1927)

mass drop when 62 parachutists jumped from three bombers. This was also the year Wiley Post made the first solo flight around the world.

1934. Floyd Smith published a magazine article describing freefall techniques for delayed (freefall) jumps. The Forest Service experimented with the dropping of fire fighters to battle forest fires. Later the *SmokeJumpers* were established. American Victor Herman set an altitude record jumping from 24,000 feet in the Soviet Union.

1935. The first free-drop parachute tower, some 125 feet high, was built in Hightstown, New Jersey. This was the year that the infamous DC-3 made its first flight.

1936. By this time, the Russians had established 559 training towers and 115 training stations. In the U.S. during the late '30s, there were some steerable canopies such as the Hoffman Triangle and the Hart designs. But designers turned back to the non-steerable models in the '40s. Colonel Wateau of France proposed the Fédération Aéronautique Internationale (FAI) accept parachuting as a sport.

1937. The first flight of the Twin Beech. This aircraft was to be used extensively for parachuting in the 1960s and lead to the formation of ten-person teams, the number of skydivers it would hold.

1938. Floyd Smith and Lyman Ford approached Henry R. Mallory at the 100-year-old Cheney Brothers Mills in Manchester, Connecticut, proposing to form a parachute company. Pioneer Parachute Co. was established and Smith designed a completely new line of parachutes. World War II was not far off. Nylon is invented by duPont.

1941. The Germans dropped 14,000 paratroopers onto the island of Crete. In the U.S., Arthur H. Starnes made a record freefall from 30,800 feet to 1,500 feet. Carefully monitored by doctors, he proved that properly equipped aviators could survive long freefalls from high altitudes. December 7th: The Japanese attack Pearl Harbor and the supply of silk to the U.S. parachute industry is shut off.

1944. Frank Derry applied his *Derry Slots* to some 28-foot military reject canopies to bolster the dwindling Forest Service inventory. This was a significant action, as he was modifying surplus canopies for steerability for the first time.

1946. The National Parachute Jumpers Association changed its name to the National Parachute Jumpers-Riggers, Inc.

1947. Charles E. Yeager made the first supersonic flight over the United States. More improvements in the parachute would be needed. Lew Sanborn was issued parachuting license A-1, A. R. Garrison B-1 and Joe Crane C-1.

1948. At the prompting of Joe Crane, the NAA proposed to the Fédération Aéronautique Internationale, the international body which governs sport aviation competition and records, that parachuting be accepted. The Commission Internationale de Parachutisme was established and Crane was appointed the first U.S. delegate. Leo "Birdman" Valentin developed the spread, face-to-earth freefall position and later the method of using the arms and legs to make controlled turns and barrel rolls. He was killed in 1956 while using large plywood wings to extend his freefall time. One wing hit the plane on exit and broke, placing him in a spin. He activated both parachutes but they tangled around him. By now, the Italians had established 48 local parachute clubs.

1949. The French government set up ten public sport parachuting centers. The techniques of stabilized freefall were further refined.

1950. Captain Richard V. Wheeler bails out at a record 42,449 feet. The first meeting of the Commission Internationale de Parachutisme of the FAI was held in Paris.

1951. Five European nations fielded teams to the First World Parachuting Championships in Yugoslavia. The Commission Internationale de Parachutism (CIP) adopts world record classifications.

1954. Fred Mason, an Army sergeant stationed in Europe, represented the U.S. at the Second World Parachuting Championships at St. Yan, France. Eight nations were represented. Richard Hart filed a patent on an extended "T" cut in standard flat circular canopies.

1955. Jacques Andre Istel visited France, learned the freefall techniques and returned home to form the first U.S. parachute team. Raymond Young coined the term *skydiving*.

1956. The first full U.S. Team was fielded for the Third World Championships in Moscow, using donated equipment. They finished sixth out of the ten nations entered.

1957. The NPJ-R evolved into the Parachute Club of America. Jacques Istel and Lew Sanborn filed for a patent on the deployment sleeve.

1958. Lyle Hoffman and James Pearson of the Seattle Skydivers made the first baton pass in Vancouver, B.C. A month later, Steve Snyder and Charlie Hillard made the first in the U.S. at Fort Bragg, North Carolina. This was the year that the Army reversed its stand against sport parachuting and actually began to foster and encourage it. Military parachute clubs blossomed nationwide overnight. The U.S. Team was picked at an elimination meet for the first time and the winners went on to compete at the Fourth W.P.C. in Bratislava, Czechoslovakia. The U.S. finished sixth out of fourteen. Jacques Istel files for a patent on the *three panel T* and *double blank* steerable canopy modifications.

1959. Lew Sanborn was issued license D-1. The Strategic Army Corps Parachute Team was formed in Fort Bragg. Two years later they were renamed the Army Parachute Team and soon after they adopted the nickname *Golden Knights*. Dave Burt developed the parascuba concept. Jacques Istel's Parachutes Incorporated opened the first commercial sport parachuting center in the U.S. in Orange, Massachusetts. In the late '50s, the sport of parachuting began to grow and equipment played a large part in this development. The sleeve, introduced from France, made opening forces tolerable, and military surplus parachutes were cheap. With a little work, a 28' Air Force back parachute could be made steerable, a sleeve could be added and D rings for the reserve attachment could be installed. At the urging of Parachutes Incorporated, Pioneer began to manufacture a line of sport equipment. Steve Snyder began work on an automatic parachute-activating device designed to meet the particular requirements of the sport parachutist. He incorporated as *Steve Snyder Enterprises* and filed for a patent on the *Sentinel* the following the year.

1960. Captain Joseph W. Kittinger, Jr. stepped out of a balloon gondola at 102,800 feet over New Mexico with only a 6' stabilizing chute. During the freefall to 18,000 feet, he reached a terminal velocity of 702 mph.; the trip took four-and-a-half minutes. Curt Hughes and Loy Brydon patented the famous TU steerable canopy modification. The Army parachutists swept the U.S. Team tryouts and competed in Sofia, Bulgaria. Barbara Gray of North Carolina and

Kittinger reached 702 mph in his plunge from 102,800 feet

Sherrie Buck of California were the first female entries from the U.S. Lew Sanborn makes the first successful camera jump.

1961. Ted Strong, coach of the West Point Parachute Team, returned to civilian life and established a parachute company in the Boston area. This was the year that the National Collegiate Parachuting League was established. In Arizona, four employees of Parachutes Incorporated, Jacques Istel, Lew Sanborn, Nate Pond and Bill Jolly, established two world records, the first for the U.S. Pierre Lemoigne filed his basic Para-Sail/Para-Commander patent.

1962. The first PCA Instructor/Examiner Conference was held in Phoenix and 19 candidates took part. PCA membership was beginning to climb and had already reached 6,000. The U.S. hosted the 6th World Championships at Orange, Massachusetts; 24 nations were represented. For the first time, the U.S. fielded a full women's team. After the meet, some northeast parachutists tried sleeving and jumping Lemoigne's Para-Sail. With the addition of some steering lines, Pioneer developed it into the Para-Commander. It was demonstrated at the 1963 Nationals in Issaquah, Washington, but conservative Pioneer was reluctant to market it.

1963. A combined Army and Air Force team bettered the Soviet Union's group altitude record of 37,000' when they exited a C-130 at 43,500' over El Centro, California. The

Federal Aviation Administration published the first formal rules for sport parachuting, thus recognizing the establishment of the activity. Lemoigne filed for another patent on the Para-Commander concept.

1964. Domina Jalbert of Boca Raton, Florida, filed for a patent on his ram-air inflated Para-Foil canopy. In the early part of the year, Loy Brydon helped Security develop the Crossbow (XBO) parachute system; the first sport piggyback, it was revolutionary. The canopy resembled the Para-Commander and its availability forced Pioneer to the market. The U.S. Team chose to use the PC in the XBO system and in 1964 they dazzled the World at the 7th W.P.C. in Leutkirch, West Germany. Six years after the first baton pass, six jumpers piled out of two aircraft over Arvin, California, and formed the first six man star. Bob Buquor caught it all on film. This was the year the Chute Shop (later North American Aerodynamics) was established in Flemington, New Jersey. The Army Parachute Team made an assault on the world records and conquered 55% of them. This was the first time that any one nation had held a majority of parachute records.

1965. The Arvin Good Guys formed the first eight-man star. This year will also be well remembered for another reason. It was at this time that the commercial airline industry ganged up on the sport by encouraging the FAA to enact very restrictive regulations. Jumpers united under PCA and argued their case by writing letters and attending the hearing. The parachutists put up such an impressive show, the Air Transport Association and others didn't even bother to show up for the rebuttal session in the afternoon. Rod Pack made the first chuteless jump.

1967. The Parachute Club of America is renamed the United States Parachute Association. The first ten-man star was completed over Taft, California. A week later it was duplicated over Elsinore. Then six months later a ten-man star competition was staged. In the '60s, most jumpers used non-steerable reserves in the belief that an unmodified canopy opened more reliably. Steerable modifications to reserve canopies hadn't been approved by the FAA and few people had them. Actually few were known until the reserve was used. Toward the end of the decade, some lofts acquired approval for single or multiple *doghouses*. Bill Newell founded the Bob Buquor Memorial Star Crest.

1968. Steve Snyder performed developmental work on the ParaWing and filed for a patent on his OSI or *Opening Shock Inhibitor*, a heavy web strap that wrapped around the lines.

The sport received a great deal of publicity that year when Bob Sinclair took Johnny Carson out at 12,500 feet on a buddy jump. Sinclair held the entertainer's harness until he pulled his ripcord. The videotape was shown on the *Tonight Show*. Strong Enterprises developed the Stylemaster harness/container system for the U.S. Team. It

Johnny Carson receives his final equipment check prior to his first jump, a freefall from 12,500 feet

incorporated a number of revolutionary design features.

1969. Steve Snyder began to market the Para-Plane, a ram-air Jalbert canopy. He and Dick Morgan made an intense marketing effort to prove that a square canopy was superior to the round one for the accuracy event. As interest in relative work increased in the early '70s, many jumpers selected squares, for their superior glide angle, to get them back to the drop zone. The round, bulky PC was dead and the squares cornered the market except for some new lightweight circular canopies. Snyder filed for a patent on his PCR or *Pilot Chute Controlled* reefing system.

1970. A four-way sequential relative work team event was introduced to the Nationals in Plattsburg, New York. Steve Snyder filed for patents on a new ram-air canopy suspension system and the Mark 2000 automatic opener. The first 20-way star is built over Elsinore.

1972. The ten-way event was introduced to the National Championships held in Tahlequah, Oklahoma. The name of the game was speed stars, or forming the circle as soon as possible after exit. Interest developed in the team events and the biggest social event of the winter jumping season was the Thanksgiving meet in Zephyrhills, Florida. The U.S. hosted the World Championships in Tahlequah, Oklahoma. The first boogie was hosted by Garth Taggart in Richmond, Indiana.

1973. The Army Team's DC-3 crashed on the way to a demonstration jump killing all fourteen aboard.

1974. A world record 31-way star was formed over Elsinore, California. North American Aerodynamics acquired the rights to the Jalbert Para Foil and began limited production. In the early '70s relative work boomed and buyers demanded parachutes which were smaller and lighter. Smaller meant the last team member would be closer to the door for the speed event. Lighter meant more freefall time, since all would fall slower and with a greater range of speed. Conventional harness/container systems were developed, such as Strong's Fastback with a sloping top so it wouldn't hang up in the top of the door on exit and the POP TOP reserve which was very thin and clean. But by 1974, the equipment pendulum was swinging again and RW jumpers were returning to the piggyback; its clean lines made the flyng better and slowed the fall. Jumpsuits grew bigger and bigger.

1975. A 32-man star was formed over Tahlequah and Snyder's Strato-Cloud went into production. About this time the FAA relaxed its insistence that manufacturers design and build entire parachute systems in order to acquire approval, and this resulted in a great proliferation of small manufacturers producing harness/container assemblies specifically for the sport. Bill Booth eliminated the ripcord on his Wonderhog assembly and substituted a throw-out pilot chute. USPA moved its headquarters from Monterey, California, to Washington, D.C.

1976. The year of the U.S. bicentennial saw a new social event at the Nationals, the *Boogie*. This was a four-day affair between major jumping events, filled with non-evaluated

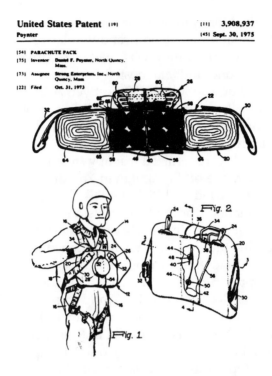

United States Patent [19]   [11]   3,908,937
Poynter   [45] Sept. 30, 1975

[54] PARACHUTE PACK
[75] Inventor   Daniel F. Poynter, North Quincy, Mass.
[73] Assignee   Strong Enterprises, Inc., North Quincy, Mass.
[22] Filed   Oct. 31, 1973

Fig. 2

Fig. 1

jumping, manufacturers' displays, seminars, canoe trips and fun. It was highly successful and promised to be an annual event. Canopy Relative Work was demonstrated at the Nationals. For the first time, every accuracy competitor jumped a square canopy.

1977. Mike Barber and Kirk Morrison made the first tandem jump over DeLand. The large group event was changed from speed stars to sequential, and team events became infinitely more popular than unaccompanied flight. Manufacturers catered to the relative worker. The throw-out pilot chute was very popular and many alternatives to the Capewell canopy releases appeared. Never before in the history of the parachute had so many users spent so much developmental effort without governmental financial inspiration. Bill Dause is first to reach 5,000 jumps.

1978. Para-Flite introduced a ram-air reserve canopy. USPA memberships continued to climb, the equipment became even more exotic and the sport continued its vigorous growth. More jumpers than ever became proficient at sequential relative work, and canopy relative work became more popular. Bill Ottley was made executive director of USPA. Richmond, Indiana, hosted the nationals for the first time and the boogie was the biggest yet. A DC-3 crashed on takeoff but all survived. Para-Flite licensed other firms to manufacture ram-air canopies. FAA extended the reserve re-pack cycle from 60 to 120 days.

1979. USPA recognized canopy relative work. BASE jumps were made off El Capitan in Yosemite National Park. Mike Truffer started a tabloid titled *Skydiving*. An all-women 24-way formation was made over Elsinore.

1980. Fuel prices climbed. Several centers adopted piggy-back gear for student use. Skydivers opened the Super Bowl. Craig Fronk and friends made the first North Pole jump. USPA adopted rules for Para-ski National Championships. Elsinore was flooded. The 1st World cup of CRW was at Zephyrhills and it saw the completion of a 14-way stack.

1981. The Nationals were held in Muskogee, Oklahoma, for the first time. Relative Work World Championships were hosted by Zephyrhills, Florida. Carl and Jean Boenish start-ed *BASE* magazine covering jumps from fixed objects. A 27-way night formation was made over Perris, California. The USPA approved the Accelerated Freefall Program. Canada initiated a Progressive FreeFall Program similar to the U.S. AFF Program.

1982. Canopy Relative Work became part of the Nationals for the first time and a 20-way formation was made. CRW had its first World Cup competition. USPA Headquarters moved to Alexandria, Virginia. Some centers began using square canopies for student training. *Mr. Bill* jumping began. Twelve skydivers died in a crash of a Twin Beech at Taft, California. U.S. fatalities dropped to twenty-nine.

1983. Ted Strong and Bill Booth began experimenting with Tandem jumping. The FAA decided not to deregulate sport parachuting. The CSPA made use of automatic releas-es by students mandatory. Rising waters closed Elsinore again. Jumpsuits got tighter for increased fall rates. A 72-way formation was built over DeLand. The FAA approved the use of auto gas in some aircraft. USPA initiated Eagle and Falcon freefall awards.

1984. USPA introduced the Pro Rating for demonstration jumpers. Frenchman Roch Charmet made jump number 10,000 in Sheridan, Oregon. The FAA adopted TSO C-23c standards for parachutes. An all-women 48-way formation was completed in DeLand. USPA approved the use of square canopies by students. B.J. Worth jumped off the Eiffel Tower for a James Bond film.

1985. Ted Strong developed a drogue to slow tandem jumpers. John Stanford and Phil Huff experimented with up-skiing: using a round canopy to tow skiers up the hill. A 23-stack canopy formation was built over Spaceland Paracenter in Houston. Dave Huber made 250 jumps in 24 hours in Issaquah, Washington. Bill Dause logged 100 hours of freefall time and 9,000 jumps. Don Kellner made jump number 10,000 in Hazelton, Pennsylvania. Annual U.S. fatalities dropped to twenty-four.

1986. Paul Poppenhager, Jr. made 60 jumps in ten hours, packing his own main. An all-female 60-way formation was built over DeLand. A 100-way formation was built over Muskogee, Oklahoma. Nearly 2,000 turned out for the Freakbrother Convention, renamed the World Skydiving Convention, in Quincy, Illinois, and a 120-way formation was built. The first Tandem fatality was recorded in Connecticut. The Olympic Committee recognized the FAI as the official representative of hang gliding, soaring and parachuting. Warning labels appeared on jump gear. Paragliding with foot-launched ram-air canopies became popular in Europe.

1987. Steve Snyder withdrew the Sentinel automatic activation device from the market after 27 years because of product liability considerations. Ram-air canopies were approved for student use in the U.K. Greg Robertson saved a jumper rendered unconscious, by diving down and pulling her reserve. A 126-way formation was built over Koksije, Belgium. Cheryl Sterns and Russell Fish each made 255 jumps in a 24-hour period in Lodi, California. USPA received assurances from major airlines that parachutes will be allowed as carry-on baggage. New York deregulated skydiving. A 32-

way CRW formation was built over Lapalisse, France.

1988. The Parachute Industry Association held its winter meeting on a cruise ship between Florida and the Bahamas. Skydiving opened the Olympics in Seoul. Rocky Kenoyer made 403 jumps in 24 hours in Snohomish, Washington. USPA changed the BSR's to require ram-air main canopies, automatic activation devices and piggyback containers for students. A 144-way formation was completed over Quincy, Illinois. Tom Pirus accumulated 132 hours of freefall time in 8,000 jumps. The Perris drop zone logged 62,041 jumps in 1988.

1989. A 73-way female formation was made over Montgomery, New York. USPA convinced the FAA not to release a detrimental update of Part 105.

1990. B.J. Worth jumped into a cave in Mexico. A 16-way female CRW stack was built over Madera, California. Helmut Cloth introduced the Cypres AAD. Bill Dause logged 156 hours of freefall time. The first freestyle meet was held in Bryan, Texas.

1991. The PIA held its first international symposium in Orlando, Florida. SSE put the Mark 2000 AAD back on the market. USPA's building was dedicated to Bill Ottley. Don Kellner logged jump number 15,000. *Point Break*, a film on surfing with a skydiving sequence, brought thousands of students to local drop zones.

1992. A Twin Otter crashed in Perris killing sixteen. This caused a major re-emphasis on the use of seatbelts by jumpers. As a result, new laws were written holding the pilot responsible for ensuring that seatbelts are fastened prior to the aircraft being moved. The CIP changed "relative work" to "formation skydiving." The Army Team got a vertical wind tunnel.

1993. Elsinore flooded again. Lyle Cameron died while piloting an airplane in Honduras. The IRS tried to collect excise taxes on fuel used in jump planes. POPS membership reached four thousand.

1994. *Drop Zone* and *Terminal Velocity*, full-length feature films on skydiving, were premiered. Airtec sold Cypres number 10,000. Bill Booth took another group of skydivers to the North Pole.

1995. Cheryl Sterns logged her ten thousandth jump. PIA set up their web site. PIA held a meeting in Germany. A Queen Air crashed on takeoff at West Point, Virginia, killing 12 plus one on the ground. Ted Strong demonstrated the Quad Pod, a seat holding four people flying under a large ram-air canopy. Sit flying became popular.

1996. USPA turned 50 and PIA turned twenty. The first USPA-sponsored Freestyle National Championships were held. USPA's Basic Instructor Course was formalized and course directors were rated. The first skydiving CD-ROM was published. An international team built a 297-way formation over Russia.

1997. Former president George Bush addressed the opening ceremonies of the International Parachute Symposium in Houston. In March, he made his second jump in Yuma, Arizona, an AFF, Level I jump. The first was in 1944 near Chi Chi Jima. USPA stops the IRS from taxing jump aircraft flights. Several jump aircraft crashed during the year.

Dan Poynter presents George Bush with a Switlik Quick Attachable Seat parachute identical to the one he used in 1944.

1998. Three die jumping at the south pole. A world record 246 formation is made over Skydive Chicago. Kurt Gaebel starts the National Skydiving League to foster competitive Formation Skydiving competition. Spaceball (a weighted tennis ball/badminton combination) makes its debut in Florida. Sub-100' canopies make their appearance. The 1st World Air games are held in Turkey.

1999. Lew Sanborn, D-1, marks 50 years of continuous activity in the sport. Blade Swooping becomes popular. Adrian Nichols uses a winged suit to track nine miles from 30,000 feet. The PIA Symposium is in San Diego; over 1,500 attend. Five skydiving aircraft crashed. 572 skydivers from 39 nations participate in the largest-ever civilian jump over Bangkok, Thailand. They included General Henry Shelton, chairman of the U.S. Joint Chiefs of Staff. The World Team '99 set a new world record by completing a 282-way in Ubon, Ratcharthania, Thailand.

2000. The USPA proposes a renovation to the training of student skydivers through an innovative and comprehensive "Integrated Student Program." Several assaults on a 300-way formation were attempted but not achieved. High performance canopy flight competitions become more prevalent.

2001. FAR 105 (Parachute Operations) underwent major revisions and for the first time in 20 years, Tandem Jumping was no longer done by exemption to the FARs as it became an officially recognized activity with appropriate federal regulations. A four point 106-way sequential dive was competed at Skydive Cross Keys, NJ. Skydiving is shut down for one weekend in the United States following the attacks on the World Trade Center and the Pentagon. The USPA was successful in persuading the National Security Council to restore skydiver access to the airspace.

2002. The USPA's Integrated Student Program is formally adopted. The first successful quadra-plane diamond CRW formation is completed. A new women's world record formation of a 131-way was completed during the "Jump for the Cause" event at Perris Valley Skydiving in California. "Jump for the Cause is a non-profit organization of jumpers collecting donations for cancer research. The magic number 300-way is finally successfully completed over Skydive Arizona. Jumpers complete a 56-way canopy formation over Lake Wales, Florida, but without FAI judges to make it official.

2003. After two years of organized league competitions in the U.S., The FAI accepts a bid from the United States to host the first World Cup of Canopy Piloting (high performance canopy flight competition) at Perris Valley, California.

The gull sees farthest who flies highest. *—Richard Bach*

Chapter Four

Skydiving Emergencies
Causes, Avoidance and Corrective Actions

In the sport of skydiving there are a number of possible emergencies, happily all are rare. But since we are dealing with machines (aircraft), new elements (air and altitude), high closing speeds (relative speeds between freefalling jumpers as well as terminal velocity approaching the ground), mechanical devices (parachutes), obstacles (trees, power lines, etc.), and last but certainly not least, the human element (you and your instructor, pilot, and others), you must be educated in these areas; you must be properly prepared.

Canopy malfunctions and other emergencies are not common in sport parachuting but if one happens to you, once may be enough. Therefore, in this chapter a disproportionate amount of discussion is being devoted to the problems and a great deal of your training time will be expended on recognizing and coping with emergencies.

Emergency procedures are being given separate treatment here in their own chapter but they are not separate on the drop zone. They are mixed in with your other jump training. In chapter two we told you to do a number of things such as to cover your reserve ripcord handle in the airplane. In this chapter we will explain in detail *why* these cautions are necessary. Not all parachuting emergencies concern parachutes but all do concern parachuting. Injuries may be caused by a crash of the jump plane or a canopy ride into an unexpected pond. In the following pages we will cover almost everything that can go wrong and explain to you what to do it if does.

Both parachute equipment and skydiving instruction have changed tremendously in the last several years. Now that most parachutists are starting off with more dependable ram-air canopies, piggyback systems, automatic activation devices and more specialized professional training, the rate of injury, both fatal and non-fatal, has dropped and is expected to drop further.

Fatal injury statistics. Some statistics will help to orient our thinking. In the United States, over the last several years, an annual average of 33 people have been fatally injured while parachuting. The number rose to 44 in 1998, mostly due to an increase in canopy mishandling.

It must be emphasized that some of the categories listed did not themselves kill; the jumper died for failure to react properly to the situation. See the fatality summary published by the USPA in *Parachutist* magazine each year for the latest statistics. Following are the numbers for 2002.

21% were involved in **freefall or canopy collisions**. Some freefall collisions happen when two or more skydivers run into each other but most occur during opening because the skydivers have not separated far enough after relative work. Jumpers sometimes steer canopies into each other as they converge on the landing area.

12% **failed to pull the ripcord or pulled too low**. Some of these fatalities can be traced to medical problems such as heart disease or a history of blacking out. Others are simply unexplainable because it is impossible to interview the deceased jumper. Some of these fatalities may be due to hard pulls on the main where the jumper simply fails to pull the reserve. Many of the malfunctions that do not result in fatalities can be traced to a lost pull-out pilot chute handle. Other reasons are accidental reserve openings, pilot chute stuck in its throw-out pouch, accidental riser release and premature main opening.

Remember when sex was safe and skydiving was dangerous?

12% had **canopy malfunctions** where the main began to deploy and an equipment malfunction began a series of events that lead to a fatality. Three of the ten malfunctions were *pilot chutes in tow* where the pilot chute was deployed but the main canopy remained in, or partly in, the main container. Fortunately ram-air *square* canopies are less malfunction prone (one out of maybe 700 jumps) than round canopies (one out of about 250 for the Para-Commander class round). In fact, Roch Charmet of France made his first 5,000 jumps on a square without a malfunction.

Reserve-use statistics. There are also some interesting statistics on reserve use. One DZ reported just two cutaways for 4,862 first jump students. And, those minor malfunctions were due to line twists. Square canopies are very reliable compared to the rounds we used to use.

Be careful of canopy malfunction statistic comparisons. Main parachutes malfunction more often than reserve parachutes due to packing and wear. Mains are usually hastily packed by jumpers wanting to make the next load. Reserves are inspected and repacked slowly and carefully by a licensed parachute rigger every 120 days. And reserves are usually factory fresh with no prior use to result in worn parts.

But squares do malfunction sometimes. Nearly half of the malfunctions were due to knotted lines or slider hang-up. The rest of the main malfunctions are due to bag lock, broken lines, streamers, canopy damage, link problems and *other*.

12% had **reserve problems** that were usually main-reserve entanglements; some due to improper emergency procedures and some due to accidental container openings.

39% were **landing fatalities.** There were numerous landing fatalities in the past five years that were totally avoidable by using proper canopy control techniques. The majority of these were due to low altitude collisions or attempts to avoid collisions between jumpers resulting from their not paying

---

To venture is to risk one's life; not to venture is to lose one's reason to live. —*Jim Palmieri*

attention to where they were headed at landing time, and from the unfortunate propensity of people to play with their super high-performance canopies close to the ground in the act of what is called a "hook turn." These turns, spectacular as they are, yield a marked increase in downward and forward speed. When done at an inopportune time or altitude, they can and have resulted in spectacular "smash" landings in which the jumpers impact the ground in excess of 45-mph, literally pulverizing their skeletons. Historically, water, power lines and even moving trains have posed as landing obstacles. Higher performance ram-air canopies may be responsible for helping jumpers to avoid landing hazards, but a lack of common sense in the control of these canopies has also been responsible for numerous serious injuries and fatalities.

The numbers. USPA figures reveal there are some 302,000 people participating in skydiving each year. 34,000 are active skydivers and the rest are students. Of the 3.2-million jumps made each year, 268,000 are by students and the rest are by experienced skydivers.

Over the past ten years, there was an annual average of 33 fatal skydiving accidents in the United States yielding a rate of one fatality for every 97,000 jumps (at three jumps per day, this will take you quite some time) and one for every 9,150 participants. USPA estimates there is one fatality for every 30,000 student jumps. These jump figures can be compared with one fatality per 2,308 hang gliding flights and the one in 2,582 Americans who die each year in all accidental deaths (91,000 out of a total U.S. population of 235,000,000 in 1983). It should be pointed out that the above figures include all jumpers, both those who observe safety procedures and those who take chances. The figures even include some documented suicides.

It is interesting to compare fatal accident numbers with

The simple fact is that reserve parachute systems (container, ripcord, deployment system, canopy and pilot chute) can malfunction. It should be used only as a backup in a genuine emergency.

—Paul Sitter

other activities: in a recent year over 105 people perished scuba diving, 856 bicycling, over 7,000 drowned (365 in bathtubs), 1154 succumbed to bee stings, four died playing basketball, 1063 while boating, hang gliding lost 13, snowmobiling 60, water skiing 47, and 300 were even hit by lightning. Then there are other transportation statistics to compare: In a recent year, 50,000 people were killed in highway accidents, there were 1,171 boating fatalities, 235 airline deaths and 1,164 light aircraft *general aviation* fatalities.

Non-fatal injury statistics. What about non-fatal injuries? Most student injuries, other than bruises and scrapes, occur to ankles, backs and wrists. These injuries are usually caused by poor landings, frequently due to an improper flare when both toggles are pulled all the way down behind the jumper's hips, allowing the wrists to contact the ground first, when he or she falls backwards. Some instructors estimate that ten percent of the students were injured in the old days of round canopies. Rounds deposit their cargo much faster because they can't be flared. The result was many more leg and ankle injuries. So 90,000 students making 300,000 jumps could expect 6,000 injuries. Today, the rate is about one twisted ankle for every 2,500 jumps.

Some injuries are serious and some are not so serious. Occasionally, a small woman over 30 will break an ankle or leg on the first jump in an apparently soft landing. She may have a calcium deficiency.

By comparison, in 1985, 7,700 people were treated in hospital emergency rooms for injuries received in amusement park rides, 395,000 were treated for baseball injuries and 581,000 for bicycle injuries. In 1985 and 1986 there were 511 *reported* jet ski accidents and the Coast Guard figures that less than 25% of the casualties are reported. In Ontario in a recent summer, three people drowned while golf-ball diving using scuba gear to retrieve balls in golf course ponds.

The risk and the reward. Thousands of parachutists find

The sky is not the limit, the ground is. *—Allen Roulston*

jumping to be a great deal of fun, the ultimate outdoor, aviation recreation sport. You must weigh the risk and the reward; it is a personal decision.

Why we jump. The explanation used to be simple: jumpers were crazy. Some psychologists talked of Freudian death wishes while others believed in fear displacement or denying fear in their lives by directing their attention to another more manageable one. Others theorized that participants in high-risk sports were acting out psychopathic fantasies in an attempt to make up for feelings of inadequacy or to demonstrate omnipotence. So much for the non-jumping, ground hog, whuffo, head shrink community.

Fortunately, in the last 30 years, the shrinks have decided that pursuing a high-risk sport is not all that bad. Perhaps more of them have tried skydiving. In 1973, Bruce Ogilvie, professor emeritus of psychology at San Jose State University, conducted a study of 293 high-risk competitors including skydivers, racecar drivers, fencers and aerobatic pilots using psychological batteries and personal interviews. Ogilvie found risk-takers to be success oriented, strongly extroverted, above average in abstract ability and superior in intelligence when compared to the general population. He found that these athletes are rarely reckless; their risk-taking is cool and calculated. He estimates that six percent of the high-risk athletes compete out of anger or out of deep feelings of inferiority or because they are trying to prove something about themselves. The other 94 percent are emotionally stable. Ogilvie feels risk-takers grow up in a *go for it* world where they are coached to believe they can only learn by trying and perhaps losing. Meanwhile their timid friends are being told: don't do that, you could get hurt.

During initial jumps, there may be a higher level of excitement but later on, most skydivers simply concentrate on the challenge. They want to learn more, skydive better

---

Skydiving is a game of odds. The object of the sport is to improve your odds as much as possible. *—Sandy Reid*

and, most of all, not let down the team.

Hazard briefings. Emergency procedures will vary from drop zone to drop zone to fit local conditions. There may be trees, rivers, power lines, hostile neighbors, prisons, highways or a girls' school. In fact, those DZ's lacking certain hazards may touch on the corrective action for every emergency but lightly. Therefore, when visiting a new DZ, it is imperative that you get a briefing on the area.

Alcohol and drugs. In order to achieve the greatest enjoyment from your skydiving experience, you will want to approach it with an unfogged mind. This means going to bed early the night before and going easy on the booze. Even the common cold will trouble you due to the changes in atmospheric pressure. If your mind and body are not operating at 100%, you will react with less efficiency in an emergency and you will enjoy the jumping less. Remember, the lower pressure at altitude amplifies the affects of alcohol and drugs.

While there are traditions of bringing a case of beer to the DZ for any major first (hence, known as the "case of beer" rule), it is important to keep the alcohol in the coolers or refrigerators until after the last jump of the day is aloft so that there will be no questions as to whether or not participants were under the influence of anything. This is both good policy and common sense.

Health concerns. Jumping with a head cold can lead to ruptured sinuses and ruptured ear drums. The inner ear and the Eustachian tubes do not take kindly to large pressure changes when they are plugged. Infections in these areas can produce debilitating pain under normal jump conditions. In a few words — if you are sick or under the weather, don't jump. Loading up on antihistamines and decongestants can cause other medical problems. There is always another day to enjoy a jump in good health.

It is one thing to be in the proximity of death, to know more or less what she is, and it is quite another thing to seek her.

—*Ernest Hemingway*

Scuba diving alert. There is no problem in descending into the water within 24 hours of jumping or flying, however, there is trouble waiting in doing the reverse. Scuba divers know to stay away from air travel for a period of 24 hours after their last descent below 30 feet (one atmosphere's increase in pressure) so as to avoid the bends (nitrogen bubbles forming in the joints and blood stream). Since skydiving involves air travel, the same rule applies.

Some fear is good for you. It has been said that the difference between fear and respect is knowledge. Most people fear skydiving because they don't understand it. Fear is the result of ignorance and it is part of nature's protective mechanism; it warns us to beware when we are on unfamiliar ground. The best way to cope with problems is to prevent them in the first place. The key is education. It is unfortunate when someone is injured while engaging in sport, but it is tragic when a second person is hurt for the same explainable and preventable reason.

Sometimes the airplane fails

Airplane problems: Engine and structural failures. If the engine is going to fail, it will probably do so when the pilot reduces power after your full throttle takeoff. If the engine quits, he will attempt the best landing he can, straight ahead off the end of the runway. Since you are helmeted, padded with gear and strapped in, you need only assume the proper position to be prepared. Draw your knees up, tuck your head down, fold your hands across the back of your neck and hold your head down to resist whiplash. As soon as the plane comes to a stop, get out FAST. If you are nearest the door, get moving. There are people behind you who want to get out. There is always the danger of fire, particularly if the aircraft has suffered structural damage on impact. Watch where you step, the plane may have clipped through some power lines. They can zap you and they start grass fires. Remember that the wings or the belly of the airplane usually contain flammable fuel.

The emergency landing position

While it is rare, an airplane is a mere machine, and may therefore break. —*J. Scott Hamilton*

Occasionally, the jump ship suffers a structural or other mechanical failure. Twisted-on parts sometimes twist off or a canopy may get draped over the tail jamming the controls. Depending upon the situation and the altitude, your instructor will select one of two commands: *PREPARE TO CRASH* or *GET OUT* (jump). The dividing line is usually set at 1,000 feet above the ground since at this altitude there may be enough time for an orderly exit and the pilot will probably be able to land his *glider* on the runway. The instructor might tell you to jump and pull your reserve on the theory that it is somewhat more reliable and may deploy faster than the main and/or he may be concerned about the setting of your AAD. His instructions will depend on the circumstances of the situation.

So, if you are below 1,000 feet when the challenge occurs, you will land with the aircraft. If you are over 1,000 feet when the rubber band breaks, your instructor may direct you to make a normal static line jump, but you will do it all a lot faster; swing out onto the step and go. Student freefallers may be directed to make a jump and pull; this is where they will open their mains as soon as they clear the aircraft, or the instructor may sit them in the door, pull their reserve and simultaneously push them out. It all depends on the altitude at the time and the nature of the emergency. Licensed jumpers are next, then the instructor and, in the case of severe structural failure, the pilot. The purpose of getting out of the plane is not only to remove you from the area of danger but to lighten the load making the aircraft easier to control. The instructor goes next to last because he must take care of those in his charge. The pilot goes last (he wears a parachute too) so that he may wrestle the jump ship to keep it flying until you are gone.

The above rules are general and are for students. Experienced jumpers may elect to exit lower. For example, if

---

The Right Stuff: Not mere bravery in risking one's life but the calculated approach to the impossible, or to death, as always controlled, seeking and passing a seemingly infinite series of tests. —Tom Wolfe

the aircraft is at 500 to 1,000 feet, an expert skydiver may elect to jump and pull the reserve (which presumably opens faster). Of course you will follow the directions of your instructor, but sometimes you have to make the decision yourself. In the excitement of solving the engine failure or other problem, the pilot may allow the airspeed to drop, stalling the plane and allowing it to spin. In this condition the aircraft drops fast and the centrifugal force may pin you against the side or ceiling. Now is the time make the decision to scramble and **get out.**

Depending on the size of your jump ship and the procedure at your drop zone, your static line may be hooked up on the ground, at 1,000 feet, or on jump run. Whether or not your main is hooked up may determine what type of escape you can make in case of an aircraft emergency. For example, if you hook up prior to boarding, and the plane crashes on takeoff, when you unbuckle and get out, you can expect to unpack your main about eight to 15 feet from the door (the length of your static line).

The final point to remember is to watch and listen to your instructor for directions. When you receive them, carry them out quickly and without panic.

Open parachute in the airplane. Several times in the past, jumpers have been pulled through the side of the jump plane when a container opened and a canopy escaped out the door. Rarely does this result in a fatality but usually there is severe damage to both the jumper and the aircraft.

If either the main or the reserve open prematurely in the aircraft, one of two things will happen; the pilot chute and/or canopy will either start out the door or remain in the plane. You have only one course of action for each situation.

If the **main** container opens in the aircraft, it is usually the result of excessive movement by a person in the aircraft.

Why would anyone want to jump out of a perfectly good airplane? The problem is that there is no such thing as a perfectly good airplane. Every plane is nothing more than an accident looking for a place to happen.

-55 IACW67 AC ACC N34621

The jumper whose reserve escaped out the door of this aircraft was lucky; he survived. Notice how close he came to taking out the control cables which run through the door channel and just inside the torn Alclad.

This could happen when you constantly shift positions, rubbing the static line and/or closing flap on an interior surface or snagging the static line on something during movement in the aircraft (from one position to another). With the Instructor Assisted Deployment (IAD) method, these hazards are real because hand-deployed pilot chutes use small closing pins. With long plastic coated cables for a main ripcord, the hazard is much less likely, especially when the ends are tucked into housings on a closing flap. If the main container opens, it is a simple matter to move backward pinning the errant canopy against a wall or flat surface. Show the problem to your instructor immediately. Once satisfied that you have it well secured, disconnect the main canopy from your harness by operating the canopy releases (the method depends on the type of system you are using — your instructor will probably do this for you as well as disconnect your reserve static line device). This is so that if it should somehow get out the door later, you won't be connected to it. Now sit on the canopy and pilot chute so they won't get away and ride the plane down.

Sometimes the reserve container will burst open while you are in the back of the plane. The pin works its way out, or perhaps since you are in the back of the plane, you are not vigilantly guarding your reserve ripcord handle and it is snagged on something and gets pulled out as you move around trying to find a comfortable position. Grab the reserve pilot chute and canopy, cover them and hold them tight. Call the instructor's attention to the problem immediately. The reserve creates a greater potential danger than the main because it cannot be quickly disconnected from the harness.

This deploying reserve canopy pulled the static-line jumper off the step.

It is impossible to make a parachute foolproof because the fools are so ingenious.

If, however, either of your canopies start out the door while you're attached to it, you will follow it out. You have, at most, two seconds, and if you hurry you will experience a near-normal canopy ride to somewhere in the vicinity of the airport. But if you are slow, the developing canopy will act as a giant anchor, extracting you not just through the door but, more than likely, through the side of the aircraft too, causing great injury to you, damage to the aircraft, and exposing others still in the aircraft to great danger.

The best solution is prevention. Always guard and protect your static line and/or your ripcord(s), canopy release handle and pins.

Exit hazards—general. If you don't stay low during your climb out, you may rub your container across something on the door that might open the container, resulting in your extraction off of the aircraft. This is not as dangerous as the parachute opening inside the plane, but certainly just as surprising. Make your movements slow, smooth, and deliberate. Let your instructors help you and guard you as you move into the proper exit position. You may end up with a normal parachute ride, or you may be in tow by the aircraft.

Exit hazards—static line or IAD. When climbing out onto a step for a S/L exit, you need to firmly plant your feet on the step so that you don't trip over yourself and fall off. If you do find yourself prematurely exiting the aircraft, merely arch hard for stability. Don't grab the pilot chute or parachute as it comes by you. To do so may cost you your life.

Exit hazards—AFF. When climbing out for an AFF exit, your instructors are supposed to have good control of you. If you start to stumble, they will probably help you into position. If you do prematurely exit, at least one of them should have a hold of you and you will need to arch hard for stability.

When climbing out, make sure your hands stay away from the instructor's ripcord handles. Occasionally an instructor has been launched off the step or off the door sill when a student grabbed for the instructor and snared a ripcord handle by mistake. (That gives the instructor a very long canopy ride.)

Exit hazards—Tandem. Equipment manufacturers and their representatives have trained the TIs to control your postion during the exit. It is important for you to put your hands and feet exactly where you have been trained to put them. If the exit process causes the container to rub against a door (such as in a Cessna exit), there is a possibility of having a premature, out of sequence deployment (a malfunction) which presents a unique set of problems. TIs have also been discouraged from performing intentionally unstable (multiple tumble) exits as there is always a possibility of getting entangled with an out of sequence deployment during that activity.

Dangling static line. After the instructor dispatches each student, he will unhook the static line and stow it in the back of the aircraft or under the pilot's seat. If he forgets to disconnect the static line, it is one ingredient for another horror story. During the scramble to exit, jumpers have managed to get those long pieces of webbing half-hitched around their ankle. The result is a surprising and abrupt halt just a short distance out the door. Due to the weight of the gear and the wind, it is impossible for the jumper to climb back up. There should be a knife in the plane to cut you loose and, of course, every experienced jumper in the plane should be carrying one. If there aren't any knives handy, you will hope the pilot is sharp enough to think of breaking some glass out of one of the instruments in the panel because your alternatives are not terribly pleasant. Either you can pull your ripcord and risk jerking your leg off, or you can wait it out and suffer severe runway rash when the plane lands. One jumper caught in this situation lucked out, he was jumping from a helicopter. The pilot set him down gently and red faced in front of everyone on the DZ.

Student in tow. One of the more dramatic problems is the static line hang-up or student in tow. It occurs when you or some part of your equipment entangles with the static line preventing separation. You wind up suspended about ten feet below the aircraft by the long nylon web. This emergency is extremely rare and if it does occur, it will probably be because the static line is misrouted (perhaps under the harness). Maybe the error was missed in the equipment check, or you and the instructor failed to keep the line high and clear as you moved into the door to jump, or you performed some wild gymnastic maneuver instead of a stable exit and became entangled in the line. Some students, despite all their training, yell arch thousand and then let go with the hands, leaving the feet firmly planted on the step, thus they perform a backloop upon exit.

If you deploy the reserve while in tow, you may not rip loose. You could slow the plane to a stall. Here, the owner, instructor, pilot and aircraft were all lowered to earth under the same 24' canopy.

The in-tow/hang-up situation presents all of you with a perplexing situation. The jump ship will be more difficult to fly. In fact, the pilot may be unable to maintain altitude because of all the extra drag. Just as with the dangling static line situation, you do not want to pull the reserve or land with the plane. As with other emergencies, there is an accepted procedure. You, your instructor and pilot must be familiar with it.

The pilot will be diverting the aircraft to a safer, open area and will be trying to gain altitude. If you relax, you will probably assume a stable towing position either face or back to earth which is better than twisting in the wind.

If you are conscious and your arms have not been injured, signal the instructor by placing both hands on top of your helmet. Your hands will show you understand the situation and are ready to take corrective action. Your instructor will signal he is ready too by holding up a knife. Now, your instructor will cut the static line and you will fall away. Pull the reserve ripcord. Be sure you are cut loose before you pull.

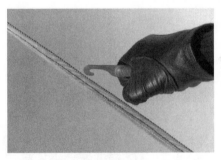

Your instructor will release you by cutting
your static line

If you are unconscious or otherwise incapacitated, you won't be able to give the OK signal to your instructor. Your static line will still be cut but your instructor (and you) will rely on your automatic activation device to deploy your reserve parachute.

A chance is what you take before you think about it. A calculated risk is what you take after you have evaluated all possible factors and have determined that risk. —Craig Elliot

Back when reserves were worn in the front, instructors could lower an unconscious student by unhooking their own reserve and attaching it to the static line. The static line had to have an extra ring for attachment to the reserve to make this method of rescue possible.

There is also a second type of main canopy in-tow emergency to be considered. Normally, you fall away from the step so quickly that it is virtually impossible to tangle your canopy in the tail, but if one of your parachutes opens when you are on the step, entanglement may occur. If you find yourself in this situation, look up and determine which parachute is fouled on the aircraft. If it is the main parachute (which will be attached to risers that can be disconnected from the harness), look at your reserve ripcord handle, jettison your main and pull your reserve ripcord immediately per the procedures that you were taught to use. If it is your reserve that is entangled on the aircraft, pulling the reserve/SOS ripcord would not change your situation but it

Many years back, this Army test jumper managed to hang his canopy over the tail. A knife was lowered to him from a second plane. He cut himself free and opened his reserve. (The canopy release was a later development.)

will make your main canopy useless as it would be discon-nected at the risers, therefore don't pull the reserve ripcord handle. The fouled canopy may just self-destruct, putting you back into freefall, in which case you will need to deploy your main parachute to save your life. (If you deployed your main parachute while the reserve is fouled on the aircraft, you can assume that major structural damage will occur to that aircraft and anyone left inside that aircraft will have to perform their own emergency procedures.)

Static line not hooked up. Occasionally, despite all pro-cedures, a student exits the jump plane without being attached to it. While hooking up the static line is the instruc-tor's responsibility, you must verify that it is attached prior to exit. If you forget to check this and find yourself in freefall, follow the procedure for a *total*: pull your reserve ripcord.

Pulling high is dangerous if you are being followed out by experienced jumpers intending to pull at their "normal" altitude. Everyone expects you to pull below 3,500 feet if you are a S/L or IAD student, 4,500 feet if you are an AFF student. (Tandem jumps traditionally go out of the airplane last because they do pull at higher than normal altitudes, espe-cially when multiple tandem jumps are made from the same aircraft.) If you pull higher, another freefalling skydiver could hit you. An open canopy descends at about 1,000 feet per minute and jumpruns are usually a minute apart. If you plan on pulling higher announce your decision to all before leaving the ground.

Freefall Emergencies

Accelerated FreeFall (AFF) emergencies. As you get ready to leave the aircraft, you are supposed to do a pre-exit check to make sure that your instructors are ready to exit too. If you make an error in your exit count, you can fool your instructors into thinking that you are about to leave and they may end up pulling you off the aircraft before you are truly ready to go. If you leave at the wrong time in the count, you could be taking your instructors in tow. This could lead to some awkward flying if you are not arched. You may be positioned in a reverse arch (like a cat standing on top of a toilet bowl) which will attempt to send your butt to earth. The exit timing depends upon you doing the exit count right so that your instructors can exit with you, not before or after you. If you find yourself looking up at the sky or tumbling, arch hard for stability. Your instructors will be doing their best to assist you in getting back to the proper belly-to-earth position.

AFF: Loss of one instructor. If you sheared off one instructor during the exit or one let go because he was not contributing to the stabilization of the formation, arch for stability and check with the remaining instructor during your circle of awareness. If you get a headshake of "NO," it may mean that the instructor holding onto you is not quite comfortable with your stability at that time. On the other hand, it may mean that he doesn't want you to go to the next portion of your tasks because the other instructor is just about to re-dock on the formation and he wants that instructor in the correct position before you continue with your tasks. You may or may not feel the other instructor re-dock. Whenever you get a "NO," simply arch a bit more, wait a few seconds, then do another circle of awareness. If you get a nod of "YES," you may continue on with your skydiving tasks regardless of whether or not you have just one of both

When you run away from fear, it grows in your mind. When you move towards fear and attack it directly, it recedes. —*John Amatt* instructors firmly holding onto you.

AFF: Loss of both instructors. You are in an extremely hazardous environment if you don't have an instructor holding onto you. The moment you realize this, arch and pull immediately.

The following emergencies apply to either AFF or S/L or IAD program freefalls. Of course, in the S/L or IAD programs, an instructor might not be in the air with you during your freefall.

Five-Second Rule for loss of stability. Here's a good rule for AFF or freefall. It is called the Five-Second Rule. If you are out of control, attempt to regain control by arching hard for five seconds. If you don't recover stability by the end of that five-second period, deploy your parachute immediately (which one depends upon your altitude). This rule is normally taught to AFF students when they start their Category C training and it is applicable to all freefall students.

Loss of altitude awareness. If you can't determine what your altitude is because you can't see your altimeter and you can't see either of your instructors' altimeters, arch and deploy your parachute immediately. The worst of all situations is to go into the ground at a high rate of speed simply because you didn't know where you were.

Goggles. If your goggles weren't tight, they may come up off of your eyes and cause sight problems. You could simulate a practice pull position and try to hold them in their proper place, but it is probably better to end the freefall once the situation occurs. There is nothing worse than a distraction to disorient you and cause you to lose track of time and altitude. When in doubt, whip it out (deploy your parachute).

Ripcord or Pilot Chute/Deployment Challenges

Common ripcord and hand-deployed pilot chute malfunctions are the lost handle and the hard pull.

Lost handle or out-of-sight hand-deployed pilot chute. Some ripcords are held in place by elastic webbing or Velcro® closures. If the ripcords come out of these places, they may be blown out of your sight. Some puds (knobs or handles for hand-deployed pilot chutes) attach with Velcro closures, and some are stowed in elastic pockets. There are pros and cons to where these pilot chutes and deployment handles should be mounted. Either one may separate from the container and be blown behind you. Search for the rip-cord (one time only) by following the harness to the ripcord housing with your hand. Search for a hand deployment device (one time only) with your hand by following the con-tainer to the area where it is supposed to be mounted — per-haps even as far as the closing grommet. If you can't locate the handle immediately, pull your reserve ripcord. Practice this on the ground periodically.

Lost handles and hand-deployed pilot chutes can also occur after the pull if you fail to pull far enough. Make sure you pull the ripcord all the way out of the housing, or if using a hand-deployed pilot chute, pull the pud to arm's length before you release it.

Hard pull. The hard pull may be caused by a bent or rough pin, a hand-deployed pilot chute bound up in its pouch, or you may have packed more canopy in the center of the container instead of filling the corners. If you feel resistance to your pull, give it two more quick tries (perhaps even with both hands if possible while maintaining the arched body position) — this really applies only to ripcord equipped gear as you can't be expected to reach around to your right rear hip area with your left hand — and then if that doesn't deploy the main parachute, pull your reserve ripcord immediately. After a number of jumps, it is normal to become somewhat complacent about the pull; you may give it a relaxed, half-hearted jerk. The pull may take as much as 10 kg (22 lbs.) of force, so pull again. If continual hard pulls are bothering you, you might choose to spray a non-petroleum-based silicone or Teflon® fluid on your rip-cord cable or your closing pin and your closing loop. This will make quite a difference and it will last for many jumps. You may occasionally have to do it again as dirt and grime builds up on your pin or ripcord cable system. Inspect your system for any signs of roughness. If they exist, get a rigger to replace the rough component with a smooth one.

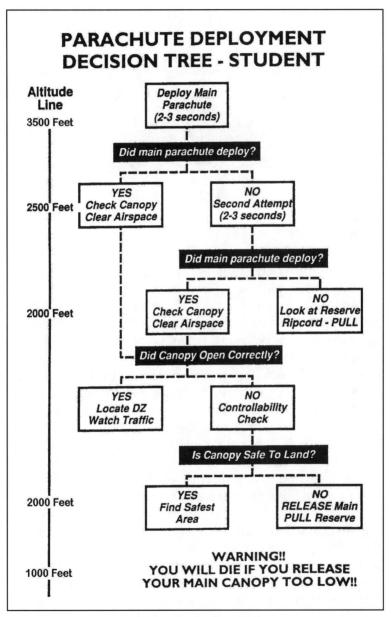

PARACHUTE DEPLOYMENT DECISION TREE - STUDENT

Altitude Line
3500 Feet

Deploy Main Parachute (2-3 seconds)

Did main parachute deploy?

2500 Feet — **YES** Check Canopy Clear Airspace | **NO** Second Attempt (2-3 seconds)

Did main parachute deploy?

2000 Feet — **YES** Check Canopy Clear Airspace | **NO** Look at Reserve Ripcord - PULL

Did Canopy Open Correctly?

YES Locate DZ Watch Traffic | **NO** Controllability Check

Is Canopy Safe To Land?

2000 Feet — **YES** Find Safest Area | **NO** RELEASE Main PULL Reserve

1000 Feet — **WARNING!!** YOU WILL DIE IF YOU RELEASE YOUR MAIN CANOPY TOO LOW!!

Skydiving Decision Tree by Paul Sitter

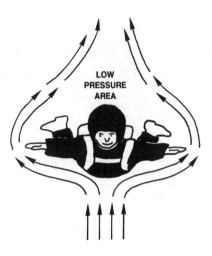

Pilot chute hesitation. A problem you could have with your *reserve* deployment, or a main with a spring-loaded pilot chute, is the common pilot chute hesitation. Hesitations can happen to hand-deployed mains but they are not as common. Hesitations occur when the pilot chute momentarily flutters in the low-pressure area behind you rather than catching air. The hesitation may be caused by a bent or weak pilot chute spring, but usually the pilot chute is just sitting in the dead air space created behind you when you are in the stable position. Sometimes the pilot chute jumps upon release but fails to travel far enough to get a grip on the air rushing past you. It may drop back down on your back and just bounce around or just lay there. If it was hand-deployed, you may not have given it a good throw.

To correct the problem, you may turn on your side during the post exit or pull count, allowing the airflow to inflate the pilot chute and pull it free, you may peek over your shoulder after pulling the ripcord, or you may sit up to *dump* (deploy your canopy). This last method of pulling, then sitting up (almost the start of a backloop) also reduces the opening forces on your shoulders, but it can lead to other problems such as trapping a tight-fitting deployment bag in its container. Consult with an instructor who is familiar with your system prior to attempting this type of maneuver.

Pull-out vs. throw-out. The pull-out and throw-out pilot chutes are preferred by experienced jumpers and more DZs are adopting them for student operations which eliminates transition training later on in their programs. However, there are still many operations that use ripcord activated, spring-loaded pilot chute deployment systems. Training for the specific system used must be ingrained into the student's behaviors so that they do things correctly each and every time. For a detailed explanation of these three systems, see the chapter on equipment.

Common throw-out malfunctions are trapped pilot chute, pilot chute in tow and the dreaded horseshoe.

Trapped pilot chute. If the pilot chute is not properly stowed in its pocket, it may bunch up and jam when you try to extract it. The trapped pilot chute results in a hard pull that may or may not be cleared. If you find you have a hard pull, try one more vigorous pull before you go for your reserve.

—**Pilot chute in tow** may be short or long. It is *short* when the pilot chute bridle is looped around something such as a harness strap. (A proper gear check could have avoided this problem.) If you have one of the rare bellyband mounted throw out models, make sure that the bellyband is not twisted. If the pilot chute bridle is wrapped around the harness (such as on a twisted bellyband or leg strap), tugging on it will only result in a (short) trailing pilot chute. Check the bridle routing during packing, have it checked in the equipment check prior to boarding the aircraft and check the routing again prior to exit. Twisted bellybands and twisted leg straps are a significant cause of pilot chutes in tow.

The pilot chute in tow is *long* when the pilot chute pulls the bridle to its full extent but does not pull the pin securing the main container. The failure may be due to a damaged pilot chute (producing insufficient drag), a rough pin, a tight main container (canopy stacked too high), or a closing loop which is too short. The long pilot chute in tow is more likely on sub-terminal velocity jumps.

Make sure the bridle-pin connection is not worn, that the pin is smooth and curved, not straight (unless it is supposed to be such as in pull-out pilot chute systems), and that the locking loop is not too short.

If you are faced with a long pilot chute in tow, never try to clear it. A recent USPA article (*Parachutist*, June 1997) stated that if you have a pilot chute in tow, deploy the reserve immediately. Therefore, it is treated as a total malfunction. Other experts in the field take the position that if there is anything out behind the container, including a spring-launched or hand-deployed pilot chute, execute a cutaway and reserve deployment immediately. Note: Most student equipment is Single Operation System (SOS) oriented. This means that pulling the reserve handle will execute the cutaway (disconnect the main risers) then deploy the reserve all in one smooth action. A two-handle system requires a separate cutaway handle to be pulled to disconnect the risers, followed by a pull of the reserve ripcord.

How to handle a pilot chute in tow has been the subject of great debate and much beer has been consumed discussing it. While there are exceptions and strong feelings about what has been stated above, time is usually too short to consider them. After the reserve starts to deploy, the main container may go slack enough that whatever kept it closed is no longer doing so, therefore the main may start to deploy. If the main was disconnected from the harness by the action of a cutaway, it will probably not be anything more than a temporary nuisance. However, one must always be prepared for possible entanglement of the two canopies whether a "cutaway" has or has not been performed.

Canopy Emergencies

Jettisoning the main canopy. Before we talk about the series of problems you may encounter with your main canopy, it is important to discuss the types of cutaway (main canopy disconnection systems) that are in common use and their procedures. The breakaway or cutaway is an emergency procedure that involves jettisoning the main canopy

---

Passing through two grand at terminal with nothing out is not the time or place to be paging through this book. Read it now.

—Curt Curtis

prior to deploying the reserve. Originally, the cutaway was performed with a knife and the lines were cut to separate the canopy from the harness. Today, we use canopy releases to *breakaway*. The breakaway procedure should be executed immediately under rapidly spinning malfunctions because ever-increasing centrifugal forces will make arm movement difficult, and may cause you to lose consciousness (red-out) due to the blood flow to your eyes.

The decision altitude for a student's breakaway is 2,500 feet. This is your safety margin, above this it is safe to try to clear the malfunction but at this point, all clearing work must stop. Watch your altitude. The breakaway must be commenced above 2,000 feet to assure you plenty of time to get the reserve out. Under high-speed malfunctions, you may be just seven seconds off the deck at this point, and it may be necessary to forget the breakaway and just pull the reserve.

To breakaway, spread your legs (for lateral stability and push them back as far as possible while bending your knees about 45 degrees (only). Arch your back and pull your head back but keep your chin resting on your chest and your eyes on the handle(s). On release you will fall into a stable, face-to-earth position.

Body position during the breakaway is very important. If you are not falling away correctly, you may become entangled in the canopy and/or lines of your deploying reserve. Even with good body position, breaking away from a violently spinning malfunction may throw you tumbling across the sky.

The breakaway procedure is as follows:

—**Two Action System**. The TAS has two handles: Pull the first one (usually a Velcro-attached pillow handle located on the right-hand main lift web), to release both risers (a single point release). Then activate the reserve by pulling the other handle (usually located on the left-hand main lift web).

Aviation is not unsafe but like the sea, it is terribly unforgiving of any carelessness or neglect.   —*C.R. Smith, Chief Executive of American Airlines' from 1934 to 1968*

A. *Total malfunction* (nothing out). Do not waste precious time breaking away; just pull the reserve.
1. LOOK at the reserve ripcord handle and arch.
2. REACH for the reserve ripcord handle with both hands.
3. PULL the reserve ripcord handle with both hands.

B. *Partial malfunction* (canopy out but not working properly).

There are two schools of thought on how to perform the breakaway action using this system. The first one presented is in the UPSA's *Skydiver's Information Manual*, Section 4, Category A, Subsection H "Equipment Emergency Procedures" under partial malfunctions.

While it states "Look at the reserve ripcord handle (step 5), it says nothing about the choice of one hand or both on the breakaway handle. It is as follows:

Note: On single-operation systems, pulling the reserve ripcord releases the main canopy first before deploying the reserve. Partial malfunction procedures for a single-operation system (SOS) are the same as for a total malfunction.
1. Check altitude.
2. Return to the arch position.
3. Ripcord systems only: Discard the main ripcord.
4. Locate and grasp the cutaway handle.
5. Locate the reserve ripcord handle.
6. Pull the cutaway handle until no lower than 1,000 feet.
7. Pull the reserve ripcord handle immediately after cutting away or by 1,000 feet AGL, regardless of stability, to initiate reserve deployment.
8. Arch and check over the right shoulder for reserve pilot chute deployment.
9. Do not cut away below 1,000 feet.
   a. If a malfunction procedure has not resolved the problem by then, deploy the reserve (requires a cutaway with an SOS system).

As in all emergencies, it would be wrong to think that they happen on every flight but it would be foolish not to prepare for them.
—*Charles Shea-Simonds*

b. In the event of any malfunction and regardless of the planned procedure or equipment, the reserve ripcord must be pulled no lower than 1,000 feet AGL.

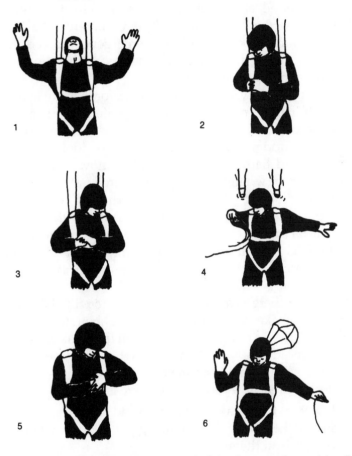

The breakaway sequence— where both hands are used on each handle

Note: For students and some other equipment, there is a device known as a reserve static line lanyard RSL (sometimes called a Stevens lanyard). This is a piece of webbing attached from the right side riser (or both risers on some systems) to the reserve ripcord cable. It is designed to pull the reserve ripcord out of its locking loop(s) as you fall away from the main parachute after that main canopy is cut away, thus allowing the reserve to deploy. When installed and operating properly, it will usually beat you to the manual deployment of the reserve. However, it should not be relied upon, for after all, along with an automatic activation device (AAD — described in Chapter 7), it is merely a back-up device to your proper execution of emergency procedures. This system can be disconnected (if necessary) by personnel who know what they are doing.

It is a possibility that when you perform a breakaway using both hands on the breakaway handle, there is a fraction of a second of disorienting instability as the maneuver is executed. Although you are supposed to be looking at the reserve ripcord handle, you still need to move one or both hands to it from whatever position you are in at the conclusion of the breakaway-handle pull. The ripcord handle may move from where it was (on the harness) under the tension of the partial malfunction to a different position during this moment. It is a possibility that there may be an additional second or more of elapsed time as you reach for the reserve ripcord handle.

Therefore, there is a second school of thought about performing the breakaway, which is, if you are about to execute a breakaway and you put your right hand on the breakaway handle and your left hand and thumb through the reserve ripcord handle, there will be no lost time reaching for the reserve ripcord after the breakaway is executed. Here is a typical scenario:

1. LOOK at the breakaway handle and arch. The arch should keep you from making a backloop when you jettison the main.

2. REACH for the breakaway handle with your right hand.

3. REACH for the reserve ripcord handle with your left hand, placing your thumb through the handle to ensure that you have a firm grip on it.

4. PEEL and PULL the breakaway handle to full right arm extension. Throwing it away is optional.

5. Immediately after you've pulled the breakaway handle with your right hand, PULL the reserve handle out to full extension with your left hand.

6. CHECK over your shoulder for a pilot chute hesitation.

7. CHECK your reserve canopy, look around and prepare to land.

In this scenario, there is no hesitation in looking for a reserve ripcord that may have moved, thus it may save a second or two of precious time.

—**The Single Operation System** is a one-handle/one-motion system. The S.O.S. has a combined handle, usually on the left main lift web, to release both risers and activate the reserve. The S.O.S. has a reserve static line lanyard (Stevens lanyard) from one riser to the reserve ripcord. The purpose of the S.O.S. is to eliminate one the motions in the breakaway sequence; that of separately pulling the cutaway handle. By pulling the reserve ripcord all the way, you accomplish both the breakaway and the reserve-ripcord pull in one complete action. With a two-action system, half a breakaway is worse than no breakaway at all unless you have an RSL.

The S.O.S. usually produces full deployment of the reserve canopy in less than 200 feet. If you find an RSL on your piggyback harness/container assembly, you should leave it on. When you and your instructor develop enough confidence that you will pull the reserve after a breakaway, you can do away with the line if you wish.

In the event of a total or partial malfunction:

1. LOOK at the combination release/ripcord handle and arch.

2. REACH for the combination handle with both hands.

3. PULL the combination handle with both hands to full arm extension.

Out of 10,000 feet of fall, always remember that the last half inch hurts the most. —*Captain Charles W. Purcell, 1932.*

4. REACH back with one hand, grasp the cables where they come out of the housing.
5. PULL AGAIN to clear the cables and
6. CHECK over shoulder for a pilot chute hesitation.
7. CHECK the reserve canopy, look around and prepare to land.

Never depend on the reserve static line device (Stevens lanyard). Always pull your reserve ripcord cable all the way out of the housing immediately after breaking away.

Canopy transfer is a third type of breakaway procedure sometimes used in Canopy Relative Work by those who believe something is better than nothing. If your main canopy becomes damaged or tangled on a jump and it is still flying forward, you may pull your *round* reserve and drag it behind you, full of air. Once the reserve canopy is inflated, jettison the main. This maneuver is extremely risky with a square reserve canopy as two squares may fly around and into each other. This type of problem is discussed later on in detail.

The canopy transfer with a round reserve

Hard pulls on cutaway handles. Sometimes a high-performance canopy will line twist all the way down to the risers, pinning the jumper's head to his or her chest. This deep involvement of the line twists into the risers can put a great deal of friction on the cutaway cables in the risers. At several PIA symposiums, Mike Turoff reported on the increased friction loadings during simple line twists as well as during high canopy loadings caused by spins both with and without line twists. Maintaining clean, well lubricated cutaway cables helps reduce the friction-induced increased pull forces, but more than that, cutaway cable channel inserts manufactured commercially by some of the equipment manufacturers greatly reduces the observed friction binding of the cutaway cables in the risers.

Also uncovered in Mike's testing was the possibility that the risers can be twisted so much behind your head that the 3-ring assembly is pinned against your helmet, preventing them from operating properly even if the cutaway cable is completely removed from its housing. A simple action here is to shake and turn your head and that should remove any blocking of the 3-ring mechanism by the helmet (or your head if you are jumping as an experienced person without a helmet).

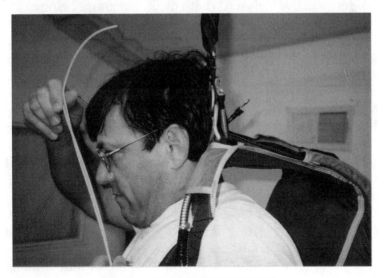

Note the twisted risers behind the head.

Harness shift. When you jettison the main canopy, your harness will shift downward taking the reserve ripcord location with it. Therefore, it is essential that you keep your eyes on the reserve ripcord handle, if your hand is not already grasping it, when jettisoning the main canopy.

Now that we have covered cutaways (breakaways), let's discuss when and where they are used.

Parachute malfunctions. A *malfunction* is any failure of the system to provide a normal rate of descent and this includes loss of canopy control. Malfunctions are normally caused by one or a combination of the following: bad packing, poor body position during canopy deployment and/or faulty equipment. There are some malfunctions, however, that just happen (Acts of God); parachutes are good but not perfect. Failures of the main parachute can be divided into two areas. Either nothing comes out and you have a *total malfunction* or the canopy starts to open but something is wrong with it and you have a *partial malfunction*. Each of these two areas will be broken down still further in this chapter.

It is because of the possibility of an equipment malfunction that the USPA's Basic Safety Requirements list the minimum container opening altitude for students and A license holders as 3,000 feet AGL (with the initial jumps being made to open at 3,500 feet AGL). For tandem jumps, the minimum container opening altitude is set at 4,500 feet AGL. For B license holders, this altitude is dropped down to 2,500 feet AGL. For C and D license holders, this altitude is dropped down to 2,000 feet AGL. The BSRs and the FARs require that a second (reserve) parachute be worn for all sport jumping. It is important that you are drilled in its use. But even with the stated opening altitude safety margin or cushion, you must be aware of the time, speed and distances involved. If you exit the aircraft at 3,000 feet AGL, for example, you will begin to accelerate; you start off at zero vertical speed and then fall faster and faster until you reach terminal velocity (more about that later). If you didn't have a parachute, it would take you about 22 seconds to reach the ground. In the case of a partial malfunction, you will have a little braking from your canopy and this means even more time. But even if you have a total, allowing for reaction time, you should be open under your reserve at well above 2,000 feet. In fact, while it seemed like an eternity to you, your friends on the ground will tell you that you performed your procedures quickly and efficiently; you will be surprised at how fast you react to a malfunction. Your main parachute takes 3-4 seconds to open and the reserve may be just slightly faster. Even at terminal velocity, which in a face-to-earth, stable position is about 120 mph, (the fastest you can fall in that position), four seconds translates into about 700 feet.

If you haven't been jerked upright by the sixth segment (second) of your exit or pull count, you should already be into the emergency procedure for a total malfunction. Static lines not hooked up, in-tow situations, lost or hard ripcord pull or pilot chute problems have already been discussed and won't be repeated here.

Total malfunctions. Of all the possible equipment malfunctions, the total (pack closure) is the safest to deal with because there is no other garbage over your head to interfere with the deploying reserve. While the total is the easiest malfunction to rectify, remember it also presents you with the least amount of time in which to act. Do not spend time trying to locate a lost handle; you do not have time. Do not waste time breaking away; a loose riser could tangle with a deploying reserve. When in doubt, whip it out. (Pull the reserve ripcord.)

Partial malfunctions. A partial malfunction is one in which the canopy comes out of the container but does not properly deploy. The canopy may not inflate (e.g. a streamer that hardly slows your descent at all) or it may take on some air and be spinning violently (e.g. a line over or slider hang-up). You could have an end cell closure that will probably slow you enough for a safe landing. So, partial malfunctions may be major and minor. An additionally important consideration is that they may be stable or spinning. Most partials can usually be attributed to an error in packing or poor body position on opening. Some partials, however, just happen.

Some partials are so minor, most instructors do not even classify them as malfunctions; they call them "nuisances."

Some of these things that just happen are line twists, end cell closures and a slider that has not fully descended. These are correctable problems which you will be trained to handle.

A good canopy is rectangular (square) and flies straight once the slider is down and the brakes are released. It is stable through the flare and turns properly with the correct toggle inputs. (Remember the controllability check?)

A good canopy

Major partial malfunctions. Ones that you don't waste time to correct.

Bag lock presents you with trailing lines, bag and pilot chute but the canopy will not come out of the bag. This problem is not likely to clear itself. Breakaway and pull your reserve.

Bag Lock

Horseshoe. This malfunction can result from bad maintenance, failure to check equipment and incompatible canopy/container systems. It can happen when the locking pin or ripcord is dislodged from the closing loop, allowing the bagged canopy to escape before you have removed the pilot chute from its stowage pocket. The horseshoe can occur if you tumble during the deployment sequence, allowing the pilot chute to catch on your foot, your arm, or some other part of your body, but these are rare occurrences today. Another possibility is a poor launch of a pilot chute from your container, allowing it to fall back into your "burble" (the partial vacuum behind you) where it can dance around and snag on something, preventing it from properly deploying. Improper hand deploy procedures can lead to the pilot chute being caught on your arm. The danger of a horseshoe malfunction is that a pulled reserve may tangle with the horse-shoed main as it tries to deploy. If you experience a

The horseshoe malfunction occurs when the main container opens prematurely

horseshoe, and you are using a hand deployment technique, pull the main's hand deploy pilot chute immediately. Then, and even if you can't pull the main hand deploy pilot chute, execute a breakaway and deploy the reserve. Chances are that there will be enough drag on the lines and canopy to separate the risers from their attachment points and present only a single line of "garbage" for the reserve to clear (rather than a horseshoed main).

Violent spin. Unless you can tell immediately that you have an unstowed brake, breakaway and pull your reserve. If you have plenty of altitude and the problem is not compounded by line twists, push the toggles down past your waist for two seconds, then let up slowly. If the spin continues, break away and pull your reserve.

Line overs can occur when a brake lock releases during the opening sequence allowing one side of the canopy to surge forward over itself, or due to a packing error or an Act of God. If you are on a very high clear and pull, you may try to pull down on the end lines (by the risers) to make the

Line over

other lines slip off. However, if you deployed at the normal pull altitude, you do not have time for this maneuver on the main. Break away and pull your reserve ripcord. If this happens on a square reserve, pulling down on the side the lines are over is your best hope, along with a great PLF.

Partial malfunctions that may be majors or minors. You may have time to make a decision as to how to handle them.

Rips and tears are not common on ram-air canopies and may usually be ridden in. Even a rip from leading edge to trailing edge on one surface can probably be controlled. Internal rips may not be visible. See whether the canopy is controllable with toggle pressure no lower than your shoulder. If your controllability check indicates a serious problem, break away and pull your reserve ripcord. If the check does not indicate a serious problem, make slow, shallow turns and flare slowly for landing.

The snivel is a slow, mushy opening. The canopy's fabric weave opens up slightly after a few hundred jumps and becomes more porous. Higher permeability leads to sniveling. Look up after pulling to watch your canopy open. Learn to distinguish a slow-opening snivel from a never-opening streamer. Sometimes replacing the pilot chute will lead to quicker openings. Try packing the nose of the canopy in different positions but check with a rigger before you experiment. Contact the manufacturer about resetting the brakes two inches higher. Then the canopy will take to the air with the tail somewhat higher giving the leading edge a better bite of air.

Slider hang-up, at the canopy. The slider may hang up at the top of the lines because it is caught in the lines or caught on the slider stops. Grommets become battered and rough as they slide down and hit the connector links at the risers. The links may be fitted with plastic sleeve, rubber, or webbing buffers. There are also several types of fabric links available now, eliminating a source of metal on metal contact. Make sure the grommets are smooth. A slider hang-up at the canopy is a high-speed malfunction and will be hard to clear. You may be upright but you are descending quickly. There is little time to deal with a slider hang-up at the canopy, so jettison (cutaway) your main and pull your reserve ripcord.

Slider hang-up, at the canopy

Slider hang-up, halfway. A slider hang-up halfway down the lines will slow you down but possibly not enough for landing. Check your altitude and if there is time (you are still above the decision altitude for emergency procedures), release the brakes and pull the toggles down past your waist for two seconds in an effort to stall the canopy and relieve some of the spanwise spreading of the canopy. Repeat if necessary, pump the steering lines up and down. If the slider descends to within 10 or 12 inches of the connector links, that is close enough. Sometimes, the slider is caught higher in a suspension line or steering line. Let both toggles up to determine whether the canopy will fly straight. If you have to pull down the opposite toggle to more than shoulder level to maintain straight flight, the canopy will probably be unstable. If you don't gain total control of the canopy by the decision altitude (sometimes called the *hard deck*), break away and pull your reserve ripcord.

What you have to do is easy. It is where you have to do it that is the challenge. —*Robert Dormidy*

If the slider comes down the lines halfway and stops, the canopy has probably changed in some way. After you are safely on the ground, measure the line lengths and compare opposite lines. Check the slider grommets for damage. Bring the canopy to the equipment manager (if it is student gear), your rigger, or send it to the manufacturer for inspection.

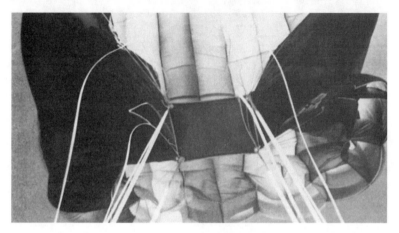

Slider hang-up, half-way

Broken suspension line(s). Most line breaks only put the canopy into a slight turn. Correct the turn with opposite toggle pressure. Occasionally the broken line causes the slider to hang up. Do a controllability check. If there is any internal damage to the canopy, it will not perform as expected. Failing a controllability check will dictate a breakaway and a reserve deployment.

Minor malfunctions are more like nuisances that can be dealt with and don't threaten you unless they get worse or are complicated by other problems.

Line twists. Sometimes, the bag rotates a few turns as it lifts off. Now you may find it difficult to get your head back to look up at the canopy. The problem is that the risers are

---

One of the great attractions of the sport to many of us is that it demands competence and skillful decision-making under pressure.
—*J. Scott Hamilton*

Line twists

closer together and twisted instead of spread. These twists can happen with or without your help. If you are kicking, rocking or twisting just as the bagged canopy lifts off, you can impart a twist to it. The principle is the same as when you give a Frisbee disc a flip of the wrist on launch. Line twists are more common on static line than freefall jumps.

Determine quickly whether the canopy is flying straight, your altitude and which way the lines are twisted. Reach above your head, grab the risers and spread them to accelerate the untwisting. If necessary, throw your legs in the twist direction. Line twists are worse on a ram-air canopy than a round because you cannot pull down on the steering lines to control the canopy until the twists are cleared and this may take up to 30 seconds. If the canopy is spinning in the same direction, you may not be able to untwist faster than it is twisting. Do not release the brakes until untwisted. While you have

Students are generally not aware of how quickly 20 seconds pass.
—*Betsy Robson*

the risers spread, check your canopy to make sure nothing else is wrong with it. A spinning canopy descends quickly. If you haven't untwisted the lines by 2,500 feet AGL (as a student), break away from your main and deploy your reserve. (As a licensed skydiver, you can make this decision altitude lower, but remember that the lower you go, the more risk you take!)

Premature brake release. Ram-air canopies are packed with their brakes set to prevent the canopy from surging on opening. If one brake releases on opening, the canopy is likely to turn rapidly which can escalate into a spin and/or an end cell closure if not corrected immediately. If the canopy doesn't have line twists, grab both toggles and pull them down to your waist. (Grabbing both eliminates having to choose which one to pull.) This maneuver will release the other brake, reduce your forward speed, stop the turn and let you see if any lines are broken. If the premature brake release is compounded with line twists, releasing the other brake may have some or no effect. Be aware of your decision altitude and try to unspin from the line twists. If you are sure that just one steering line is still set in its deployment setting, you might try to release it.

Broken steering line. When you find one of your steering lines has snapped or floated out of reach, release the other brake and steer the canopy by pulling down on the rear risers. Do not try to steer with one control line and the opposite riser. The turns will be inconsistent and you may find yourself in a dangerously low turn when you flare for landing. Pulling down on the risers may be hard but it will steer the canopy. The canopy will probably want to turn in the direction of the good control line. If you cannot make the canopy fly straight with the opposite riser, break away and pull your reserve. If the broken line wraps around the slider, do not try to pump the slider down any further. It will only make the turning worse. Reserve some energy to pull down on both risers at about ten feet from the ground to flare the landing. You want to start this flare lower because pulling down on the risers results in a more pronounced flare.

Steering line(s) won't release is similar to dealing with a broken steering line, except that one may release while the other won't. If neither steering line releases, simply fly the canopy to a safe landing using the rear risers. If only one releases, then you can pull that steering line down to the point at which the canopy will fly straight, then control the direction the canopy flies by either using the rear risers or using the one working steering line. Quite often, you will have time to grab the riser of the steering line that won't release and work towards getting it released. Be mindful of your altitude as you work on the problem. You don't want to steer yourself to a hazardous landing while you are distracted with this release challenge.

Pilot chute "under/over" problems. The pilot chute may fall over the leading edge of the canopy and re-inflate underneath, usually causing a turn in the distorted canopy. Attempt to stall the canopy slightly so that it backs up, possibly allowing the pilot chute to come back up and over the front of the parachute. If the canopy cannot be controlled with toggles, break away and pull your reserve ripcord.

End cell closures occur when the pressure outside the canopy is greater than the pressure inside. They usually happen during canopy surge on opening but they can also be caused by radical turns or turbulent air. Turbulence can occur on hot, no-wind days, on windy days downwind of trees and

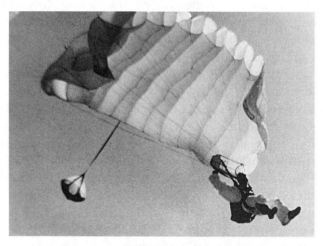

End cell closure

buildings, and during stormy conditions. Lightweight jumpers under large canopies (called *low wing loading*) will experience end cell closure more frequently. To avoid end cell closure, fly with one-quarter to one-half brakes. To counteract end cell closure, push the toggles down past your waist for a few seconds, until the cells inflate, then let the toggles up slowly. Repeat if necessary. End cell closures are not a major concern. Keep the canopy and land it if it is not spinning. If the end cells collapse below 200 feet, do not try to reinflate them. Pull to half brakes to stabilize the canopy. When you flare for landing, the cells will probably pop open.

Combination malfunctions. When confronted with more than one malfunction, correct for line twists first. The canopy will be uncontrollable until the twists are removed. When in doubt, whip it out, especially if you are at or below decision height (2,500 feet AGL).

Two canopies open. You may find yourself confronted with two fully open canopies. This can happen in several ways: The automatic activation device on your reserve could fire when you are happily flying your canopy through 1,000 feet; you may have reacted very quickly to a pilot chute hesitation without effecting a breakaway; or the main release system may have failed to separate during an emergency procedure.

If the two canopies take off at different times, they may not deploy into each other, but you need to be prepared to handle that possibility. At the Parachute Industry Association Symposium in Houston in 1997, a detailed report was presented on the performance of two ram-air canopies out — a very dangerous situation.

First, quickly check the condition and position of the main and reserve canopies, then make your decision based upon the following:

- If two canopies are out and flying side by side without interference or the possibility of entanglement exists and you are high enough (above 2,000 feet AGL) that the altitude permits, disconnect the RSL and cut away the main parachute. Steer the reserve to a normal landing. If you choose not to cut away the main or you have descended below the action altitude listed above, then steer yourself to a safe landing area by using gentle control inputs on the larger and more overhead canopy. Due to the nearly doubled surface area supporting your weight, the effective lift of the parachute system will make flaring the canopies unnecessary. Flaring one could create a hazardous situation, especially close to the ground.

Jettison the malfunctioned main canopy

- If the two canopies are both flying downward towards the ground (called a *downplane*), jettison the main. **Note:** Certain reserve static line lanyards may have to be disconnected so as not to foul the reserve parachute when the main is disconnected. Ask your instructor about the specifics concerning your system.

- If the canopies are flying one behind the other and in the same direction (called a biplane), make gentle steering inputs with the lead canopy (which is usually the main). Do not release the rear canopy's deployment brakes. Do not flare the landing.

- If the reserve container has opened but the reserve canopy has not yet, or not completely deployed, make gentle steering inputs with the main and try to haul in the reserve and stick it between your legs.

- If the two canopies have spun up so tightly around each other that you can't effect a cutaway, prepare yourself for the best possible PLF as you will undoubtedly be hitting the ground very hard.

Tandem jumping malfunctions may be aggravated because the weight is doubled while the effective drag area of the two falling bodies is not. As long as the drogue pilot chute has been deployed properly, freefall speeds are about the same as a single skydiver. If the drogue is not deployed or fails to work properly, the terminal velocity will be much faster than that of a single skydiver (120 mph); perhaps as much as 160-170 mph. The greater speed places a much greater strain on the parachute system and on the jumpers.

Large ring and ripcord handle. Older harnesses used a plain round ring for the largest of the rings in the 3-Ring canopy releases. When the main canopy is jettisoned, the largest of the riser-release rings remains on the harness. If the rings flop down on the lift web, the one near the reserve handle may be mistaken for that handle. Both are large silver rings and the reserve handle may have shifted from its normal position. Some jumpers have broken away only to tug on the wrong ring. Some never lived to tell about it. Newer equipment may have a shaped large ring or a smaller (mini) ring that is more difficult to confuse with the reserve handle. If you have older equipment, you should be aware of this potential problem.

Change of emergency procedures. Anytime you change your equipment or emergency procedures, make sure you are thoroughly trained. Practice in a suspended harness until proficient on the new equipment. Each corrective procedure is different and you must not waste precious seconds in an emergency thinking about what you should do. You must act automatically and quickly. Review your emergency procedures prior to each jump and touch all your handles before you proceed to the door.

Breakaway training is essential to assure that it will be accomplished completely, quickly and well. Training must take place in a suspended harness that is easy to rig up. Simply tie an old set of risers to an overhead beam and attach them to your harness. The drill must be repeated again and again until it becomes mechanical and automatic so that you will perform correctly and without hesitation should the time come. When you take your reserve in to be repacked, ask your rigger if you may practice the breakaway to include the reserve pull. It is a valuable experience and in this controlled environment, it is safe for your gear.

Emergency priorities. Think about and review the seven priorities of skydiving:

1. Pull—Open the parachute.
2. Pull by the assigned altitude or higher — whether stable or not.
3. Pull with stability — to improve canopy-opening reliability.
4. Check the canopy—promptly determine if the canopy has properly opened and is controllable.
5. If necessary, activate the reserve—perform the appropriate emergency procedures if there is any

doubt that the main canopy is open properly and is controllable.

6. Land in a clear area—a long walk back is better than landing in a hazardous area.

7. Land safely—be prepared to perform a PLF with the feet and knees together to avoid injury.

Canopy collisions. Let's assume that your canopy has just opened properly and you are reaching up for the toggles when suddenly, you look ahead and see another canopy coming directly towards you. What should you do? If the collision is avoidable by steering to the right or left, choose the right. The turn to the right is virtually universal in all forms of navigation. If the collision is unavoidable, spread your arms and legs out to absorb the impact over the most surface area possible, but don't spread your fingers. Keep your fists clenched so that lines won't have a chance to cleave through individual fingers, cutting them to the bone. Chances are that spreading out will allow you to bounce up and over the lines and canopy you will be colliding with. You may get a bit hurt, but you will be alive so long as you don't make full body contact with the other jumper. If you find yourself entangled with another parachute, the general rule of thumb is that the lower person has the right to perform emergency procedures first. Communicate with each other as to what you want to do, what you're going to do, then do it while you still have enough altitude to do it safely.

Most canopy collisions occur during the landing phase of the skydive, when too many people are trying to get into one tiny area all at the same time. Vigilance in canopy control and choosing a less congested area can help avoid this emergency. If you do end up tangled at an altitude too low to break away (less than 500 feet AGL), ride about half brakes and get set to do a fantastic PLF.

Landing challenges. Most of your landings will be normal and in the center of the drop zone, but unusual things do happen like landing in water, in sudden high winds, descending through power lines or trees.

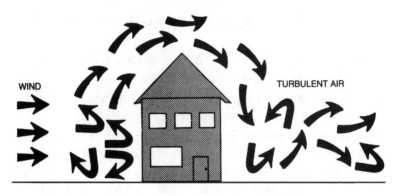

WIND

TURBULENT AIR

Obstacles may produce wind turbulence

Turbulence. As mentioned earlier, bumpy air may be encountered at any altitude and it has been known to close end cells and upset canopies. Jumpers have been robbed of their wings to be left back in freefall at 75 feet. Bumpy air may occur on windy days and on hot, no-wind days. Keep your canopy inflated during turbulence by flying at one-quarter to one-half brakes and make gentle turns. If turbulence causes a partial canopy collapse of your canopy, bring the steering lines down to half to three-quarters brakes to help the canopy to reinflate. This procedure may not apply to highly loaded elliptical canopies. Consult the equipment manual or equipment manufacturer for their recommendations on those types of canopies.

Turbulence near the ground may be caused when wind flows over obstacles such as buildings and tree lines. Avoid landing on the downwind side of any obstacle. The air may be bumpy or descending. The stronger the wind, the farther downwind the turbulence will exist and the taller the object, the higher the turbulence will be. Turbulence can be significant downwind as far as twenty times the object's height. For

> Asking students to make any transition early in their jumping career is asking for trouble. Expecting them to adjust to a different type of deployment device, a different type of canopy, or even a different type of jump (e.g. RW) early in their jumping career is not realistic and can lead to problems. *—Paul Sitter*

a fifty-foot tree line, that could mean 1,000 feet downwind turbulence. Turbulence also occurs behind other ram-air canopies. Stay away from the area directly behind another canopy about 45 degrees up from the trailing edge.

Dust devils are very dangerous. They can rob you of your canopy when you need it most — near the ground. Look for the spinning dust clouds. Unfortunately they can't be seen over grass.

One jumper landed, his canopy deflated and then it was reinflated by a dust devil. The swirling wind picked him up and then threw him back on the ground. He died from the impact. In windy conditions, pick up your deflated canopy immediately. In bad conditions, stand on it or cut it away.

High winds. If you find yourself in high winds, look behind you as you back up. Many jumpers back into power lines and fences. When landing in high winds, let go of one toggle as soon as your toes touch the ground. Keep the other toggle at the flare position and quickly pivot 180 degrees in the direction of the depressed toggle. Steer the canopy into the ground. Run toward and around it to collapse it. If necessary, continue pulling on that toggle and reel in its line to pull the canopy out from under itself.

Once you are on your feet, stand on the canopy and remove your harness. Don't let it reinflate and start dragging you all over again.

Thunderstorms are a violent vertical lifting of air masses, a phenomenon which can build cumulonimbus clouds from near the ground to anywhere from 50,000 to 75,000 feet. Thunderstorms possess violent updrafts and downdrafts along with lightning. While the West Coast of the U.S. has only around five thunderstorms each year, the northeast has 20, and Florida 80 to 90. Jumpers have been caught in cumulonimbus clouds for some pretty scary and wet rides. When the storm clouds appear, put the gear away.

The tree landing is rarely hazardous if you "center" the tree. Your canopy will lower you gently into and through the trees as you slow further, breaking the thinner branches. You will probably go all the way through to the ground and make a normal parachute-landing fall. On the other hand, if you clip a tree with a wing tip, your canopy may collapse, dropping you to the ground.

If you can't avoid the trees, face into the wind to minimize your ground speed, pull half brakes, and place your feet and knees tightly together so you won't straddle a branch. Do not attempt to brake your descent by grasping limbs; you are better off going all the way through to the ground slowly than ending up sitting in the top of the tree. Prepare for a PLF. If you come to rest short of the ground, check your position. Students should wait for DZ personnel to come to their aid.

Trees, power lines and water hazards: Elbows to the chest, hands with steering toggles in front of face and throat, feet and knees together. Look down.
Horizontal trainer

If you are within five feet of the ground and have a solid saddle (which is common on military surplus equipment), you may choose to unfasten your chest strap and then your leg straps after which you would slide forward out of the

It's not a real sport unless you can die from massive internal trauma.
—*Allen Roulston*

The tree landing

saddle and drop to the ground. If you do not undo the chest strap first, you could injure you neck as you fall away. If you are in a sport rig which has a split saddle, this procedure is far more difficult as you will have to prevent yourself from falling out of the equipment sideways once the first legstrap is released. It is probably far wiser to wait for help to arrive rather than risking an uncontrolled fall to the ground.

Stay clear of buildings, trees and other solid objects that might be likely hiding spots of turbulent air or no air at all. —*Daryl Hedges*

If you are up quite a way, relax and wait for help. If help does not arrive, you may have to climb down. Perhaps you are way off the DZ and dusk is approaching. It's hard to shout continually, and it is nice to have a whistle in times like these. You may deploy the reserve canopy without activating the cut away mechanism (for S.O.S. type equipment, pull the metal cable out of its housing without disturbing the plastic-coated breakaway cables), let down the canopy and lines and then, after disconnecting yourself from the harness (a risky operation as stated in the preceeding paragraphs), climb down hand over hand. If you let the narrow lines slip through your fingers and aren't wearing gloves, you will receive painful friction burns, so go hand over hand.

Keep your helmet on until you have both feet firmly on the ground. Its purpose is to protect your head from takeoff to touchdown, and you aren't down yet.

Power lines. You must avoid power lines at all cost; the danger is just too great. Look for the high-tension wires. If you are at an unfamiliar DZ or land off target, look for poles; wires run between them invisibly. Keep power lines continually in mind from the time you open so you can avoid them. High-tension lines don't look dangerous, but they strike with the speed and power of lightning. They may electrocute you in an instant or put you in the hospital with severe burns; it isn't at all pleasant. If there is any question about clearing the lines, turn and run with the wind until you are past them and make the decision high enough. It will be better to land downwind than to land in power lines.

If landing in the wires is inevitable, it is essential that you avoid touching more than one wire at a time. Any bird will tell you that it takes touching two wires to get zapped. If you are going into the wires, face your canopy into the wind to minimize horizontal drift and drop any ripcord and anything else in your hands (except the toggles). Pull the toggles to at least the half-brakes position to make your final descent as close to vertical as possible. Place your feet and knees firmly together with the toes pointed to avoid straddling a wire. Look for wires and wriggle and squirm as necessary trying to avoid touching more than one at a time. If you come to rest near the ground, check below to see what is underneath you. If there is no hazard below you and it is less than five feet to the ground — and assuming it is the main canopy that is hanging you from the wires you might decide to execute a breakaway and get away from the danger area as quickly as possible, but it would be better to wait for calmer heads to give you guidance in this matter. If there is a hazard below you or if it is your reserve parachute that is hanging you from the wires, you must wait calmly for competent, professional help. Any movement on your part may force an electrical contact. If a local resident walks up desiring to help you, ask them to call the power company and the DZ in that order. Warn would-be rescuers not to touch you or your gear until the power has been turned off. They could complete a circuit between you and the ground with fatal results.

Leave the canopy retrieval to the power company

Once you get to the ground, be alert for broken power lines, they are like snakes hidden in the grass and they not only strike, they sometimes start fires. Never pull on a canopy attempting to remove it from the wires, it may be your very last good deed. Let the power company do it; it is their kind of work.

Water landings. There are two types of water jumps — those you plan and those you don't. An intentional water jump is an exciting, rewarding combination of aviation and water sports. But being unexpectedly blown out over a body of water is cause for great concern. In fact, while few jumpers have perished in a planned water jump, 48 perished in unexpected water landings between 1967 and 1984. These figures have dramatically decreased now that the use of ram-air canopies has become universal and floatation devices for operations within one mile of water are mandated for students by the BSRs and any skydiver using a round reserve. (This BSR [Section 2-1, K. 5.] is waiverable by at least a Safety and Training Advisor.)

Do not subject your main to an intentional water jump

The procedures for these two very different types of landings are not the same.

In an intentional water landing you will slide back in the saddle, undo the chest strap, the bellyband (if there is one), and loosen both leg straps slightly (unless you have a full saddle harness, in which case you can release one leg strap up high, then the last leg snap upon splashing down). This procedure is also recommended if you find yourself being blown unexpectedly out over the ocean or other immense body of water. When there is absolutely no question that you are going for a dunking, you should inflate your floatation device. Don't get out of your gear until you get wet. Don't break away when you think you are about to get wet. Depth perception over water is deceptive. You may think you're at 20-feet, but you're probably much higher. Without knowing how deep the water is, you almost guarantee yourself a landing injury if you don't steer the canopy all the way to the surface. For landing purposes, assume the water is just a few inches deep. Take a deep breath and prepare to do a PLF. Line up your landing into the ground winds (you may have to use the sun's position for a reference) and once you are wet, swim or work your way forward out of your gear. Don't try to save the gear at first. Remember that it is replaceable, you aren't. Worry about the gear later, when you are safely away from it. Better yet, let someone else (such as your water landing crew) worry about it.

When making an intentional water jump, conditions are good, the jump is planned and the necessary flotation equipment is worn. The ingredients for tragedy, on the other hand, are born by being unprepared for the unexpected.

The *Basic Safety Requirements* mandate the wearing of flotation gear when parachuting within one mile of any water deep enough to take a life, but there are times when one mile is not enough. A bad spot on a big load with high upper winds, sudden radical wind changes, or a popped

---

A superior skydiver uses his superior judgment to avoid situations in which he has to demonstrate his superior skill. —*Anon.*

round reserve as you exit at twelve grand, for examples, may carry you far from the friendly DZ. Some water requires more protection than just flotation gear, such as when a jumper punches through the ice in the wintertime. Most unintentional water landings are also unexpected. They take place in narrow rivers and small ponds; so small that you don't know you are going into them until just a short distance from splashdown. There is no time to do much water-landing preparation, particularly if you are trying to avoid trees. As a result, you are going into the water in all your gear and your chances are poor.

On the other hand, if you go through the intentional water landing procedure just in case and then miss the water only to land in the trees because you couldn't spend enough time steering, you may subject yourself to other dangers.

The greatest danger in water landings is becoming entangled in the net-like canopy and lines. In fact, we should think of: panic-canopy-entanglement-drowning. All are challenges, very much related, and either of the first two can lead to the others. If there is little wind in the small tree-protected pond, the canopy will deflate and fall straight down on you in a huge mess of tangled nylon fabric and lines. If you panic, you are sure to become caught in the trap. It seems logical, then, to try to avoid the canopy, or better yet, avoid the water landing.

The procedure recommended for unintentional water landings is as follows: You are at 1,000 feet and the wind is backing you toward a water hazard. If you continue to face the wind, you may land short of it and if you turn to run, you may land on the other side of it, but one thing is for sure: you will land in the vicinity of it. So, take the action outlined below and then at double to triple the height of the trees, face into the wind to minimize your ground speed, pull your toggles to half brakes, and place your feet and knees firmly together in preparation for a PLF.

Two Action System (TAS). Continue to steer, activate your flotation gear if you have it, undo your chest strap and your bellyband if there is one. Loosen your leg straps so that you can slide the saddle forward a bit. Disconnect the RSL.

Then, just before touchdown, reach for the canopy release handle. At the moment your feet get wet, not one moment sooner, activate the releases. The tensioned canopy will recoil upwards and even a mild wind will carry it away. Altitude is very difficult to judge, especially over flat ground or a large body of water. One is always tempted to drop out of the harness just before touching down, but what appears to be just a leg length may really be building height, so don't break away until your feet are in the water.

This procedure will leave you floating with your harness and reserve on but with the dangerous unpacked main canopy gone. Roll over on your back and take off the harness. The harness won't hurt or restrict you and the packed reserve will even provide positive flotation. In fact, the reserve won't become negatively buoyant for about three minutes. So, you can use it for temporary flotation. The AAD may open the reserve container once it gets wet.

Single Operation System (S.O.S.). With the S.O.S. system, if you jettison the main canopy, the Stevens lanyard will activate the reserve unless you disconnect it. Allow yourself to get wet, bend forward and then swim or work your way forwards out of the loosened leg straps as quickly as possible. Get clear of the canopy.

If the canopy does land on top of you anyway, grab it and follow/hand walk a seam to the edge of the canopy. There is no reason to panic as you can always lift the porous fabric to form a space to breathe. Once clear of the canopy, swim away using mostly your hands until you are clear of the lines. Keep kicking to a minimum, as pumping legs tend to draw lines and fabric toward them.

If you should land in a river, even a slow moving one, you want to jettison your main as soon as possible. If it catches in the current it will drag you under and/or downstream away from your rescuers.

Besides your reserve, certain other pieces of your gear may provide some flotation. Pneumatic soled jump boots, full shell helmets, knotted jumpsuits, etc.; they are all there for those who think to use them.

You must undergo (dry) unintentional water-landing

training for your USPA A license and (wet) live water training with full gear for the B license. These requirements have probably saved hundreds of lives so far.

Buildings. Landing on a building presents two distinct hazards. First, you might go through the roof of the building, which may lead to a broken or cut extremity. Second, if it is windy, you might find yourself being dragged off of the building and going for a second extremely hazardous landing. If you feel your life is in danger (such as being dragged off a high building), break away from the main as quickly as possible. Don't worry about the reserve inflating — it won't have enough of a chance to do so. If it is your reserve that put you on the building, try to collapse it as quickly as possible. If that doesn't work, you're going off the building in the wrong position for a second landing and there probably won't be much of a chance to get into a PLF mode, but try to anyway.

Many building landings do not end this well.

Other obstacles. There are many other landing obstacles that are potentially hazardous to parachutists such as ditches, fences, hard roads and even some unique ones like hot water geysers. These hazards at your DZ will be pointed out to you in your first jump course, probably with a marked aerial photograph. When visiting a new drop zone, be sure to check in with an instructor or the Safety & Training Advisor for a briefing on their local hazards and recommended alternate landing areas.

When you are in the air, look for the danger areas. *Invisible* barbed wire runs between visible fence posts, power lines run between power poles, isolated buildings are served by electricity. Power lines, ditches, and fences often border roads, airplanes land on runways, etc. This should all be obvious, but sometimes it's not. It is all new to you and the view is different: you are looking down at the terrain now, not horizontally.

Since nature abhors a straight line, consider anything on the ground that looks like it has a straight line to be a hazard area (such as where a cutting of a field stops at a fence line). If an obstacle presents itself, steer your canopy to avoid it. Turn your canopy to *run* and land beyond it, if necessary. If you are going to strike an object, hit it feet-first. Successful landings under a parachute are like those in an airplane: *the ones you walk away from are good*. It is far better to land outside the target area and walk back than land on a fence and be carried back. Don't let *get home-itis* get you. If you pass over the obstacle very low, you may not have sufficient altitude to turn into the wind for landing. It is then preferable to crab the canopy slightly and try to do your best forward PLF. But, obviously, the best solution is to think and plan ahead to avoid the obstacle in the first place. The most important rule about landing hazards is: Continually make efforts to avoid them. The second rule is: It is better to land flying downwind than to hit an obstacle.

Airport safety. Never smoke around aircraft, hangers or pumps. Both aviation fuel and aircraft fluids present a great fire risk.

When moving light aircraft, be careful where you push. They are covered with very light fabric or metal

and are easy to damage. The
pilot will show you where it is
safe to apply pressure.

Beware of the prop. It is difficult to see and will make quick
mincemeat of anyone who walks
into it. Always walk around the
back of fixed-wing aircraft and
in front of helicopters. Stand
where the taxiing pilot can see
you; his or her forward visibility
is not good. Get into the habit.

Children and dogs may find
airplanes attractive

Leave the dog and the children at home, the airport is not a
nursery. If a play area is made
available to children at the DZ, remember that they are
still your responsibility.

If your airport has more than one runway, stay off the
active one. It will normally be the one running the closest
to the direction of the wind. Remember that planes usually takeoff and land *into* the wind so look for them
downwind. Rules change from airport to airport and at
some you will not even be allowed to cross the active. Do
not walk down any runway and do not fly your canopy
over one under 500 feet.

Be nice to all the pilots, they have a lot of clout at the airport and you may need one to fly the jump ship. Be patient
with the whuffos (spectators), they *are* public opinion.

Stay off the runway

Warning

- Read and follow all operating instructions and all manufacturer specifications, instructions, advice and requirements for use of the equipment.

- Use only manufacturer-recommended, compatible components.

- Examine and replace ANY defective, worn, or deteriorated component of all equipment.

- Examine all gear and equipment, including all fittings, buckles, snaps or other fasteners, before each use of any parachute product.

- Use only those products designed for parachute use.

- Do not exceed recommended or stated forces, speeds or other factors regarding safe use of the equipment.

- Read and follow all warning labels, manuals, instructions, training or experience requirements and recommendations, and all recognized parachute use procedures.

- Check and calibrate all altimeters, timers or other similar equipment before each jump or use.

- Never attempt to use equipment packed, prepared, assembled or fitted by others unless he or she is a certificated parachute rigger. Know and examine your equipment before each use.

FAILURE TO FOLLOW ALL WARNINGS, INSTRUCTIONS AND REQUIRED PROCEDURES MAY RESULT IN SERIOUS INJURY OR DEATH.

UNITED STATES PARACHUTE ASSOCIATION PUBLICATIONS
Section 2-1: Basic Safety Requirements

Note: Each paragraph in the BSRs has a marginal notation of S, E, FB, or NW, which identifies its waiverability as indicated in Section 2-2.

A. Applicability [NW]

1. These procedures apply to all jumps except those made under military orders and those made because of in-flight emergencies. Voluntary compliance with these procedures will protect the best interests of both the participants and the general public.

2. A "skydive" is defined as the descent of a person to the surface from an aircraft in flight when he or she uses or intends to use a parachute during all or part of that descent.

3. All persons participating in skydiving should be familiar with the Skydiver's Information Manual and all federal, state, and local regulations and rules pertaining to skydiving.

B. Compliance with Federal regulations [NW]

1. No skydive may be made in violation of Federal Aviation Administration (FAA) regulations.

2. FAA regulations include the use of restraint systems in the aircraft by all skydivers during movement on the surface, takeoff, and landing.

C. Medical requirements [NW]

1. All persons engaging in skydiving must:
   a. Carry a valid Class 1, 2, or 3 Federal Aviation Administration Medical Certificate; or
   b. Carry a certificate of physical fitness for skydiving from a registered physician; or
   c. Have completed the USPA recommended medical statement.

2. Any skydiver acting as parachutist in command on a tandem jump must possess an FAA Class 3 medical certificate or the equivalent.

D. Age requirements [NW]

1. For jumps with a single-harness, dual parachute system, skydivers are to be at least, either:
   a. 18 years of age [FB]
   b. 16 years of age with notarized parental or guardian consent [NW]

2. For jumps with a tandem parachute system, skydivers are to be at least the age of legal majority. [FB]

E. **Student skydivers**

Note: All references to USPA instructional rating holders apply to higher rating holders in that training discipline.

1. General [E]

   a. All student training programs must be conducted under the direction and oversight of an appropriately rated USPA Instructor until the student is issued a USPA A license.

   b. A person conducting, training, or supervising student jumps must hold a USPA instructional rating according to the requirements which follow.

2. First-jump course [E]

   a. All first-jump non-method-specific training must be conducted by a USPA Instructor or a USPA Coach under the supervision of a USPA Instructor.

   b. All method-specific training must be conducted by a USPA Instructor rated in the method for which the student is being trained.

3. All students must receive training in the following areas, sufficient to jump safely [E]:

   a. equipment

   b. aircraft and exit procedures

   c. freefall procedures (except IAD and static-line jumps)

   d. deployment procedures and parachute emergencies

   e. canopy flight procedures

   f. landing procedures and emergencies

4. Advancement criteria

   a. IAD and static-line [E]

      (1) All jumps must be conducted by a USPA Instructor in that student's training method.

      (2) Before being cleared for freefall, all students must perform three successive jumps with practice deployments while demonstrating the ability to maintain stability and control from exit to opening.

   b. Harness-hold program [NW]

      (1) All students must jump with two USPA AFF rating holders until demonstrating the ability to reliably deploy in the belly-to-earth orientation at the correct altitude without assistance.

    (2) All students must jump with one USPA AFF rating holder, exit safely, maintain stability, and deploy at the planned altitude without assistance prior to attempting disorienting maneuvers.

  c. All students must jump under the direct supervision of an appropriately rated USPA Instructor until demonstrating stability and heading control prior to and within five seconds after initiating two intentional disorienting maneuvers involving a back-to-earth presentation. [E]

  d. Tandem training jumps [E]

    (1) All tandem training jumps must be conducted by a USPA Tandem Instructor.

    (2) For progressive training requirements following tandem jumps, refer to "Crossover training."

  e. Other tandem jumps [E]

    (1) Jumpers not rated as USPA Tandem Instructors who successfully complete a tandem instructor course in accordance with FAR 105.45 may act as a parachutist in command on tandem jumps.

    (2) Any jumper acting as tandem parachutist in command must meet the recent experience requirements for USPA Tandem Instructors.

    (3) Intentional back-to-earth or vertical orientations that cause tandem freefall speeds exceeding that of droguefall are prohibited.

  f. Tandem equipment experience: [E]

    (1) Before acting as parachutist in command or instructor on a tandem jump, a skydiver must satisfactorily complete an FAA-approved course of instruction on that equipment.

    (2) Tandem equipment instruction must be conducted by an individual approved by the tandem equipment manufacturer of that system.

5. Crossover training [E]

  a. Students may transfer after the first or subsequent jumps to another training method after demonstrating sufficient knowledge and skill in the areas of equipment, aircraft, exits, freefall maneuvers, deployment, emergency procedures, canopy control, and rules and recommendations to enter into that program at a comparable level of proficiency and training.

    b. Students previously trained in a tandem program may continue in a harness-hold program or must demonstrate a solo exit and practice deployment with stability in the IAD or static-line program prior to advancing to freefall.

    c. Students previously trained in a harness-hold program must have exited stable without assistance or performed a stable IAD or static-line jump with a practice deployment supervised by a USPA IAD or Static-Line Instructor prior to performing freefall jumps with any non-AFF-rated USPA Instructor.

6. Students training for group freefall [S]

    a. All student freefall training for group freefall jumps must be conducted by a USPA Coach under the supervision of a USPA Instructor.

    b. All students engaging in group freefall jumps must be accompanied by a USPA Coach until the student has obtained a USPA A license.

7. Instruction of foreign students [E]

    a. Foreign non-resident instructional rating holders appropriately and currently rated by their national aero club may train students from that nation in the U.S., provided the instruction is conducted in accordance with the USPA Basic Safety Requirements.

    b. Appropriately and currently rated USPA instructional rating holders may assist in this training.

8. No skydiver will simultaneously perform the duties of a USPA instructional rating holder and pilot-in-command of an aircraft in flight. [NW]

9. All student jumps must be completed between official sunrise and sunset. [NW]

F. Winds [S]
Maximum ground winds

1. For all solo students

    a. 14 mph for ram-air canopies

    b. 10 mph for round reserves

2. For licensed skydivers are unlimited

G. Minimum opening altitudes [E]
Minimum container opening altitudes above the ground for skydivers are:

1. Tandem jumps-4,500 feet AGL

   2. All students and A-license holders-3,000 feet AGL

   3. B-license holders-2,500 feet AGL

   4. C- and D-license holders-2,000 feet AGL

H. Drop zone requirements

   1. Areas used for skydiving should be unobstructed, with the following minimum radial distances to the nearest hazard: [S]

     a. solo students and A-license holders-100 meters

     b. B- and C-license holders-50 meters

     c. D-license holders-unlimited

   2. Hazards are defined as telephone and power lines, towers, buildings, open bodies of water, highways, automobiles, and clusters of trees covering more than 3,000 square meters. [NW]

   3. Manned ground-to-air communications (e.g., radios, panels, smoke, lights) are to be present on the drop zone during skydiving operations. [NW]

I. Pre-jump requirements [NW]

The appropriate altitude and surface winds are to be determined prior to conducting any skydive.

J. Extraordinary skydives

   1. Night, water, and demonstration jumps are to be performed only with the advice of the local USPA S&TA, Instructor Examiner, or Regional Director. [NW]

   2. Pre-planned breakaway jumps are to be made by only class C- and D-license holders using FAA TSO'ed equipment. [E]

   3. Demonstration jumps into level 2 areas require a D license with a USPA PRO Rating for all jumpers, including both tandem jump participants. [E]

   4. Contact canopy formation activity is prohibited on tandem jumps. [E]

   5. Tandem jumps into stadiums are prohibited. [E]

K. Parachute equipment

   1. Each skydiver is to be equipped with a light when performing night jumps. [NW]

   2. All students are to be equipped with the following equipment until they have obtained a USPA A license:

     a. a rigid helmet (except tandem students) [NW]

    b. a piggyback harness and container system that includes a single-point riser release and a reserve static line, except: [FB]

        (1) A student who has been cleared for freefall self-supervision may jump without a reserve static line upon endorsement from his or her supervising instructor.

        (2) Such endorsement may be for one jump or a series of jumps.

    c. a visually accessible altimeter [NW]

    d. a functional automatic activation device that meets the manufacturer's recommended service schedule [FB]

    e. a ram-air main canopy suitable for student use [FB]

    f. a steerable reserve canopy appropriate to the student's weight [FB]

    g. for freefall, a ripcord-activated, spring-loaded, pilot-chute-equipped main parachute or a bottom-of-container (BOC) throw-out pilot chute [FB]

3. Students must receive additional ground instruction in emergency procedures and deployment-specific information before jumping any unfamiliar system. [NW]

4. For each harness-hold jump, each AFF rating holder supervising the jump must be equipped with a visually accessible altimeter. [NW]

5. All skydivers wearing a round main or reserve canopy and all students must wear flotation gear when the intended exit, opening, or landing point is within one mile of an open body of water (an open body of water is defined as one in which a skydiver could drown). [S]

L   Special altitude equipment and supplementary oxygen
Supplementary oxygen available on the aircraft is mandatory on skydives made from higher than 15,000 feet (MSL). [NW]

Skydiving Rules of the Air

These right-of-way rules are extracted from Federal Air Regulation Part 91, *General Operating and Flight Rules* (shown here in regular type). They are further explained as they apply to freefalling skydivers and gliding parachutes (shown here in **bold** type). These are the general rules; local rules may be different.

91.67 Right-of-way rules; except water operations.

    (a) *General.* When weather conditions permit, regardless of whether an operation is conducted under *Instrument Flight Rules* or *Visual Flight Rules*, vigilance shall be maintained by each person operating an aircraft so as to *see and avoid* other aircraft in compliance with this section. When a rule of this section gives another aircraft the right of way, he shall give way to that aircraft and may not pass over, under, or ahead of it, unless well clear.

    (b) *In distress.* An aircraft in distress has the right of way over all other air traffic.

    (1) A reserve canopy has the right-of-way over all main canopies.

    (c) *Converging.* When aircraft of the same category are converging at approximately the same altitude (except head-on, or nearly so) the aircraft to the other's right has the right of way.

    (1) The canopy (on your level) to your right has the right of way.

    If the aircraft are of different categories

        (1) A balloon has the right of way over any other category aircraft;

        (2) A glider has the right of way over an airship, airplane or rotorcraft; and

        (3) An airship has the right of way over and airplane or rotorcraft.

    However, an aircraft towing or refueling other aircraft has the right of way over all other engine-driven aircraft.

(1) The less-maneuverable aircraft has the right of way over the more-maneuverable. A balloon would have the right of way over a parachute and a parachute would have the right of way over sailplanes, hang gliders, airships, airplanes and rotorcraft, in that order.

(2) A tandem pair has right of way over a solo jumper both in freefall and under the canopy.

(3) A cameraperson has the right of way over solo jumpers both in freefall and under the canopy.

(4) A less-maneuverable round canopy has the right of way over a square.

(d) *Approaching head-on.* When aircraft are approaching each other head-on, or nearly so, each pilot of each aircraft shall alter course to the right.

(1) Approach other freefalling skydiver(s) slightly to the right. If you misjudge the closing speed, you will miss the formation or jumper.

(2) Canopies approaching each other head-on should turn to pass on the right. If you find yourself heading for another canopy after opening, veer to the right. If you cannot avoid a collision, spread your arms and legs to avoid going through the lines.

(e) *Overtaking.* Each aircraft that is being overtaken has the right of way and each pilot of an overtaking aircraft shall alter course to the right to pass well clear.

(1) Pass other freefalling skydivers to the right.

(2) Pass other canopies to the right.

(f) *Landing.* Aircraft, while on final approach to land, or while landing, have the right of way over other aircraft in flight or operating on the surface. When two or more aircraft are approaching an airport for the purpose of landing, the aircraft at the lower altitude has the right of way, but it shall not take advantage of this rule to cut in front of another which is on final approach to land, or to overtake that aircraft.

Remember that it is easier to see below you than above you.

(1) In freefall, the lower person has the right-of-way. If someone is flying under you, especially at pull time, it is your responsibility to move away.

(2) Anyone in the process of opening has the right-of-way. A wave-off is a signal that the skydiver is about to pull.

(3) Under the canopy, the lower canopy has the right-of-way. Give way to the lower canopy at altitude and near the ground. Lower canopies should not make hook turns in front of other canopies on final approach. If you are the low canopy, do not assume others see you. Shout to let them know you are there.

(4) Approach the target in a left-hand pattern unless local rules dictate otherwise.

(5) After landing, clear the target immediately for the next canopy.

(g) *Inapplicability*. This section does not apply to the operation of an aircraft on water. (See 91.69).

We fly through the air (together) with the greatest of ease.
    —Andrew Haines

Chapter Five

Your Freefall Progression

Your progression in our sport after your first jump will depend upon which training program you enrolled in. The first jumps in these training programs were briefly mentioned in chapter 2. Once you are ready to make a second, third, and many more jumps, you need to progress through a well designed training program which will fulfill your wants and desires to get into the air.

The USPA has (with the help of much input from the field) designed an Integrated Student Training Program (ISP). What does the ISP look like? The ISP is a block-charted comprehensive attempt to give students and instructors a "road map" of training objectives in eight specific categories regardless of what type of training program is being used with good suggestions as to where a student would be (jump-number wise) in the various programs in each of these categories. Your ground school instruction will come from a certified instructor with a S/L, IAD, AFF, or Tandem rating specific for the classwork you are taking, and a certified instructor with the appropriate rating will directly supervise each of your jumps until you no longer require formal instruction.

A detailed write-up of the program is available from the USPA in the Skydiver's Information Manual (SIM) in either hard copy or downloadable form from their website (http://www.uspa.org). Since programs have a tendency to evolve and change, we won't bother retyping all of the

USPA SIM Section 4-1 — Student Skill and Knowledge Sets

Categories, Jump Numbers and Supervision	Exit and Freefall	Canopy Flight	Equipment
CAT A: AFF: 1 (Two Als) S/L & IAD: 1-2 (S/L I or IAD I) TAN: 1 (TI)	Adaptation to skydiving environment; principles of deployment	Steering; Intro to pattern: wind line; landing procedures	Altimeter and operation handle orientation; instructor gear checks
CAT B: AFF: 2 (Two Als) S/L & IAD: 3-5 (S/L I or IAD I) TAN: 2-3 (TI)	Relaxed body position; leg awareness; unassisted stable deployment (simulated for S/L & IAD)	Assisted pattern' assisted flare; written flight plan; review PLF	Handle operation and protection
CAT C: AFF: 3-4 (Two Als, then one), S/L & IAD: 6-7 (S/L I or IAD I) Former TAN: 4-5 (AI)	Solo controlled, relaxed freefall; heading awareness; wave-off	Solo pattern and flare; wing loading; turbulence; downwind landings	Complete orientation (main closed); observe pre flight
CAT D: AFF: 5-6 (AI) S/L & IAD: 8-11 (S/L I or IAD I) Former TAN: 6-7 (AI)	Solo exit (AFF); heading control; freefall speeds and times	Back-riser control with and without brakes; stand-up landing within 50 meters of target (assisted)	Assisted pre-flight; AAD operation; AAD owner's manual
CAT E: AFF: 7-9 (AI) until cleared from AFF, then Coach S/L & IAD: 12-15 (S/L I or IAD I until 45-sec. Delays, then Coach) (Merge Tandem Students into a suitable program)	Door exit; aerobatics; unsupervised freefall	Stalls; traffic avoidance; unassisted landing within 50 meters of target; finding the "sweet spot" of the canopy; performance of rectangular vs. elliptical canopies	Complete orientation (open canopy); component identification; unassisted pre-flight; comprehensive RSL discussion
CAT F: AFF: 10-13 S/L & IAD: 16-17 (Any program's I or Coach)	Tracking; two clear and pulls for former AFF students	Braked turns, approach, and landing; maximum glide; unassisted landing within 25 meters of target on two jumps	Assisted packing; pin check (others); parachute system and canopy owner's manuals
CAT G: AFF: 14-16 S/L & IAD: 18-20 (Any program's I or Coach)	Group exits; forward motion; docking; break-off and separation	Collision avoidance review; reverse turns; unassisted landing within 20 meters of target on two jumps	Solo packing; rigger's responsibilities; maintenance orientation; ADD review
CAT H: AFF: 17-20 S/L & IAD: 21-24 (Any program's I or Coach)	Diver exit; swooping; traffic awareness during swooping, tracking and deployment	Front riser control; landing within 20 meters of target on three jumps	Owner maintenance (three-ring system closing loop)

detailed information of those programs here. What we will concentrate on in this chapter are the fun things you can do as you progress through the ISP along with some of the different ways to do those fun things.

USPA SIM Section 4-1 – Student Skill and Knowledge Sets

	In-Depth Emergency Review*	Rules and Recommendations	Spotting and Aircraft
CAT A:	Passive aircraft emergencies (instructor leads)	FAR 91.107 (seat belts); SIM 2-1 (First jump course topics)	Propeller avoidance; movement in aircraft
CAT B:	Training harness: deployment problems; partial and total malfunctions; stability recovery; and altitude awareness	SIM 2-1 (students); SIM 5-1 (malfunctions); FAA AC-90-66A (illustration of aircraft traffic patterns)	Airport orientation and recognition; runway and approach incursions; aircraft patterns
CAT C:	Open parachute in aircraft; off-airport landings; obstacle recognition and avoidance; turbulence; collapsing the canopy on landing	SIM 2-1 (student equipment); FAR 105.43.b.1 (equipment); local laws; canopy owner's manual	Pattern selection
CAT D:	Training harness: routine opening problems; instant recognition and response; building landings	SIM 5-1 (buildings); SIM 5-3 (AADs); FAR 105.17 (cloud clearances)	Jump run observation; looking below for aircraft
CAT E:	Training harness: two canopies out; high-wind landings; independent response to aircraft emergencies	SIM 2-1 (winds); SIM 5-1 (dual deployments); SIM 5-3 (RSLs and Altimeters); FAR 91 (pilot responsibilities); FAR 105.43.a & b (packing authorization and interval)	Aircraft orientation; airspeed; weight and balance; winds aloft; intro to exit spot selection; assist with jump run
CAT F:	Power line landings	SIM 2-1 (all); SIM 5-1 (power lines); SIM 5-2 (recurrency recommendations); SIM 5-7 (group separation); parachute system and reserve owner's manuals	Group separation; assisted jump run; calculating exit point from winds aloft
CAT G:	Canopy collision response; tree landings	SIM 5-1 (trees and collisions); SIM 5-5 (weather); SIM 6-1 (group freefall); FAR 105.43.c (AAD maintenance)	Unassisted jump run; weather
CAT H:	Water landings; low turn recovery	SIM 5-1 (water, low turns) SIM 6-2 (breakoff); FAR 105.13 (aircraft radio usage); FAR 105.15 (notification of jump requirements); AC 105-2C Approvals (aircraft)	Notification to FAA of jump activity; review STCs, Form 337, etc.

*After training recommended in the USPA Integrated Student Program for solo students coming from the tandem training program

Just as planning prepares you mentally, ground practice helps your body get used to going through the motions.

If you are in the Static Line or Instructor Assisted Deployment programs, your last instructor controlled deployment jump and your first freefall should be on the same day, so plan your weekend considering the number of jumps you plan to make.

Most students make two jumps per day, and three is the recommended limit. Sport parachuting requires a lot of ground preparation and is quite tiring so, unless you are jumping at a commercial center where they take care of the carrying and packing of the gear, you will probably find that three jumps take all day and wear you out. Experienced jumpers may make a dozen jumps in a day while doing their own packing, but most call it a day after five.

There is very little freefall time during your initial training in the S/L and IAD programs, especially during those short delays, so you will only have time to perform your planned maneuver once. In fact, the jump is more of a practical skills test than a learning experience, so a lot of thought and practice on the ground is required. Use the training aids, think about what you plan to do on each jump, and make dry runs over and over. With this approach, you will progress faster because you will make fewer mistakes in the air. Quicker progress will provide you with a greater sense of accomplishment and you will have more fun. It is always nice to do well especially in an exciting new challenge such as sport parachuting.

Ripcord pulls or Pilot Chute Throws. You will probably become more sensitive to the pull time as you progress up the freefall delay ladder. During your instructor controlled deployment jumps and early delays, you will leave the step in a poised exit or the strut in a hanging exit, almost standing head-up. Later as you approach terminal velocity (after ten seconds), your head will drop more until your body is parallel to the ground and your airwork will become more important than your exit. Now, for the first time, you will have the time and air resistance to make bodily corrections. Stability, especially in pitch (head up-down), will be much more noticeable. If you go head down on the pull, you will probably find it terribly unnerving. (It may hurt your neck and shoulders during opening due to a "crack the whip" effect and on the next jump you won't be looking forward to this part of freefall.) You may find yourself counting down and making a quick grab for the handle in order to avoid going head-down. There are easier, more satisfactory ways to combat the problem.

Position. The best approach to deploying the main canopy involves reaching for the main ripcord handle or hand-deployed pilot chute with the right hand while bringing the left hand over the head as you were taught on your practice deployment jumps. This method not only counteracts the tendency to go head down, it will allow you to correct any problems in the other axes (turns and rolls). If you can think to bend the legs at the knees a little more at the time you come in to pull, you won't go head down and the pull will be a very satisfying one.

Put your left hand over your head for stability

Ripcord trained students. Some students have trouble locating the main ripcord handle. Every piece of rental or club gear is adjusted a little differently; you can't expect the handle to be in exactly the same place every time. It is, therefore, essential that you look for the handle prior to reaching for it. The technique is to push the head back (to help you arch) while bringing the chin down to the chest and lowering the eyes to visually locate the handle. Depending upon the location of the handle, it may also help to turn the chin to the side. Look at the ripcord and you won't miss it when you reach for it with your hand.

Hand deployed pilot chute trained students. For hand deployed pilot chute rigs, you will have to thoroughly train yourself to reach for and throw the pilot chute per your training. You can't look for it as it is behind you, in your rear-right hip pocket area.

Eyeball the ground. Learn what 4,000 feet AGL looks like.

Altimeters are mechanical and, though they may be relied upon most of the time, are subject to failure. Learn to eyeball the terrain, learn what 4,000 feet AGL (Above Ground Level) looks like so you will recognize it the next time you encounter it. That is a routinely assigned pull altitude when you are in early freefalls.

Longer delays. After devoting a lot of time to your ground practice and mastering your jump and deployment procedures, you will be advanced to longer freefall delays.

During your increasing length of freefall, you will become conscious of wind, noise and speed while you begin using your altimeter more than your count in freefall. The

When the people look like ants—pull,
when the ants look like people—pray.

needle of the altimeter doesn't move very fast during the first ten seconds of freefall, so you may still have to concentrate on your count.

Your exits are important on your early freefalls as you are still falling relatively slowly (sub-terminal) and initially have little airspeed with which to work. The direction of your exit will determine your body attitude in the air; there isn't enough time or airspeed to correct for a bad exit except by arching hard!

The real excitement will come with relative work when you hold stable as base for your first hook-up. You will learn to wave off, prior to pulling. Experienced jumpers always wave off to alert any other skydiver who might be above them that a parachute is about to be deployed. You will also learn how to brief the pilot on the plan of the jump. On 30-second delays you will be flying your canopy to land within 25 meters of the target center.

Wave off. The action of bringing both hands from the relaxed arch position at the side of the head to a position crossing each other above the head, then back. This is usually performed as two cycles with the accompanying action of the jumper looking from side to side to determine if anyone is crossing over his back (the deployment area). It is a signal to those above you that you are about to pull. It is a chance for you to ensure that you won't hit anyone above you by deploying your parachute. (If someone was crossing over your back, you could wait another second or two prior to deploying your parachute, or slide to the side so that the danger of deploying into another freefalling skydiver is minimized, but don't wait too long...the ground is a harsh mistress!)

Supervision. All of your jumps will be made under the direct supervision of a USPA rated instructor (even while jumping with a coach) until he or she is satisfied that you can

---

Any deviation from the horizontal plane is just plain poison for most people. Many people like to go fast and do things but, for some obscure reason, their ingrained fear of doing it straight down still persists.

take care of yourself and signs you off as being off formal instruction. This isn't the end of your learning; it is just the end of your being under their direct supervision. Once you have been certified as capable of supervising yourself, you will be allowed to board the jumpship without an "instructor in tow" and may even jump from a small two-place plane carrying just you and the pilot.

Class A License. Finally, it is time for the magic jump called the USPA A-License Check Dive. On this jump, you must determine the spot to exit the aircraft on your own and use it. You can use any exit position you want; hopefully one you're comfortable with. You do an assigned aerobatic maneuver of a figure-8 (left and right 360-degree turns in succession with altitude checks), and then perform a backloop. Then your coach moves to within 20 feet of you and allows you to dock on him without his assistance. Remembering your key altitudes, you can keep playing in the air until about 6,000' AGL, then you must turn and track on your own initiative by 5,000' AGL, gaining at least 100 feet of separation between you and your coach. You must wave off and deploy your parachute system by 3,000' AGL. Then, you get to play around with your canopy again and follow your pre-selected landing pattern to a landing within 20 meters of the target.

With your oral quizzes done and your A-License card filled out, you become a genuine 100% certified licensed skydiver! The A license is another great milestone in your parachuting career and a time to celebrate. Now you may take part in your jumping future, which is unlimited. You will be eligible to participate in small group relative work once you have your A-License in hand. Don't rush into big group RW until you are comfortable with small group work.

Your relative work jumping will become more and more exciting as the number of people in the air with you increases. This is where the fun really begins in parachuting; this is what makes the first 20 or so jumps worth all the hard learning. Now let's get down to some other specifics of skydiving such as things you can do once your formal training is complete.

Distance Fallen Each Second to Terminal Velocity

Seconds From Exit	Meters Per Second	Feet Per Second	KMS Per Hour	Miles Per Hour
1	4.8	16	17.5	10.91
2	14	46	50.4	31.36
3	23	76	83.3	51.81
4	31.5	104	114.0	70.91
5	38	124	136.0	84.54
6	42.5	138	151.4	94.09
7	45	148	162.4	100.91
8	47.5	156	171.1	106.36
9	49.5	163	178.8	111.14
each additional second	49.5	163	178.8	111.14

General Rule:
After terminal velocity is reached (about 10 seconds), it takes 15 seconds to free fall each 1000 feet, depending on your height, weight and jumpsuit.

Cumulative Distance Fallen in Free Fall Spread Position

Second of free fall	Meters	Feet	Second of free fall	Meters	Feet
1	4.8	16	15	612.5	2010
2	19	62	20	884	2900
3	42	138	25	1150	3770
4	74	242	30	1415	4650
5	111.5	366	35	1685	5530
6	153.5	504	40	1955	6410
7	198.7	652	45	2220	7290
8	246.5	808	50	2490	8170
9	295.5	970	55	2760	9050
10	347.5	1140	60	3025	9930
11	399.5	1310	65	3295	10810
12	452.5	1485	70	3565	11690
13	506	1660	75	3830	12570
14	561	1840			

Recommended Exit Altitude For Pack Opening of 2500′ Above Drop Zone

Type of Jump	Above DZ Feet	Meters
Static line	3000	984
Clear & Pull	3500	1148
5 sec delay	3500	1148
10	3800	1246
15	4500	1475
20	5500	1803
25	6500	2131
30	7500	2459
40	8500	2787
45	9500	3115
50	10500	3443
60	12500	4098
65	13500	4426
70	14500	4754
75	15500	5082

Freefall tables

Freefall Speeds Chart

MPH	Variable
102	camera suit (Garry Carter data)
104	"slow" Strong Tandem
104	very slow face-to-earth formations
108	"average" Strong Tandem
108	overall average face-to-earth formation skydiving (Garry Carter and barographic data)
110	"fast" Strong Tandem
110-115	"fast" recreational face-to-earth formation skydiving
114	competition team face-to-earth formation skydiving (Garry Carter data)
114-120	"fast fallers" in face-to-earth formation skydiving
118-122	sit-flying in a laid back or relaxed position with a standard design sit-flying suit
125-135	sit-flying in a straight-backed sitting position with a standard design sit suit
125-130	skysurfing with normal wing sit-flying suits
150	standing up in a sit-flying suit
125-160	head down flying

Freefall table for various fall rates

Exit altitude with opening at 2500 feet	Length of free fall in feet	Time of freefall with 120 mph terminal velocity (seconds)	Time of freefall with 109 mph terminal velocity (seconds)	Time of freefall with 96 mph terminal velocity (seconds)
3000	500	6	6	6
3500	1000	9	10	10
4000	1500	12	13	14
4500	2000	15	16	17
5000	2500	18	20	21
5500	3000	21	23	24
6000	3500	24	26	28
6500	4000	26	29	31
7000	4500	29	32	35
7500	5000	32	35	38
8000	5500	35	39	42
8500	6000	38	42	45
9000	6500	41	45	49
9500	7000	43	48	52
10000	7500	46	51	55
10500	8000	49	54	59
11000	8500	52	57	62
11500	9000	55	61	66
12000	9500	58	64	70
12500	10000	60	67	73
13000	10500	63	70	76
13500	11000	66	73	80
14000	11500	69	76	83
14500	12000	72	80	87
15000	12500	75	83	90

Speed. Distances fallen are calculated for freefall in a stable spread position with average temperature and pressure conditions for a sea level drop zone. The tables assume you are wearing about 35 pounds of equipment and a trim but not tight, jumpsuit providing a fall rate of about 115 mph or 170 feet per second. Also see the Conversion Table in Chapter Two. Caution: your rate of descent increases with (1) other body positions, (2) higher temperature, (3) lower pressure (e.g., higher field elevation). Use these tables with extreme caution at field elevations over 1,000 feet, especially during long delays. Tight jumpsuits will speed up the descent. A good rough rule of thumb is that the first 1,000 feet takes ten seconds and each 1,000 feet after that take five seconds.

Stability and body positions: *Stability* is the result of a balance of forces. It occurs when you are falling in a selected position (e.g., face-to-earth) without requiring constant correcting movements. You are relaxed, at ease and not rotating on any axis. Because of the distribution of your body and parachute weight, it is difficult for novices to freefall for any length of time in a standing position, so we must select another acceptable comfortable alternative such as lying face-down. This position is familiar, easy to learn, allows a good field of view and gives you the feeling of flying like Superman. Other positions you could maintain easily are back-to-earth and the head-to-earth delta, but they can build up excess speed or be more disorienting. Using your arms and legs as control surfaces in the face-to-earth position, you can do most anything an airplane can do—except go back up.

Since we are trying to learn stability, it should be mentioned that it is possible to become unstable or Z out (go out of control). Buffeting (oscillating about one axis such as pitch; head up-down) can be corrected by relaxing and moving the arms back or in just a bit. Buffeting doesn't happen often and may not occur until you have several jumps, so the greatest problem may be in recognizing buffeting before the jump is over. Uncontrolled turns, slow or fast, are caused by unequal alignment of the legs, arms and/or trunk. Most students have no idea what their legs are doing because they can't see them; the legs must be in identical positions. If you go unstable at altitude, go ahead and attempt to correct it. If you are unstable at pull time or become disoriented, pull anyway. It is better to be stable during deployment, but it is best to be deploying regardless of position.

To deal with unintentional instability above normal pull altitudes, there is a rule of thumb called the five-second rule. It is: if you become unstable and didn't intend to, arch very hard for a count of five seconds. If you don't recover stability in that time, deploy the main canopy immediately. At opening altitude, you are running out of time fast. Even if a poor body position causes a malfunction, you are still slowed to about a tenth of your freefall rate of descent, so you will have more time to execute emergency procedures.

The spread stable position

The spread stable position or *cross* is the basic position for the beginning static-line program skydiver. The arms and legs are straight out and the back is arched hard to provide a shuttlecock shape.

The basic freefall position

The basic freefall position or *box* is a relaxed, stable, face-to-earth freefall position with a medium arch, with the legs bent upwards and the arms bent into a 90 degree or less U-shape. This position used to be called a frog. It is the common advanced flying position from which you will make all maneuvers. To practice the basic freefall position, start from the basic spread and then gradually relax it by bending the arms at the elbows and legs at the knees. Feel your way into it and make mirror-image limb movements so as to maintain balance. You won't be able to watch your legs but you can keep your hands in view out of the corners of your eyes. If you relax at terminal velocity, your body will naturally flow into the basic freefall position.

The basic freefall position may be further modified by tightening it, especially at the shoulders and hips. Bend your knees more and move your elbows closer to your sides. Also try arching more and rolling your shoulders further back. Your reduced drag will cause you to increase your rate of descent without going head-down into a delta position.

Spider. The opposite maneuver or position is called the *spider* or *reversed arch* and is used to slow the descent. The "spider" is accomplished by spreading out as far as possible and reversing the arch as though you were on top of a large beach ball. Some people even do what is called a "turtle" where they keep their arms in a bit and roll their shoulders forward cupping the air. The basic freefall positions: tight, regular, spider and turtle are common in relative work. They allow you to alter your vertical descent speed relative to other freefalling jumpers without creating unwanted horizontal movement. You can expect these positions to take many jumps to find and perfect.

The back to earth or *rocking chair* position. Note the reversed arch.

The stable back-to-earth position is a lot of fun and some jumpers can actually perform relative work this way. Getting over, holding it and getting back will provide you with the confidence that if you ever do find yourself out of visual contact with the ground, you can correct the situation. The easiest way to get over is with a barrel roll (discussed later in this chapter) and it is easy to maintain the SDB (Stable Delay, Back) with a reverse arch. Now you will be able to see both your hands and feet at work. To return to the face-to-earth position you can arch hard but this takes some time. You might do half a forward loop or half a back loop, but you must master the loops first. The simplest way to return is with another barrel roll. While you are over on your back, do not trust a chest-mounted altimeter. Positioned there, it is in a partial vacuum area, and will often read 1,000 feet too high.

The delta position

The delta is a stable fall position with the head down providing a much increased descent rate. It is normally used in relative work to swoop down to the action. In the delta, the arms are swept back and maneuvering is done with the shoulders, hands and/or legs. The arms may be spread or tight against the sides and the legs may be spread or pressed together.

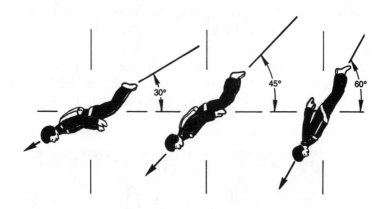

The angle of your delta is adjusted with the arms

Altitude and speed are two things to watch in the delta. You may accelerate from 120 mph in the face-to-earth basic freefall position to some 190 mph in a delta and this speed, plus the head-down body position, will make your opening something to remember if you fail to return to a proper body position for opening! So, flare out to a stable spread position and slow down for a few seconds before dumping your main. Since you are eating up the altitude so much faster, you will want to keep an eye on the altimeter. A good, tight delta is a lot of fun; you can feel the great increase in speed as the wind pulls at your jumpsuit.

Vertical speed. With simple movements of body surfaces, the freefalling skydiver may increase and decrease his or her vertical speed, cover a significant amount of ground horizontally and perform every aerobatic maneuver as though suspended by invisible threads. This is true flying, the closest you will ever come to imitating the birds without large cumbersome wing-like equipment.

Short, fat people freefall faster at terminal than tall, skinny ones; your speed is easily noticeable by others around you in relative work. Your vertical speed in freefall is determined by your weight and your air resistance

At pull time, you pull—regardless of body position. *—Mike Truffer*

Your attitude does not change your weight but it does affect your drag
and resulting air speed. As you alter your profile to the relative wind,
you alter your air resistance (drag).

(drag). If you wish to fall faster, you must increase weight
or decrease drag. Conversely, if you wish to fall slower, you
must lose weight or get bigger in area. Relative work is flying in relation to other fliers. In freefall it isn't practical to
add and shed weight so you are left with changing your
drag area. Fortunately this is rather easy; by simply sweep-
ing back your hands to drop your head into a delta position, you can increase your vertical speed by more than
50% and you may reach a horizontal speed of as much as 40
mph. Look around. You do not want to run into another
skydiver.

By arching more and bringing your arms in and bending
your legs up in a coordinated fashion, you reduce the
amount of surface area exposed to the relative wind. This

The other relative-work definition is the one where you do work for
your relatives. This has been known to decrease your potential for
making skydives, thus, it may be something you choose to avoid during good jump days. —*Mike Turoff*

will increase your straight-down fall rate. Conversely, by arching less (getting flatter) and extending your legs out in a coordinated manner, you increase the amount of surface area you have exposed to the relative wind and decrease your straight-down fall rate.

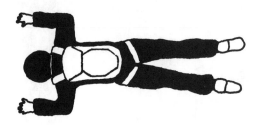

Arms up—body level

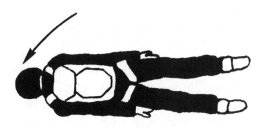

Arms back—head down

In the spread stable face-to-earth position, your body's weight is concentrated in the center and your limbs are both vanes and control surfaces, very much like an airplane. You are balanced with an equal amount of air resistance on your limbs all around your weight in the center. Now, if you move your hands and arms rearward, reducing the supporting drag on the upper part of your body, you will go into a head-down attitude. Or, if you put your hands straight up over your head and draw your knees up to your chest, you will start into a backloop. You can even turn (yaw axis) by simply dropping a shoulder, as this places a twist in the body so that it takes on a shape somewhat like a propeller. So, by altering your flying surfaces, you can perform most any aerobatic maneuver.

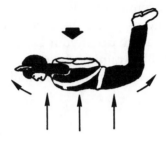

Level: the air flows around the body evenly

At an angle: the air is deflected around the body producing horizontal movement.

When you are freefalling in a face-to-earth position, your body plows through the air forcing it to flow evenly all around you. But when you angle your body, such as in a delta, the air is deflected and this imparts some horizontal movement; your body acts like a sled.

So, it can be seen that all your aerial maneuvers are initiated and achieved through the alteration of your control surfaces (hands, legs, etc.). These alterations change the attitude of your body, varying its effective surface area with respect to the relative wind, and cause a deflection in the air flowing past your body.

> The air! Man has visions of flight—not the roaring progress of heavy sinking machines, but that silent loveliness of gliding on outstretched arms that comes to everyone in dreams.
> —*Frank S. Stuart*, "City of the Bees"

Once again, ground practice and review will increase your chances of success in the air. It helps to know what you are doing before you go up. If your DZ does not have a horizontal hammock-like training device, a lot of these maneuvers may be practiced on the floor, a small table or even a bar stool.

The track is a modified delta, a position used to cover lots of ground

The track position is sometimes used by the parachutist who discovers he has erred in spotting or has drifted in freefall; he uses the track to get back to the opening point. Even more important, it is used to turn and track when jumpers separate after relative work to achieve maximum horizontal separation for opening. The track is a further refined delta which forms the body into a rough airfoil like the profile of an airplane's wing. This position is designed to produce some lift, in addition to the force of the deflected air, to move the body through the air horizontally. It has been theorized that in a max track, one can achieve an angle of 35 degrees or more from the vertical, or approaching 1:1. This means that on a sixty second delay from 12,500' providing 10,000' of freefall, one could cover 7,000' of ground, that's 1.35 miles!

To learn the track position, start with a delta on a 45-second delay to build up some working speed. After accelerating head-down for 15 seconds, bend slightly at the waist, roll your shoulders forward, bend your arms to follow the body, cup your hands, force your head back, straighten your legs while keeping them together and point your toes. You should be able to feel and see the difference but remember, it takes time to build up speed so accelerate for 15 seconds and then get into position and hold it for 20 more. When you are really starting to develop lift, you will feel your dive flatten out quite a bit. The track can be steered by gently guiding with your arms, hands, shoulders or head. The track is not only fun, it is one of the most important positions. It should not only be tried, it must be mastered.

Turn and track before pulling

Turns are a movement about the vertical (yaw) axis and are the most elementary of your basic maneuvers.

When you are ten seconds out and falling at terminal velocity, you have a lot of relative wind (the wind or air striking your body) to work with, a lot of air to push on. From the basic freefall position, even angling both hands 45 degrees the same direction will produce a slow turn. Study this phenomenon on your next drive to the DZ by sticking your hand

Even minor tilting of the palms will cause a turn

To turn, twist your body like a propeller

out the window of the car. At 60 mph, you are doing only half the speed of face-to-earth freefall but it is enough to demonstrate wind deflection. In freefall, your body is riding on a slick cushion of air. Very little pressure is required to make it turn.

There are many ways to effect a turn; in fact, the trick is in not turning. Any alteration in the position of your hands, arms, legs or body will produce a turn unless counteracted by another body part. Some of these specialized turns such as the push turn are used for certain types of jumps such as style competition. In turning, the twist is the trick. Turns are made in the same way from the basic freefall, delta or track positions; just lower a shoulder. In the basic freefall position, the hands and arms are lowered too.

If you can start a turn, you can stop a spin. *—Ted Strong*

To learn natural turns, exit the aircraft, assume the basic freefall position and build up speed to near-terminal; turns will be sluggish if you start right off the step. Bring your hands back just a bit so you are very slightly head low then look in the direction you wish to go. Bend your head that direction and dip that hand and shoulder. Your body will follow your eyes. Soon, turns will become second nature, automatic. Like riding a bicycle or swimming, turns need not be deliberated over before every movement. In time, even stability will become automatic. When moving an arm, one leg will compensate subconsciously. You won't even know it. To stop the turning, just straighten back to your basic freefall position. If you are turning fast, you may have to position yourself briefly for a turn in the opposite direction so as not to overshoot your heading.

Two 360-degree turns in opposite directions are combined and called a figure eight. Mastery of this maneuver is one of the requirements of the USPA A license.

There are a few more important points worth remembering. Turns are not immediate; it takes some time to build up turning speed. So hold the position until it takes effect and then be prepared to stop your turn just before you come around to your heading. Use a ground reference point for a heading and make it something that will be easy to find when you come around. Remember that sub-terminal turns are slow and mushy, unlike the turns you will make after nine seconds out. If you should get into trouble practicing turns, and can't stop one with an opposite correcting turn, assume the delta position. Once straightened out, go back into the basic freefall position. You can always delta out of a spin. But remember to keep track of your altitude and pull at pull time whether you are stable or not.

The barrel roll should be one of your earliest aerobatic maneuvers because it is easy, not as potentially frightening as a front loop or back loop, will help you practice SDB (Stable Delay Back-to-earth) and mastery of it is good insurance in case you ever find yourself on your back unexpectedly.

The barrel roll

To make a barrel roll from the basic freefall position, spread out to a cross position. Straighten your legs and pull them almost together while sticking your arms straight out to the side. Then bring one arm in across the chest while dipping (rolling) that shoulder. The sudden loss of drag on that side of your body will cause it to drop, and roll you onto your back. To complete the roll, extend the folded arm and bring in the outstretched one. Then resume the spread-arm cross position as soon as the ground comes into view again. Do another roll with more coordination and it will be smoother. Once you feel confident about barrel rolls, try one from the basic freefall position and accelerate it by throwing your arm and shoulder under and into the roll. Because your arms are in, you will do the complete roll in an instant.

Forward loops are easy, though at first, going head down may make you a bit anxious. Just as we learned the barrel roll, we will start with a safe and slow method and then we will clean it up into an improved loop.

Assume a cross position. Extend your legs straight back and spread them just slightly. Then put your arms straight

First forward loop   Improved forward loop

out. Your spread arms will give you lateral stability so you won't fall off to one side. Now simply bend way forward at the waist. The sudden loss of drag on the upper part of your body will cause your head to drop and you will go all the way around. When the ground comes into view again, straighten your body. You may wish to throw the arms high in a flare to stop on the level. Once you feel confident about these elementary forward loops, try them from the basic freefall position by bringing your hands in to your shoulders, bending at the waist and throwing yourself into it. You should be able to perform two independent forward loops with ease on a 20-second delay, even if you wait to begin until you are near terminal velocity, nine seconds from exit. If you find yourself on your back having completed only half a loop, you may wish to use a barrel roll to get back over.

The backloop

The backloop is just like doing a gainer into a swimming pool but you don't have to worry about hitting your head on the diving board. First we will try the safe and slow method and then the improved loop.

Assume a cross position. Extend the legs straight back, spread just slightly. Then spread your arms straight out to the sides. This position will provide you with lateral stability so you won't fall off to the side. Now quickly bring your knees up to your chest. The sudden loss of drag on the lower part of your body will cause it to drop and you should go all the way over. When the ground comes into view again, straighten the body and flare. Once you feel confident about this elementary method, try the backloop from the basic freefall position. Simultaneously push forward and down with your arms as you pull your knees up to your chest and throw your head back. The momentum should carry you all the way over. Flare when the ground comes into view again.

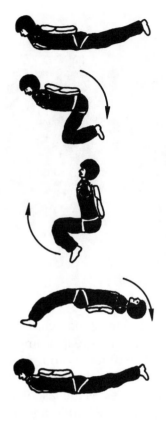

First backloop   Improved backloop

A sloppy or incomplete backloop may leave you on your back. A barrel roll is probably the easiest and fastest way to return to the familiar face-to-earth position should this happen.

Front loops and back loops are much easier out of an aircraft than off a diving board because you have more time and do not have to worry about entering the water at the right angle.

Other positions and maneuvers. There are other freefall positions and maneuvers such as the style tuck, backslide, T, daffy, layout backloop, twist through, knee turn and so on which you will want to attempt after mastering the above-mentioned basics. Once you can handle the above, all others will be easy.

The unpoised, door exit is a prerequisite to relative work

Door exits are a thrill. They are one of parachuting's training milestones and provide you with a great feeling of accomplishment. The satisfaction you will feel is equivalent to your first freefall and your first sighting of another jumper in the air. You must master the door exit as it is the last of the basic skills required for beginning relative work and for most skydivers. RW is what jumping is all about.

Now that you feel confident about your loops and rolls, you know you can recover if you should suddenly find yourself on your back. There is no reason to be apprehensive about an unpoised exit. There is no need to exit the aircraft face-to-earth, or even stable, as long as you are in complete, continual control.

Let's start with a warm-up jump—a modified poised exit from a Cessna. Get in the door and when you are ready to go, reach for the strut with your left hand, put your left foot on the step and then just swing out and go. As you leave the step, your position is just like the old poised, stable one, but your right hand and right foot never make contact with the plane. This exit looks cool and is a great confidence builder.

Now a real door exit; straight out perpendicular to the

fuselage. Just dive out with your arms swept back, do a forward loop and flare. Nothing to it and it happens so fast! You might get flipped by the prop blast and relative wind, but it isn't likely because your profile is very small. You will be out of the prop blast by the time you flare out face-to-earth.

Next, try the same exit without the front loop. Once you clear the door, arch, throw your hands high and bring your feet together to counteract the loop. (This looks like a Superman swoop.) Try some exits straight out and try some with turns into the direction of flight. Make corrections by adjusting your body position and avoid kicking or attempting corrections by throwing your body around. From large aircraft, dive back and down to minimize the effect of the prop blast. You will love door exits and will never go back to the poised type, except for some specialized, hanging-on group exits.

To practice for RW and be ready to learn big formation work, try exiting headfirst and transitioning smoothly from the Superman swoop into a tight delta. Gradually move your hands and arms down close to your body and spread your legs about shoulder width. It will take several jumps to get the feel of this but you will use it a lot later.

There are many things to do in the short time you have in freefall, so don't spend all of it on the exit. After leaving the aircraft, get on with your other airwork, canopy work, etc.

Relative work is the intentional maneuvering of two or more skydivers in close proximity to one another during freefall. Rapid precision freefall relative work is fun, fast, and exciting; there is something to learn and enjoy on every jump. RW is an activity that requires teamwork; it is a coordinated balancing act requiring maximum effort from each and every participant. The preparation is great while the flying time is short, and anyone in the air can blow the jump by taking out the fragile formation. When successful, relative work is an incomparable joy to be shared by all. Whereas relative work was once a hit-or-miss affair between two jumpers, it is now an exact aerodynamic science often involving 100 or more participants.

Relative work: group jumps

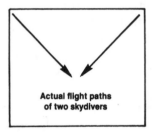

**Actual flight paths
of two skydivers**

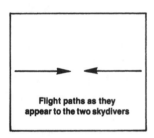

**Flight paths as they
appear to the two skydivers**

RW was born in 1958 when Lyle Hoffman and James Pearson made the first baton pass in Vancouver, BC. Later that year, Steve Snyder and Charlie Hillard made the first baton pass in the U.S. In subsequent years, the stick was abandoned but small star formations were being accomplished routinely. Size was usually held to four, the capacity of most jump planes. In 1965 at Taft, California, the Arvin Good Guys put the first 8-man together. Taft was also the site of the first 10-man in 1967, and the Center even hosted a 10-man competition later the same year. Credential type recog-

All motion is relative to the observer. —*Albert Einstein*

nition also began that year when Bill Newell established the Star Crest Awards and began issuing patches to those who had been in stars of eight or larger. In 1970, a 4-way RW event was added to the National Championships; it wasn't large star work, but it was RW. Ted Webster led an RW team to the 1970 World Championships in Bled, Yugoslavia, to make demonstration jumps, and this turned on the world to RW.

Recognizing that many women participated in relative work, the term *man* soon gave way to *way*, as in 10-way event. A 10-way speed star event was introduced at the 1972 U.S. Nationals; interest in large star RW was booming. The Commission Internationale de Parachutisme accepted RW in 1973, and both 4-way and 10-way were now world-wide events. Interest soared! Equipment changed, big planes were located, and jumpers drove great distances to get together to jump the big birds. Everyone was doing RW. Novices aspired to it and old timers learned something new; RW put the fun back into jumping. At the end of 1976 in Zephyrhills, Florida, over 100 10-way teams entered the annual meet. Through 1975 and '76, the large star interest turned to sequential RW; the plain old star was passé. Now they were doing snowflakes, accordions, donuts and even flying back-to-earth. When the CIP met in 1977, it adopted the 8-way sequential event for world competition. Then jumpers began doing the impossible: zipping around formations, crossing over other bodies intentionally and using the drop in the burble to position themselves. They made three-dimensional formations with one or more members standing up! It was incredible. RW is obviously limited only by the imagination.

You will be eligible to participate in relative work once you are on 30 second delays in the static-line or IAD program, or are enrolled in an AFF program and are able to perform all the elementary maneuvers mentioned previously, including turns, loops, door exits and tracking.

The exultation of seeing fine relative-work flying is surpassed only by the joy of being part of the jump yourself. —*Pat Works*

Dirt dives are used to plan RW jumps

Pre-jump planning is even more important in RW than in solo leaps. When you are on your own, lousy flying hurts only you. In a group, mistakes may take out the formation or even cause injuries, and this is no way to make friends. Freefalling jumpers can collide in the air or one may open below the other. High speed collisions occur when one jumper stops (under an open canopy) and the other is still at terminal. So it pays to plan the jump.

Your initial RW training will probably be with an instructor or coach, one-on-one. He or she will help you with the basics. Your first hookup will be followed with practice in exits, dives, vertical and horizontal maneuvers, the approach, docking and the breakoff.

If you find trouble getting on the loads with the big guys, it's only because you are a novice and not yet ready to soar with the eagles. Remember that the other jumpers have a lot of time and money riding on the jump; they want a successful formation. They dislike being targets for the less experienced, and have a right to be selective.

Relative work puts the fun, comradeship and excitement back into the sport. *—Ned Luker*

Rehearsing the exit

You would probably only make a mistake and be embarrassed anyway, so develop your own skill by working in small groups. The best RW practice may be performed with just two participants. Solicit the help of a qualified RW instructor from your DZ staff. Often he or she will offer you a lesson for only the price of a lift ticket. Form your own 4-way team of big-load rejects and work together. Once you are making hookups consistently, switch the exit order. Is the link-up smooth? Can you do it sub-terminal? Six seconds out the door? Can you fly side-by-side without touching? Ask an eagle to coach your team. When you are good enough, when you have tried hard enough, the eagles will notice. Then you will have to remember to be kind to novices.

Many of the people asking to get on 10-way loads aren't capable of making consistent 2-ways. —*Bob Iverson*

RW flying positions: Fall rate in relative work used to be controlled by adjusting the jumpsuit: pulling it in to go down and extending it to go up (relative to the other skydivers). During the wing war of the seventies, everyone wore huge jumpsuits with wings, vents and swoop cords. Today the teaching has changed and most jumpers are wearing slicker, tighter jumpsuits. Everyone is falling faster, and fall rate is controlled though body shaping; the curve in the shoulders, hips and back. We fall faster by placing more curve in our back and we fall slower by straightening our body with the elbows and knees down slightly. Fall rate is a very important part of relative work and it seems to be difficult for new jumpers to master.

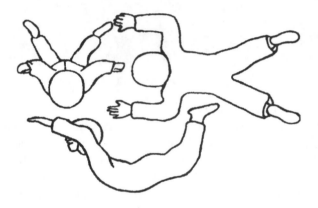

The boxman position

The boxman position is a basic freefall position with 90 degree angles: Your back is arched 90 with your head up, your legs are spread 90, your arms are up 90, your elbows bent 90 and your knees are bent almost 90. You will have to do some stretching exercises to master this position in the air. Think about your body shape in freefall, relax and let your arms and legs blow back. Close-in maneuvering is done with slight torso movements, with the lower back and shoulders aided by small leg movements. Your hands and arms are used to dock but not to maneuver.

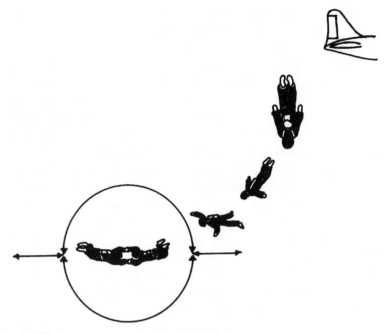

Delta down and flare

Use the delta position to close large vertical distances. If you are the last one to exit, you will have to get down to the base formation of one or more other jumpers. Sweep back your arms, press your legs together and aim toward your target. The farther the distance, the steeper your delta will be. Now think about energy management. You must delta to accelerate and move down as quickly as possible but you must slow down before you arrive at the level of your target. If you flare too soon, you will have to readjust to accelerate again. If you flare too late, you could collide with or over-shoot the base. Perfecting your swoop through energy management takes practice. You must be fast when you are far from the formation and slow when you are close. You must perfect your timing and be smooth. So hold this tight delta

---

You'll find there are two ways to get noticed: Doing real good and doing real bad. —*Roger Nelson*

until halfway to your objective and then slowly and smoothly relax the track by letting your legs and arms spread. Look, time, and adjust your descent to a smooth, gentle dock.

As you approach the base, extend your arms if you are going too fast and extend your legs if you are not closing fast enough. These movements will alter your body angle placing you slightly head-low or slightly head-high. Adjusting your body does not bring immediate results. A second or two are required to change your direction and momentum.

If you flare too soon and find yourself above the base, you will have to pull in your arms and legs to move down. Do not use the delta when close to the base. A radical acceleration will make you overshoot your objective.

If you find yourself below your target (or base), you will have to spread out to try to go back up (relative to the other skydivers). This is a bad place to be because forward movement usually means increased descent speed. It is also difficult to close on a target from below.

Most jumpsuits have grippers

Grip. When you reach your objective, you will hook-up or dock with a grip. This should be a no-tension grip, as though you and the base were flying in close proximity but not touching. Do not hang on a formation. The point is that the base is not a place to land and relax. You must join the formation—on level and actively fly your part of it.

Do not reach for a grip. Reaching down will make you float, while reaching up will probably disturb the person you grab or even make the whole formation slide. Do not carry any momentum when docking. Reaching out, gripping and pulling yourself in will move the base. Similarly, if you dock too hard, you will push the formation. These are simply cases of action and reaction: The formation is reacting to your push or pull.

Make your grip where it will provide the maximum amount of stability with the least amount of disruption. Gripping too high or too low on an arm or leg may apply too much leverage. In large formations, it is best to grip arms between the elbow and shoulder so your gripee can use his or her lower arms to grip and fly. Grip legs at the knee. Gripping a foot will pull it downward which will put tension into the formation and/or cause the group to slide.

For advanced relative work instruction, see the books listed in the Appendix of this book.

Freestyle skydiving consists of creative movements by one or more skydivers. The positions are limited only by the imagination. Freestylists are performing positions and movements we used to think were impossible, such as standing up, and they are performing in synchronized groups. See the videotapes listed in the Appendix.

Tamara Koyn performs a Chinese Split

Sitflying and freeflying

Skysurfing

Birdman suit-front
(photo by Jussi Laine)

Birdman suit-back
(photo by Jussi Laine)

Continuing education. Skydiving is evolving so rapidly that there is always something new to learn; nobody knows it all. Once you finish the static-line course or the AFF course, you will want to progress to Level 8 to develop your freefall skills. See USPA's *Skydiver's Information Manual* for full details.

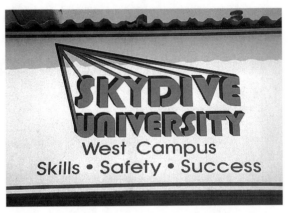

Advanced skydiving schools are spreading across the country

Anytime you lay off for more than 30 days between jumps, you will have to undergo refresher training and make a basic jump. For example, if you took the static-line training and do not have your Class A license, you will have to make a static-line jump. If you have your Class A license but not your B, you will have to make one clear and pull.

Every relative work dive should end the same way: Turn, track away, clear the air over your head, wave-off and pull. —*Bill Dause*

Chapter Six

Your Canopy Progression

Flying a ram-air canopy is a great deal of fun. In fact, students today cannot appreciate how good they have it. Modified round canopies have a forward speed of only 5 to 7 mph, depending upon your weight, and they let you hit the ground so hard your feet sting. Sport round canopies such as the Para-Commander class have a forward speed of between 10 to 14 mph, depending upon your weight and their construction. Ground contact with them is not as hard as a round when they are handled properly. Rear risers can be pulled down during the last few feet of the descent to get some minor decrease in the descent speed. Fortunately, you will not be using rounds or even PCs as main canopies during your training.

Flying the ram-air canopy. Basic canopy flying was covered in Chapter Two, and during your progression through the USPA's ISP, you will have many canopy flight tasks to perform to help you gain a full understanding of your canopy's flight characteristics and behavior/performance. You should ask for and read the flight manual of the type of canopy that you are using as well as talk to the experience jumpers and instructors at the dropzone, read this chapter, and look into some of the books and videos listed in the Appendix.

During your training, you will get to know your canopy and its capabilities. You will learn to turn your canopy using not only the steering lines/toggles, but also with the risers, both front and rear. You will learn to flare you canopy with the rear risers, make the canopy dive with the front risers, and make diving turns by pulling on a front riser. You will also learn braked turns and flying in partial and deep brakes. Try a fast 360-degree turn by holding one toggle full down. Fly at full glide (toggles up), one-quarter, half and three-quarter brakes. Hold each position for several seconds and notice the amount the canopy slows down. Hold both toggles at chest level and then let one up. Compare this turn to one in which you push one toggle 3/4 to all the way down while holding

Airspeed verses ground speed and the ram-air canopy
Para-Flite drawings

the other toggle in the half brakes position. These turns from half brakes will be flatter, slower, and more stable than a fully depressed toggle turn from the full-flight position and they will lose less altitude. Canopy familiarization should be conducted above 2,000 feet (and breakaway altitude). At 1,000 feet you should be entering your landing pattern.

If you would like to check your angle of glide at each brake position, spit into the air and watch its angle of fall. Spit with the toggles up and spit again with the toggles down. Always spit to the side — never *into* the relative wind — otherwise your saliva will just come back on you!

A ram-air canopy flying through the air may be thought of as a boat moving through a wide river. Think of the wind as the current and the canopy as a boat. A boat moving upstream might have the throttle wide open and yet make little headway relative to the shore because of the strong current. On the other hand, when the boat turns to run downstream at the same throttle setting, its speed relative to the shore is quite high. The same principle applies to parachute canopies holding against the wind or running with the wind.

Spotting is the selection of the course to fly on jump run, directing the pilot on that course and deciding on the correct point on the ground over which to leave the aircraft in order to land in the target area. There is more to spotting than just looking down since a good spot depends upon the direction and speed of the wind as well as several other factors.

It is also the responsibility of the spotter to check for traffic below to ensure the safety of both the jumpers and the people in those aircraft who are sometimes oblivious to jump activities (which is a violation of the FARs on their part!) Never leave the aircraft if there is any question as to the safety of the jump on its way down!

Now that everyone is using high-performance canopies, spotting has almost become a lost art. Exit point selection is sometimes so bad that even ram-air canopies are unable to

---

The more advanced a canopy is, the more gentle you must be when controlling it. —*Charles Shea-Simonds*

bring the team back to the drop zone. Knowing how to spot will make you a lot more popular while it adds to your skydiving education.

To begin with, let's think of the total descent as being in three separate phases: the *throw forward,* the *freefall drift* and *the canopy ride.* As you exit, you are traveling the same speed as the jump plane and are thrown forward in the direction of flight. Your trajectory is dependent mostly upon the speed of the aircraft at the time of exit. The freefall drift is that distance you are moved by the upper winds (those between the aircraft altitude and the canopy deployment altitude). The third segment consists of the effect of the wind on you during the two to four minutes you spend descending under your canopy to the target area.

So, we must locate and consider four important points: 1. the landing point (target), 2. opening point (by compensating for ground winds), 3. exit point (by compensating for the winds aloft and *forward throw),* and 4. the engine cut point (to allow the plane to slow down and to compensate for the *exit lag — the* time you need to climb out).

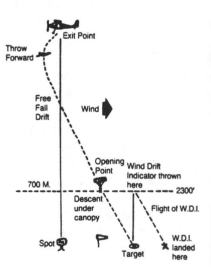

There is more to spotting than simply looking straight down

Because both you and your canopy have a horizontal movement capability, you can make up for an imperfect spot to some degree, as well as compensate for changing conditions. The ever-decreasing margin is called the *cone of maneuverability* and you must stay inside it in order to return to the target area. If you stray just one meter outside, there is no way you can get any closer to the disc than one meter unless the wind changes. As you descend, the maneuvering area becomes smaller and the canopy control strategy becomes more critical. Stay inside and you always have a chance at the disc. Most of your jumps will be made in lower wind conditions. When your canopy is able to penetrate the wind, you have a lot more options to work with in order to get to a safe landing area. The cone of maneuverability is not very distorted to the upwind area. If you go somewhat downwind of the target while up high, you can probably still get back to the target area.

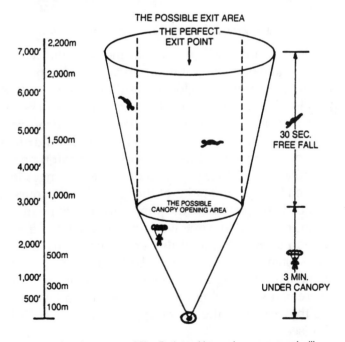

The cone of maneuverability. Both tracking and canopy speed will make up for bad spotting to some extent.

You should always spot as though you were jumping an unmodified round canopy and aim for the very center, the perfect exit point, unless you are spotting for a "several group pass." In that case, plan the first exit point where the aircraft enters the "good" possible exit area so that the last group out can still exit in the possible exit area. Each group leader should take a moment to check their exit point lest they be beyond the "envelope" of a good exit area. This will allow you and the other leaders the maximum compensation for errors and may be a blessing to the jumper on your load who has to use his or her round reserve.

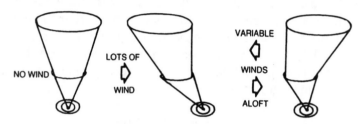

Now, crank in some wind and the cones take on their real shapes

There are four practical ways to measure the wind for determining the opening point: observation, balloon system, wind drift indicator and global positioning system (GPS). Observation is the one most often used and it works satisfactorily with ram-air canopies on large open drop zones. The balloon system is rarely seen today. The wind drift system is very accurate but it uses expensive aircraft time.

Observation is an easy way to determine changes in the spot. Watch the opening point of the group before yours and even ask their spotter where the jumprun and exit point were. Obviously, observation won't work on the first lift of the day.

Balloon system. Some of the larger centers have used a balloon system. They release a balloon, track it with a theodolite (a surveying instrument) and note its azimuth in time increments. Knowing the rate of ascent and consulting a chart, they can plot the opening point on an aerial photo for all to see.

Wind drift indicator. Another way to determine wind speed and direction is by dropping a wind drift indicator or *streamer* over the target at opening altitude. The WDI is normally a weighted piece of crepe paper designed to descend at the same rate as an open canopy. The wind will differ in intensity and direction at different levels and the specifics are nice to know when shooting an accuracy jump. Otherwise, it is sufficient to pick a point from the streamer drop and accept the mean effect of the wind.

Throwing the wind drift indicator

Accurate spotting requires the ascertainment of the opening point and the exit point. On low jumps, these will be virtually the same, but on high ones there are many additional factors to consider.

Before takeoff, the pilot will select an approximate wind line based on the windsock or wind tee. Ordinarily, he will

---

Some people spot 'em as they see 'em, some people spot 'em as they are, but there is no spot until you step out the door; and by then it really doesn't matter anyway. —*Lynn Levengood*

fly the streamer drop by approaching the target directly into the wind to minimize ground speed and give you as much time as possible to select the spot. This approach will also minimize *side drift*; drift is when the aircraft is not both moving and pointing in the same direction.

Make sure you have at least two WDIs aboard; keep one in reserve. Unroll the streamer a short distance, bunch it up and don't grip it tightly with a sweaty hand; you want it to unwind when you release it. Give course corrections to the pilot by direction and then amount, such as *right-five*, and wait a few seconds before spotting again so that the plane can level back out. If you are off course, remember: The closer to the exit you are, the greater the correction you will need. If the pilot is on the radio or otherwise occupied, use hand signals. Throw the streamer down and back forcefully so as to miss both the step and the tail.

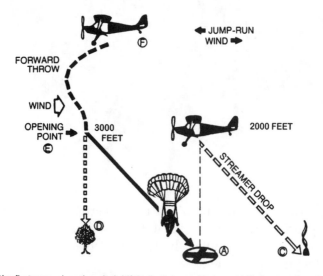

On the first pass, drop the wind drift indicator over the target (A). Draw an imaginary line from its landing point, (C) through the target (A) to a point 1.5 times the distance upwind (D). This becomes the ground reference for the opening point (E) and the exit point (F).

Good judgment comes from experience, and experience?—well, that comes from poor judgment.

Make sure the wind drift indicator has unrolled properly and keep your eyes on it. If the pilot is not skilled at flying jumpers, remind him that you want to keep an eye on it, so that he will remember to fly the aircraft in such a manner that you will be able to see it. This requires him to make climbing circles towards the WDI without blocking the view of the WDI with the lowered wing. If you take your eyes off the streamer, it is sure to disappear against nature's camouflage, especially as it nears the ground. The WDI should descend at about one thousand feet per minute.

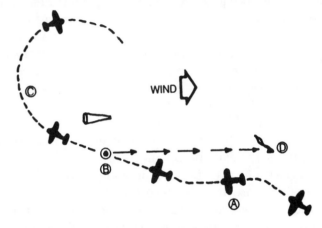

The streamer run: A. Direct the aircraft over target center, B. Throw the wind drift indicator directly over target. The pilot makes shallow turns to the right keeping the streamer in view through jump door, C. The streamer lands, D.

At some drop zones, they throw the WDI at exit altitude. They eyeball the WDI on the ground, then the target, and then an equal distance upwind of the target. This is the opening point of an *airborne parallelogram*. Unfortunately, this uses up three or so minutes of aircraft flight time so at most DZs, the WDI is thrown at 2,000 feet AGL for an opening point of 3,000 feet AGL. To arrive at the right exit point, they simply multiply the ground travel distance by 1.5.

Always take advantage of all the wind speed and direction indicators available to you, rather than relying solely on the WDI. If the last lift made the target, how did their spot compare with the direction indicated by the windsock?

When the smoke leaves that chimney, does it change course after rising a bit? At what angle does it leave the stack? Which way are those small puffy clouds moving? When you are in the air, check the shadows from the clouds on the ground. Is anyone down there kicking up dust? Look for farm machinery, cars on dirt roads, etc.

The opening point will be upwind from the target about 1/4 mile for each five mph of ground wind velocity. In fact, the true opening point may be even farther since the wind usually blows faster as you go higher, due to the friction provided by the ground. The distance to the correct opening point adds up fast.

There are other complications too. Heat waves create a mirage and make the target appear to be farther downwind than it really is. Mirages contribute only about 15 feet for each knot of ground wind, but this will make a difference if there is a *dog leg* in the wind, i.e., the ground and upper winds are up to 90 degrees different.

The next consideration is the selection of the *exit point* so that you will reach the *opening point* when it is time to pull. For low jumps, the exit and opening points will be the same, but there is quite a difference on longer freefalls. When going up for more than a 15-second freefall, you should check into the *winds aloft*. You can always check the jumpers ahead of you and compare their exit points with their opening points, call aviation weather or ask the pilot, prior to exit, if he senses any changes in the winds aloft. Above 9,500 feet, compensate 1/4 mile for each 15 mph of wind. Below 9,500 feet, cut the correction in half. The effect of the winds aloft on your fall will depend on how much time you are in freefall. Falling slowly, spread and stable, you will drift farther than in a full delta position.

Having just given the guidelines above for exit points, let us examine some of the mathematics behind these statements. The selection of the "cut" point and the exit point will be affected by the amount of time it takes for the jumpers to get into the exit position (small group and small aircraft) or to line up in the door (large group, large aircraft), the forward throw upon exit (due to momentum), and the upper winds' speed which causes freefall drift.

Global Positioning System (GPS). At more and more skydiving centers, the pilots use GPS to find the exit point. They adjust the point throughout the day based on experience from the previous drop. The little "black box" calculates position from three satellites and is very accurate. With GPS, pilots are doing the spotting today.

Cut point. Estimate the number of seconds it takes for your group to get into position based on several "dirt dives" on the ground. Then, figure the distance of the aircraft's travel across the ground and call the "cut" short of the intended exit point.

Forward throw and freefall drift. As you exit, you are traveling the same speed as the jump ship (about 80 mph) and are thrown forward by momentum. This forward speed bleeds off in about 15 seconds due to air resistance on your body. Your trajectory through the air is dependent upon the speed of the aircraft at the time you leave the step. However, your travel across the ground will be dependent upon two forces; that of your forward throw and that of the wind speed across the ground. Look at the table below for wind speed accumulated over a period of 15 seconds to figure your forward throw, and remember that although you start out at 80 mph, you end up at zero mph. Therefore, you should consider the average speed across the ground during the forward throw period as 40 mph (we're not going to delve into the physics of deceleration resistance here).

Wind Speed MPH	Feet / Second	Feet /15 Seconds	Feet / 30 Seconds	Feet /40 Seconds
0	0	0	0	0
5	7	110	220	293
10	15	220	440	587
15	22	330	660	880
20	29	440	880	1173
25	37	550	1100	1467
30	44	660	1320	1760
40	59	880	1760	2347
50	73	1100	2200	2933
60	88	1320	2640	3520

You should have found the forward throw to be about 880 feet. Now consider the effect of the winds aloft on your trajectory across the ground. If, for example, the wind speed aloft was exactly 20 mph and that wind acted on you for a total of 30 seconds (allowing some time for it to accelerate you downwind), you would be pushed downwind the exact same amount as your forward throw, therefore your exit point and opening point above the ground would be identical. As you jump in higher winds aloft and make longer freefalls, the wind's affect on your geographical position across the ground increases. For higher exits and higher winds, some formations have been observed to be blown almost a mile from the exit point! So remember, forward throw, wind speed, and exit lag all play a part in the decision of where to call the "cut" and exit the aircraft.

Here is a graphical representation of what is being described. Remember that these are just general guidelines.

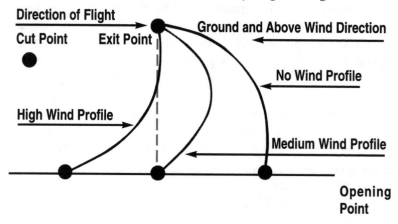

Direction of Flight

Cut Point   **Exit Point**

Ground and Above Wind Direction

No Wind Profile

High Wind Profile

Medium Wind Profile

Opening Point

So, what do you use for the exit point? You want it to be sufficiently far upwind to allow for the combined effects of forward throw and freefall drift to put you where you deploy your canopy so that you can make it back to the DZ safely. It was previously stated that the exit point should be about 1/4 mile upwind of the target for every 5 mph of ground wind. Let us examine that based upon the number of minutes of the canopy ride, the wind speed, and a given canopy speed across the ground. The table below shows the distance traveled across the ground due only to wind speed. A canopy speed of 20 mph would be used for travel both upwind and downwind, so let's negate its total effect for the first example. Imagine that you are jumping in a ground-wind speed of 10 mph and you want to deploy your canopy at 3,000 feet AGL, allowing a maximum hang time of 3.0 minutes. Looking at the table, you notice that the value of 2640 feet of travel (1/2 mile) is exactly what has been suggested (1/4 mile for each five mph of ground wind). If you wanted to plan for a longer canopy ride (such as a cross-country ride), multiplication of these values is straightforward. You can also figure-in canopy speed on top of wind speed to compute the increased travel capabilities of running downwind. For example, if you wanted to travel downwind for two minutes with your canopy doing 20 mph, a two-minute travel distance using the wind speed (10 mph) and canopy speed would yield a full mile's worth of ground travel.

Wind Speed MPH	Feet 1/2 Minute	Feet per 1 Minute	Feet per 1.5 Minutes	Feet per 2.0 Minutes	Feet per 2.5 Minutes	Feet per 3.0 Minutes	Feet per 3.5 Minutes
0	0	0	0	0	0	0	0
5	220	440	660	880	1100	1320	1540
10	440	880	1320	1760	2200	2640	3080
15	660	1320	1980	2640	3300	3960	4620
20	880	1760	2640	3520	4400	5280	6160
25	1100	2200	3300	4400	5500	6600	7700
30	1320	2640	3960	5280	6600	7920	9240

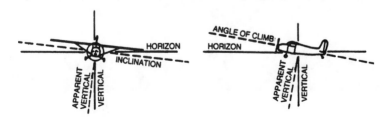

Make sure the plane is flying level

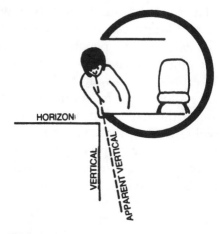

HORIZON

VERTICAL

APPARENT VERTICAL

Don't use the side of the plane as a reference point

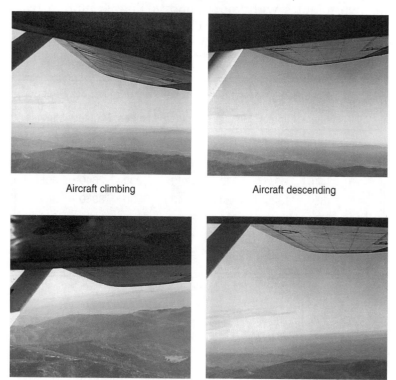

Aircraft climbing

Aircraft descending

Right wing low

Correct

Check the attitude of the plane by comparing the wing tip with the horizon

Now that you can calculate the cut point and exit point, the next task is to direct the jump ship over it. To do this well, you must first learn to look *straight down*. This is especially important just before you call for the *cut* (requesting the pilot to throttle back the engine to slow the airplane) because once the cut occurs, there is usually no more time to call for course corrections. Just where is *straight down* anyway?

Check the attitude of the plane. If the nose is high as you approach the exit point, you may be looking too far forward and may exit too soon. If your pilot is flying with one wing low, you may be looking down at an angle and be way off the wind line. If you cock your head forward during spotting, you may exit too soon.

Glance at the artificial horizon and the needle-ball indicator in the instrument panel. If they aren't centered, bring them to the pilot's attention and ask him to *level the wings*.

Don't use the side of the aircraft as a reference point. If it is curved, you probably won't be looking straight down. Keep the corrections small, in five-degree increments. Big corrections almost always require a banking turn and it takes a while to get the plane back to level. The pilot will try to make uncoordinated, flat (skidding) turns to help keep you oriented. If he made normal coordinated banked turns, you would have difficulty determining which way is straight down. Stick your head out, look straight ahead at the horizon and then look down, visualizing the drawing of a perpendicular line from the horizon to straight down. Then look at the horizon under the wing and repeat the visualization process to check your ground progress and determine the exact "straight down" point. Avoid using the aircraft as a reference; the horizon is always level.

Most common spotting errors place the jumpers in the air short and too far left. To be safe, go long. Everyone would rather run a little than have to hold, bucking winds and wondering if they are going to be blown past the DZ.

When you are at the predicted cut point, call *cut!* to the pilot, wait a few seconds for the plane to slow, then climb out; your spotting is finished. You don't have time for any more course corrections. You can't spot properly from out-

Check the artificial horizon to see if the plane is level

side the door after the cut, with the airplane going nose-low and people hanging everywhere. Besides, no correction can make much difference at this point.

If you find yourself under the canopy much too far upwind, you will have to run for the target immediately and with maximum efficiency. Pull your toggles to one-quarter brakes to minimize your sink rate. Next, decrease your parasitic drag by making your body as small as possible. Draw your knees up to your chest. This will be easier if you slide your leg straps toward your knees. Hold your hands in front of you and suck your head down.

Spotting sounds difficult but it really isn't. Start learning to spot as early as you can, so your instructor can observe and correct you.

Flying the pattern. Your approach to the target is quite similar to an airplane's approach to a runway. You will fly a *left-hand pattern* unless local rules are otherwise. Everyone should fly the same pattern to keep the air traffic orderly. Within the pattern, you will fly four *legs*: a *crosswind leg,* a *downwind leg,* a *base leg* and a *final approach.* Check your position and altitude on each leg. Fly the pattern the same way on every jump, continually adjusting and refining it.

While up high, turn into the wind to check the speed and direction of the upper winds. If they are not in the same direction as the lower winds, you are faced with a *dogleg* situation. Do these checks on every jump.

In light wind conditions (zero to five mph), the staging area is usually about 500-800 feet upwind of the landing area. In higher winds, it will be further upwind. You can play around with your canopy in that area until about 1,000 feet AGL. You may be flying *upwind* and *crosswind leg*s of the landing pattern prior to this altitude, or you may be doing any other control actions to get to and/or stay in the staging area.

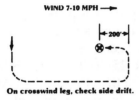
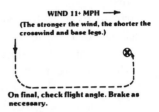

WIND 7-10 MPH ➤

|← 200' →|

On crosswind leg, check side drift.

WIND 11+ MPH ➤
(The stronger the wind, the shorter the crosswind and base legs.)

On final, check flight angle. Brake as necessary.

Fly the pattern

The following systematic landing pattern is suggested for light-wind conditions. As wind speed increases, distances upwind of the target for specified altitudes above the ground are generally increased. Remember that the canopy travels about three feet forward for every one foot down. The wind may contribute to or detract from ground travel distance depending upon which direction the canopy is facing.

Turn on the *downwind leg* at 1,000 feet AGL with your toggles up. Fly parallel to the wind line, passing about 200 feet abeam (to the side) of the upwind portion of the target area at an altitude of about 800 feet. Flying downwind, you should be moving rapidly across the ground. Keep an eye on the target and the windsock. If you are going too fast on the downwind leg, cut it short and turn on base leg sooner.

Turn on the *base leg* at about 600 feet AGL. This should be 500-600 feet past the target. As you fly downwind, check your approach angle to the target. If winds are high and your angle is too shallow, cut your downwind leg short and initiate your crosswind leg sooner to intercept *final*, closer to the disc. If your angle is too steep, fly the base leg past the wind line and then

Don't land with the wind unless you have no other good choice

make a 180-degree turn to fly back to the wind line. Check your approach angle again and repeat to the opposite side, if necessary.

Turn on *final* at 400 feet or higher. Keep the toggles up and adjust your angle to the landing area with S-turns. If it appears you may overshoot the target (it seems to be moving under your feet), make gentle 45- to 90-degree S-turns, first to one side of the wind line and then to the other. At 200 feet AGL, you are about 12 seconds from ground contact. At this point, commit yourself to your current course and your final landing area. Shift your eyes quickly from the target to the windsock and back while keeping your peripheral vision alert for other incoming canopies. If you start drifting, make small corrections. Do not make any quick toggle adjustments. If you are going to undershoot, just fly full flight until it is time to flare for landing.

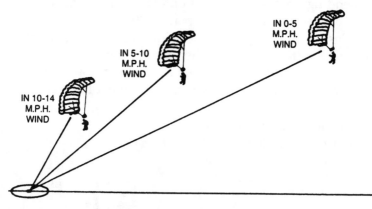

Glideslopes you can expect for given winds

When you are allowed to jump in higher winds — over 14 mph — you may enter the landing pattern at a lower altitude (your staging area will be farther upwind), and you will fly tighter to the target on the other legs. The higher the winds, the steeper your final approach will be. If you go too far downwind of the target, you may not be able to get back.

Attack the ground, do not let the ground attack you. —*Jim Wallace*

If the winds are faster than the forward speed of your canopy, you probably shouldn't be jumping! If you are, you may have to *back in* to the target. Position yourself just to the right or left of the wind line so that you can see the target by turning your head. If the target is directly behind you, it will be difficult to see the target and fly the canopy properly at the same time. Use brakes and S-turns to decrease your forward progress and increase your rate of descent. If you are not backing up enough, S-turn (*fishtail*) by turning alternately to each side.

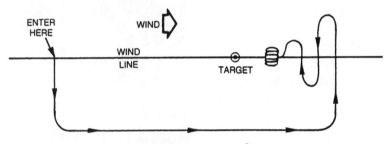

If your angle is too steep, use S-turns

When the winds are low, you will be able to venture farther downwind of the target area. Check the windsock frequently. If the wind is light and you are coming in too high on final, make some gentle S-turns or apply some brakes to lose some altitude.

Try flying the pattern with some brakes on. To turn, let *up* on the opposite toggle. For example, to turn right, let up on the left toggle. Steering this way from half brakes will give you a more stable turn. Remember that sudden or radical turns will increase both your horizontal (swing-out) and vertical speed, which is very dangerous to do near the ground.

Your landing approach will depend upon your canopy. Nine-cell ram-airs react differently from seven-cell squares. Consult your instructor and the canopy manufacturer.

Accuracy approaches, like normal landings, are made facing into the wind but much closer in to the target area than normal. Your target approach should begin at 200 to

500 feet on 1-10 mph wind days and at 500 feet or more on marginal to high wind days. Higher winds produce turbulence that may collapse your canopy and you want as much time to reinflate it as possible. Your accuracy approach should be with the brakes on and as steep as possible to lower the margin for error. But be careful; the farther down you pull the brakes, the greater the possibility you will not just *sink*, but *stall*. Stalling the canopy during landing can lead to serious injury.

If you have the toggles pulled down so you are near the stall and then you see you are going to overshoot the target, forget the target. Keep the canopy flying straight ahead and land safely. If you bury the toggles at this point, you will probably drop out of the sky. If you try a *hook* or fast low turn, the canopy will bank, you will swing rapidly to the side and you will probably be injured. Several jumpers have been killed making hook turns too close to the ground.

Landing on the disc in accuracy competition

Keep toggle movements to a minimum and do not shift around in the harness. Let your legs hang below you relaxed until the last second or two. Then depress the toggles just to the stall point to sink the canopy down to the disc in a near vertical descent. Do not jab your foot at the disc; just place it there. If the disc is in front of you, place your heel on it. If it is below you, use a heel or toe; and if the disc is behind you, use your toe.

In warm air, your canopy will sink more quickly and it may not react immediately to toggle movements.

Canopy relative work, *CRW* or *Canopy Formations* is the intentional maneuvering of two or more open parachute canopies in close proximity to, or in contact with, one another during descent. When two or more canopies hook up one above the other in flight, the formation is called a *stack* or a *plane*. Good CRW is smooth formation flying. Bad CRW results in collisions, deflated canopies, entanglements, injuries and even death. While ram-air canopies move fairly slowly, they owe their rigid shape to inflation. They lose their shape and flying ability when stopped or when the lines lose their tension.

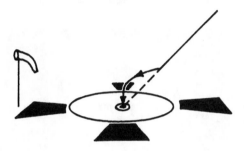

Sink down to the target

Canopy relative work: A side-by-side

CRW, like so many other activities in parachuting, began as a stunt. First practiced in 1976, it was demonstrated to the world at the U.S. National Championships in Tahlequah, Oklahoma. A few months later, Dan Poynter, an author of this book, penned a parody article reflecting the growth and growing pains of canopy relative work, and illustrated it with a couple of CRW photos he had taken. Some liked the joke, but some took it seriously and many decided to try this new form of aviation. The new activity caught on and soon demanded its own place in the sport.

A four plane

Canopy relative work began with, and was touted as, something for relative workers to do after the skydiving was over. But it soon carved its own niche and developed its own following. Jumpers began making clear-and-pulls from ten thousand feet for CRW only. They talked about it, they wrote about it, they spread the word and it caught on. Soon manufacturers were responding with equipment especially designed for canopy relative work. CRW soon became a world-class competitive event.

Canopy RW is accuracy with an aerial moving disc, and it is relative work in slow motion; many of the basics of freefall RW apply. The excitement of being in the formation lasts minutes, not seconds.

Like freefall relative work, CRW requires training and practice. The novice should learn one-on-one with someone skilled in CRW. You will start practicing planes rather than

A stack: each flier sits on the leading edge of the lower canopy

stacks, as planes are much more stable. See the USPA *Skydiver's Information Manual*, "Section 6-6 Canopy Formations," and the books listed in the Appendix of this book for more information. The two most experienced fliers usually hook up to form a CRW *base-pin*. Then the rest dock in their assigned slots. Never fly in front of a formation or your wake will disturb the formation's stability. Dock from behind and below with a moderate approach angle. If you are docking third or later, aim your center section for the person who you are trying to dock on so that he or she can hook his or her legs behind and around the lines of the center cell. If you are the recipient of a dock and the canopy docking on you collapses, release it immediately. If the flier yells *DROP!*, he or she wants you to let go immediately. Keep conversation to a minimum and verbal commands concise and direct. Minimize control movements to minimize oscillations: It is easier to dock with a stable canopy. Approaches and docking should stop by 2,500 feet. Only very experienced CRW pilots should attempt to land a formation in calm to moderate winds. Formation landings should not be attempted in high or gusty winds!

To take part in CRW, you must have logged at least 20 jumps on ram-air canopies, have a thorough knowledge of ram-air canopy flight characteristics to include riser maneuvers, and be able to land within five meters of the target consistently. You will need some special equipment: a hook knife for canopy entanglements, ankle-high socks to protect from line burns, a short or retractable bridle on your main canopy so it will not catch on another flier's gear, and cross-connector straps between front and rear risers for building planes. You should also carry an altimeter, wear a helmet with ear holes to allow hearing, soft toggles to avoid entanglements, trim tabs for equalizing descent rates, at least two rows of crossports in your canopy to aid canopy reinflation, and non-cascaded A (front center) lines. Lanyards or straps for hand planes should not be used.

At one point in time, a third or "tertiary" reserve was recommended as a means of tossing a round canopy on a lanyard out of a "collapsed stack" to save the jumper from certain injury. Most experienced CRW people shy away from this, but as a novice, it certainly adds a bit of "insurance" for your training jumps. Several "saves" have been attributed to the use of such a device.

The best times of the day to make CRW jumps are early and late. Winds are normally lower and less turbulent, so you are less likely to encounter thermals and other bump causers. Turbulence makes CRW difficult, if not impossible, and it certainly increases the danger.

Whenever you plan to deploy your canopy more than 3,500 feet above the drop zone, inform the pilot of the jump ship and everyone on board. If there are two or more aircraft in the air, make sure your pilot radios the message to the other pilots.

Exposed steering loops can be grabbed while the canopy is deploying

What Ye Sew, So Shall Ye Leap. *—George Galloway*

Chapter Seven

Skydiving Equipment

Skydivers wear two parachutes, a main and a reserve. The reserve, which is usually worn on the back above the main, is carried along in case the main malfunctions.

Main parachutes are not 100% reliable; if they were, there would be no need for the reserve. But, like the automobile, there are very few unexplainable mechanical failures. Parachute malfunctions can usually be traced to the human element, specifically: packing, body position at pull time, or poor pre-jump inspection. Consequently, while you may be packing your own main parachute, your reserve will be inspected and repacked every 120 days by an FAA (government) certified parachute rigger. Your instructors will carefully supervise your progression. They will train you, test you, and you will undergo a rigid equipment check prior to boarding the jump ship. The key to success and enjoyment in sport parachuting is knowledge; you will want to learn as much as possible about the equipment right from the very beginning.

The parts of a parachute. The parachute assembly is a train of interrelated parts that are carefully engineered into a chain. To keep the weight and volume to a minimum, each part is made just strong enough (plus a safety factor) to handle its share of the opening forces.

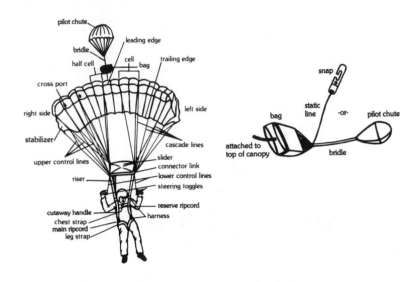

The components of the sport main parachute

The six *major* components of the **sport *main* parachute** are:

1. Pilot chute, with bridle.
2. Deployment device: bag with retainer line, diaper, etc.
3. Canopy, including suspension lines, slider and risers.
4. Harness, including hardware, ripcord pockets, etc.
5. Container.
6. Actuation device: ripcord, pull-out handle throw-out handle, static line, etc.

The six *major* components of the **sport *reserve* parachute** also consist of a pilot chute, deployment device, canopy, harness, container and actuation device, but the harness and (two compartment) container are shared with the main parachute. Technically and legally (according to the Federal Aviation Administration) the harness and container are part of the *reserve* assembly and the six reserve components are tested together. The non-certificated main pilot chute, deployment device and canopy are going along for the ride.

Piggyback containers and front mount assembly

Piggyback verses front reserve mounting. You will begin jumping with a parachute system where the reserve container sits piggyback above the main container. Most jumpers prefer the piggyback but the main and reserve can be positioned most anywhere. Through the fifties and sixties, the reserve was worn in the front like military Airborne equipment.

Incidentally, piggyback packs were formerly called *tandem containers*. Since *tandem containers* can be confused with *tandem jumps* (two jumpers under one canopy), and tandem containers are even used for tandem jumps, we use the term *piggyback* to describe the equipment and the word *tandem* to describe a type of jumping.

Static-line parachute assemblies for students are fitted with static lines and Practice RipCord Pull (PRCP) handles.

Parachute manufacturers are responsible, caring people. They guarantee their products for life.

Tandem jumping equipment consists of an oversize main canopy (360 to 500 sq. ft.) engineered to carry two people, and individual harnesses designed to snap together. Because the passenger and instructor are hooked together in tandem (passenger in front and instructor in back), their weight is doubled while their wind resistance is not. Consequently, their potential terminal velocity is greatly increased. A four-to-five foot diameter drogue chute is deployed soon after exit to trail about 15 feet above and behind, slowing them to around 120 mph from the 170 mph they would be traveling without a drogue. The drogue has other advantages too: It acts as a stabilizer for the two skydiving bodies while ensuring positive canopy deployment by pulling out the main when the drogue release is pulled.

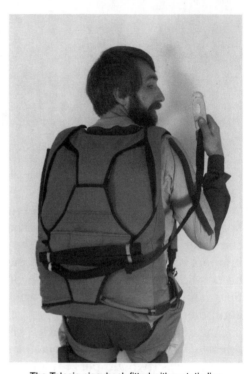

The Telesis piggyback fitted with a static line

Ted Strong of Strong Enterprises in Orlando, Florida, and Bill Booth of the Relative Workshop in DeLand, Florida pioneered tandem equipment. These two companies plus John Sherman's Parachute Labs and Dominique Marcu's Parachutes de France manufacture slightly different variations of equipment based on the same basic principle.

Equipment regulations. The design, maintenance and alteration of parachute equipment is regulated by the Federal Aviation Administration of the U.S. Department of

Transportation, which publishes the *Federal Aviation Regulations* (FARs). The following FARs apply to parachuting in whole or in part:

Part 65 — *Certification of Parachute Riggers*
Part 91 — *General Flight Rules*
Part 105 — *Parachute Jumping*

In addition, the FAA publishes *Advisory Circulars* from time to time to explain the regulations. For example, AC-105-2C explains in detail various areas of parachute equipment maintenance and modification.

TSO. *Reserve* parachutes must be *approved* prior to use under the government's *Technical Standard Order* (TSO) system either as modified military surplus or through rigid tests on newly designed and manufactured civilian equipment. Reserve parachute assemblies must be (1) tested and certificated and must be (2) manufactured under an approved quality control system.

The *main* parachute assembly—canopy, container, risers, etc.—does not have to be *approved* but *only qualified, licensed parachute riggers may make any further alterations or repairs.*

TSO C-23d dictates that all *certificated* parachutes (reserves and those used by pilots) must meet the performance standards set forth in AS-8015A published by the Society of Automotive Engineers. FAR Part 21 outlines the procedures for certifying a parachute or a component part. For complete details on the regulations, testing and the TSO system, see *The Parachute Manual* by Dan Poynter.

Repairs. *Minor repairs* (those that, if done incorrectly, *would not* materially affect the airworthiness of the parachute) may be performed by a licensed *senior* parachute rigger while *major repairs* and *alterations* (those that *would* affect the airworthiness of the parachute) may only be performed by *master* parachute riggers.

Parachutes should not be rented or loaned to persons unqualified to carry out an intended skydive or to persons of unknown ability.
—USPA's Skydiver's Information Manual

Jump pilots and *observers* (those going up for the ride—not jumping) are also required to wear parachutes in the aircraft (when specified in the aircraft's operations manual or its STC), but they usually wear regular, round, unmodified emergency gear, not sport models, and they only wear one parachute. The pilot is using the plane as his or her primary source of transportation, and he or she wears a parachute in case it might fail. The sport parachutist uses the plane as an *elevator*, a main parachute as his primary source of transportation and a reserve for use if the main fails. Hence the difference.

The deployment of the sport main parachute takes about three seconds and is divided into three separate phases: activation, deployment and inflation.

1. Activation: The container is released from its locked position by pulling a ripcord, hand-releasing a pilot chute or withdrawing the static line, depending on the system design and use.

2. Deployment: The pilot chute *anchors* itself in the air and lifts the bag with the packed canopy out of the container. As the jumper falls away, the lines pay out from their rubber band stows until *line stretch*. (The last stow or stows lock the canopy into the deployment device.) When the last stow withdraws, the *trap door* closing flap opens and the canopy is pulled out of the bag.

3. Inflation: The ram-air canopy inflates from the underside and tries to expand in a span-wise (side to side) direction. At the same time, the center cells get a bite of air and inflates. A slider retards the expansion of the canopy until the jumper has slowed. Then the slider slides down the lines, allowing the canopy to fully inflate. The opening sequence is in the reverse order in which the canopy was packed.

The ram-air canopy is a true flying machine. Before using one, you must complete a controlled program of instruction, and should read and understand all appropriate flight manuals and packing instructions. If you do not have the manuals, send to the manufacturers for them.

The bagged main canopy lifts off

The slider slows spanwise expansion of the canopy

The *ram-air* **sport reserve** operates in the same manner. *Round* reserves are activated and deployed in a similar manner but the inflation process is different.

The pilot chute is a small round canopy which enters the airstream to anchor itself there and withdraws the main or reserve canopy from its container, then keeps the lines extended until the canopy begins to spread.

The first personnel parachutes were used while flying in balloons and, since they were static line operated, a pilot chute wasn't necessary. With the perfection of the manually-operated parachute in 1919 came a collapsible, spring-loaded pilot chute. The hemispherical, conical or flat octagon, spiral spring *vane type* pilot chute has been used for years and has proven to be an excellent design.

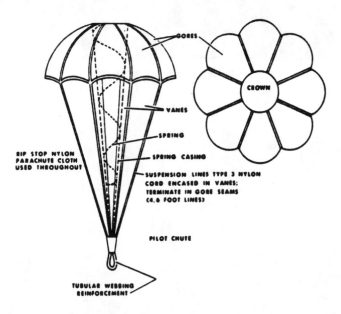

The spiral spring, vane type pilot chute

We are the first generation to have the possibility to fly with our own wings. —*Magnus Mikaelson*

Most sport main pilot chutes are hand deployed and are shaped like a beach ball with a solid fabric top and a mesh fabric bottom. This simple design will not catch on the feet. Main parachute pilot chutes are usually limp and must be pulled from their stowage pocket by hand, while reserve pilot chutes have a spiral spring to launch them from the pack. Removal of the spring reduces both weight and volume. Without the coiled spring, main containers are simpler to build and easier to close.

Pilot chutes wear out. As their fabric becomes more porous, canopy deployments can become less dependable. See the pilot chute discussion under *Snivels,* later in this chapter.

Some pilot chutes are completely enclosed on the bottom with marquisette mesh

It has been found that an increase in pilot chute area (increased drag) usually improves the dependability and effectiveness of the deployment system. However, larger and multiple pilot chutes also increase the *snatch force* and add to the stowage problem. Multiple pilot chutes were used in some back style containers with large round canopies and sleeve systems.

The *ripcord activation system* has a pin and loop arrangement to lock the container closed. When the ripcord is withdrawn, each pin slides out of its loop and the spring-loaded pilot chute jumps from the container, withdrawing the canopy. This system is commonly used in student mains, sport reserves and pilots' emergency parachutes.

The ripcord releases the spiral spring pilot chute

The *throw-out* hand-deployed pilot chute is stowed in a pocket on the bellyband, on the back of the right leg strap or on the bottom of the main container. Most throw-outs are located BOC (bottom of container). The BOC location prompts you to arch during your pull.

Early throw-outs were mounted on the bellyband and this is still the easiest place to see and grasp, but it is not *idiot proof*. Some jumpers put a twist in their bellybands when they donned their gear that trapped the pilot chute bridle.

A legstrap-mounted throw out

Adding stiffeners to the bellyband solved that problem but made the bellyband awkward. The leg strap location is not quite as easy to see but it reduces the chance of a misrouted bridle and it allows for a pull in a comfortable direction.

The throw-out pilot chute doesn't have a spring; you simply pull it out of its stowage pouch by hand to full-arm's length and let it go. The handle, usually consisting of a 2" length of 1" diameter plastic tubing or a Hacky Sack®, is mounted on the apex of the pilot chute and sticks out of the stowage pocket. The pilot chute does not inflate in the

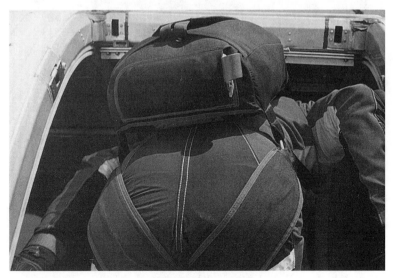

A BOC-mounted throw-out

airstream until the jumper lets it go because it is upside down. When the jumper throws the pilot chute away laterally and vigorously, it rotates 180 degrees and inflates. The inflated pilot chute now acts like a skyhook to extend the long bridle, pulling the bridle-mounted curved pin out of the main container's locking loop which unlocks the container, then lifts the bagged canopy out of the container.

The throw-out pilot chute system in use

Stow the pilot chute with the fragile mesh inside and the slippery fabric outside. Neatly fold the excess bridle and place it inside the pilot chute. The whole bundle should slide easily into the pouch. The throw-out pouch should be sized to match the pilot chute and have an elastic opening, or be made of elastic fabric. Only the plastic handle should peek out of the pouch. The pilot chute will pull the curved pin more easily if you leave a couple of inches of loose bridle near the pin. After you put the parachute on, run your fingertips along the bridle to make sure it runs straight from pouch to pin. Press any separated Velcro back together. You do not want to snag your bridle on a doorframe.

The pilot chute pulls the curved pin locking the pack

You may test your throw-out system by placing the packed parachute on the ground. Extract the pilot chute from its stowage pouch and pull straight up. The bridle Velcro should unpeel. Then the main pin protector flap should open. There will probably be enough friction between the locking pin and the locking loop for the containers to start lifting off the ground. If you are able to lift the packed parachutes completely off the ground without clearing the pin, consult your rigger.

Collapsible **pilot chute systems** eliminate the dragging of an inflated pilot chute behind the flying main canopy. These pilot chutes may have a *kill line* or a length of bungee cord to collapse the pilot chute within itself once the canopy is open.

The model with the conventional kill line must be cocked (reset to opening function conditions) before the container is closed in order for it to work properly. It has the advantage of being able to work at low exit airspeeds. It does not reinflate accidentally during high-speed spiral turns.

The type with a *bungee cord kill line* does not need to be cocked, but it does require a higher exit airspeed to function normally. Of course, in freefall, the airspeed far exceeds the minimum requirements for operating this type of pilot chute. In steep spiral turns, this type of pilot chute may tend to reinflate, but that action really won't have much effect on the performance of the parachute.

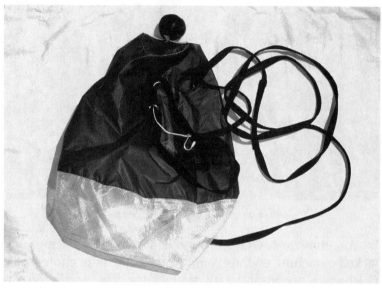

Some pilot chutes are designed to collapse once they perform their job

The *pull-out* hand-deployed pilot chute has a pillow type handle or *pud* of foam-filled fabric mounted on the lower right-hand corner of the main container. The handle is connected directly to a straight metallic pin on an 8-10" line. This short line passes through a grommet that is mounted at the base of the pilot chute. As the handle is pulled, the pin clears the main container's locking loop and allows the container to open. As the pull continues, the pilot chute is withdrawn from the container. The pilot chute inflates in the airstream next to the jumper because the handle is at the base of the pilot chute. Then the pilot chute/handle is released. The inflated pilot chute pulls from above to extend the bridle and lift the bagged canopy from the container. Today, less than 10% of the rigs have a pull-out system.

The pull-out pilot chute system

The principal advantage of the pull-out is that the shorter bridle keeps the pilot chute closer to the top of the inflated main canopy, where it is less likely to fall over the leading edge to entangle with lines when the canopy is braked.

The principal disadvantage of the pullout is the location of the handle—behind the jumper where it is out of sight and is more difficult to locate and grab. If the handle is attached to your container with Velcro, have the hook and pile strips replaced regularly to avoid a floating handle.

Hand deploy pulls must be vigorous and to full arm extension to get the pilot chute out into *clean* air. About 90% of the experienced jumpers use the throw-out while 10% prefer the pull-out. The choices vary from region to region.

Whenever you change equipment and main parachute activation systems, you must train with it thoroughly. Start in a suspended harness and then make a solo jump which includes several practice pulls and an actual pull at a higher than normal altitude. The challenge is to break an old habit (reaching for where the ripcord was) and to learn a new one.

Pack closure loops. Nylon pack closure loops wear out.

Yours will last longer if during packing you slide your pull-up cord out slowly and position it under the pin so that the cord does not rub on the closure loop. Check to make sure that the locking pin is smooth. Lubricate the locking loop with a little Teflon® or Silicone containing, non-petroleum based spray to extend its life and make pulls smoother. When replacing closure loops, check the owner's manual for correct material and length. Do not just duplicate the loop in the pack—it may have stretched. A piece of elastic webbing sewn over the washer will keep the loop from being lost when the container opens, or you may even use a piece of adhesive tape to hold it in place. Always bench test the system after replacing a loop.

The bridle, or *pilot chute connector* cord, is a piece of line, tubular nylon, or nylon tape that connects the pilot chute with the canopy or the deployment device. Bridles come in various lengths and strengths and may be either tied on, sewn on, or sewn and looped on.

Deployment devices, sleeves, bags, diapers, etc., offer several advantages over straight deployment. They are found on virtually all main and reserve canopies. Deployment devices reduce the *snatch force* of the deploying canopy by reducing its inflated size at line stretch. A parachute with a deployment device will open more reliably because the lines pay out stow-by-stow, and then become more evenly loaded prior to canopy inflation. They tend to save the canopy from damage by making the deployment more orderly.

—**The sleeve** is a long tube of cotton fabric that encases older, round sport canopies. The sleeve was one of the important basic ingredients that figured in the growth of sport parachuting. Without the availability of inexpensive surplus equipment, its modification for steerability, and the use of the sleeve to greatly reduce the opening forces, it is highly doubtful that the sport would ever have appealed to more than a few rugged individualists.

—**The bag** is like a pillowcase and the canopy is S- folded inside of it. Bags can be found on both rounds and squares.

—**The diaper** is a low-weight, low-volume deployment device which wraps around the round canopy and is locked with two or more line stows.

—**The Free-Pack Strap** was an adaptation of the principle of the diaper. It was a simple piece of 2″ wide webbing that performed the same function as the bigger diaper. It never became very popular.

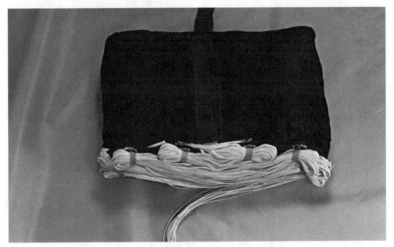

The deployment bag

The Slider is a rectangle of nylon cloth with a ring or grommet in each corner, each of which encircles one of the four groups of lines on the canopy. The slider slows the opening by staying up the lines near the canopy, restricting the canopy's size until inflation exerts enough force to push the slider down. The slider works very well to ease the opening forces, while it is easy to pack and cheap to manufacture.

Sliders come in several designs. Some are solid and some have a hole in the center. *Split sliders* can be released to separate after opening. Accuracy jumpers like this feature, because it allows the canopy to spread a bit spanwise. A flattened canopy will turn slower and accuracy performance is otherwise improved. Canopy Relative Work (CRW) jumpers like the split slider because it removes an obstacle to their upward sight. Sliders are designed for individual canopies. Do not change sliders except with manufacturer's approval.

The slider: At the canopy and coming down

Snivels. New canopies usually inflate crisply. Older canopies may open more slowly or *snivel*. The trick is to distinguish a slow opening snivel from a no-opening streamer. Canopy fabric opens up, or becomes more *porous*, with use. It happens slowly, jump-by-jump, and snivels can start between 100 and 200 jumps. But age and use are not the only causes of canopy snivel.

If your ram-air canopy is sniveling, compare the line lengths. Compare each line with its opposite, on the other side of the canopy. The differences in length should not be more than one inch. Check the *slider stops* on the canopy. If any are broken or missing, the slider grommet could be hanging up on the fabric. Check the pilot chute. It should be at least 34″ in diameter, unless the owner's manual says differently, and in good condition. If it is worn out, replace it. Any pilot chute with 500 jumps on it is probably too porous to do its job properly. The pilot chute must do more than just lift the canopy off your back: It tensions the canopy during deployment. Packing affects opening time. Check the owner's manual for the manufacturer's recommendations. If your openings are still slow, ask your rigger about ways to spread the nose during packing.

Check the *brake settings* against the owner's manual. If the brakes are set too deep, the canopy will open with the trailing edge farther down. Ask your rigger.

Check the slider against the owner's manual. You may have an assembly problem. If the slider is the wrong size, it may be slow to come down the lines. When your canopy is new, the slider will probably come all the way down to the connector links. In fact, it may hit the links rather hard, damaging the slider's grommets; and rough grommets damage suspension lines. This is why connector links are usually covered with *slider bumpers* made of plastic or rubber tubing. Some connector links have rigid plastic washers mounted in between the lines instead of the tubing. Make sure the bumpers are secured in place with tacking thread. Check that the grommets are still firmly set in the reinforcement tape. Watch for tears in the fabric, broken stitch rows and loose reinforcement tape.

Slider bumper

If your slider does not descend all the way down to the connector links at the top of the risers, pump the brakes to encourage it. Just pull both steering lines all the way down and then let up. Repeat if necessary. Many jumpers like to pump the brakes in two-second cycles.

You may have your slider modified by cutting a hole in the center. A hole will decrease the drag, allowing the slider to start downward sooner and more easily. Modifying the slider should proceed in cautious steps. Start with a five-inch diameter hole and gradually increase it to no more than ten inches. The optimum amount will depend on the original size of the slider. Some riggers make the slider smaller by sewing in a tuck. This modification may also restrict the spread of the lines. Ask your rigger.

The risers are pieces of webbing that connect the harness to the suspension lines. Years ago the risers were part of the harness and the lines were sewn directly to the risers. Now the lines are threaded onto connector links and the risers are fitted to the harness with metal riser releases. Main risers are sold with the harness, not the canopy, as both parts of the

Main canopy risers

riser-release hardware must mate. Risers on sport parachutes are fitted with guide rings for the steering lines.

The brakes are set by pulling down on the steering lines and threading the toggle loops through the *control line locking loops,* or brake set loops. Then the toggle is seated on a Velcro strip on the riser, while the loose loop of line is stowed in a Velcro® wrap pouch or in an elastic band on the connector link. Another type of toggle is the "Zoo" toggle which contains its own locking pin and loop which is inserted in the finger-trapped eye of the steering line and around the locking ring.

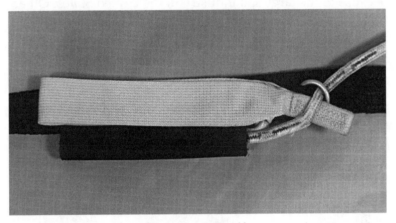

The brake set assembly

Check the brake set loops. This finger-trapped loop in the line must not be worn and the stitches must be secure. If a loop should break during opening, the canopy will surge forward on that side, will turn hard and may malfunction. At the very least, it will give you some quick turning excitement until you release the other toggle to gain full control of the canopy.

Canopy. The working part of a parachute assembly is the canopy and today's canopies work very well. Picture yourself in freefall at terminal velocity hurtling toward terra firma at 120 mph. You pull out your pilot chute, release it and your canopy deploys. At this point your weight doesn't change but your air resistance does, and dramatically at that. Under the canopy, your new terminal velocity (vertically) is just over 10 mph, and when you flare the canopy, the downward velocity will be nearly zero for landing.

Canopies are made of nylon; in the U.S. they have been since 1941, when the Japanese suddenly cut off the silk supply. Nylon turned out to be a better material than silk since it is elastic and resistant to mildew. In fact, nylon is resistant to almost everything, except sunlight and acid. Later, the entire parachute, including the container and harness was made of nylon, too.

There are many different weaves, weights, strengths and colors of nylon fabric available for canopy manufacture because of the large sail industry in the United States. Other materials, such as Dacron®, Spectra® and Kevlar® also offer some interesting possibilities. The parachute designers are trying them all.

Canopy types. Sport canopies can be divided into five general classifications: unmodified round (usually military surplus), modified round (military surplus or newly manufactured), Para-Commander class, single-surface wings, and ram-air. Only the ram-air *square* is common in the sport today.

STANDARD ROUND 28' CANOPY	PC CLASS CANOPY	RAM-AIR CLASS CANOPY
5-7 mph forward	14 mph forward	20 mph forward
18 fps down	16 fps down	10 fps down
38 degree glide	54 degree glide	72 degree glide

Performance figures are approximate and are for a 170 lb. person

Round canopies. Modified round canopies glide at about 38 degrees. Cutting the holes larger, increasing the weight or using a smaller canopy results in greater descent

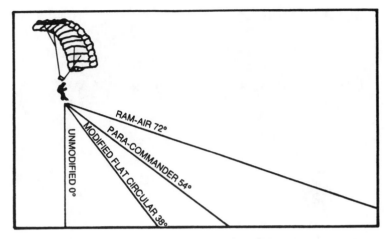

Glide comparison in no wind

and a correspondingly greater forward speed; the angle of glide remains the same.

With rounds or squares, changing the weight of the load (you and all your gear), within reason, will not alter the glide angle of the canopy, but will change the descent and forward velocity. So, for a given canopy, a heavier jumper will descend faster and have a greater forward speed than a lighter one. However, an extremely light or heavy load may alter canopy shaping to the extent that performance is altered.

Para-Commander class canopies. This canopy category is named for the Para-Commander that dominated sport jumping in the late sixties, and is characterized by the addition of centerlines to pull down the apex. The centerlines spread and flatten the canopy. The Mark I PC, the first to be marketed in 1964, was far more popular than any of its successors or competitors. Pioneer also built the Mark II, Competition model, Russian PC, RW PC, etc., while other manufacturers produced the Papillon®, CrossBow®, Starlite® and others.

The wing class canopies are characterized by a single-surface airfoil, and are very low in both weight and volume. Their performance approaches that of the ram-air canopies. There were only a few wings, such as the Delta II ParaWing®, and the Paradactyl, made in any quantity but there may be more in the future.

The Mark I Para-Commander   The Thunderbow

Ram-air class canopies have a double surfaced configuration, which is inflated by the *relative wind* flowing into the leading edge of the canopy to produce an airfoil shape. The performance of the square canopy is significantly better than round parachutes and they may be *flared* to make the landings very soft. It was Steve Snyder who put the ram-air principles, originally conceived by Domina Jalbert, to work and put the canopy on the market. Snyder designed the steering system, figured out how to make the opening shock acceptable, and then taught classes to convince accuracy jumpers that upwind approaches were superior to downwind landings. That last part may seem obvious today, but it was revolutionary in the early seventies.

The Para-Plane has a smooth lower surface. Many versions have evolved from this basic design. The Para-Foil distributes line loads to the canopy with a *catenary* (curved) structure. Note the flares on the underside (see pg. 274).

These higher performance canopies perform more like the wings of an airplane than conventional parachutes and have to be *flown* until the landing is completed. This is quite

A round will get you down but a square will get you there.

The single surface Paradactyl canopy

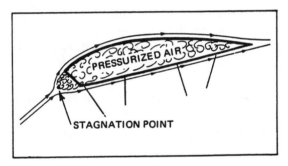

Ram-inflation

different from the standard flat circular canopy, which will bring you down safely even if you let go of the toggles and cover your head.

Canopy size selection depends upon the performance you want and your *exit weight* (your total weight including equipment when you leave the aircraft).

Jumpers wishing increased ram-air performance should switch to a smaller canopy. If your canopy is too zippy, try a larger one. Smaller ram-air canopies with similar shapes have a greater rate of descent and forward speed, but their glide angle is still about 72 degrees.

The Para-Plane   The Para-Foil

Aspect Ratio (AR) is the *span* measurement (wing tip to wing tip) compared to the *chord* measurement (the distance from the leading edge to the trailing edge) of the canopy. More specifically, AR is the square of the span divided by the area and expressed as a ratio, such as 3:1. On a rectangular wing, AR is easier to figure, as it is simply the span divided by the chord.

Higher aspect ratio canopies are said to have a *higher lift to drag ratio* or L/D (called *L over D*). The higher the AR (longer span, shorter chord), the greater the lift for the existing drag.

The *lift to drag ratio* increases 8% for each unit the aspect ratio is increased. If the wing area is increased by 20%, the lift will increase 20%, and the minimum flying speed will be reduced by 9%. Speed is the most important element of lift: Double the flying speed, and lift and drag are increased four times.

Most of the lift comes from the top surface of the wing, just back of the leading edge, so it stands to reason that to increase lift, this surface should be enlarged. A greater span results in a more efficient canopy. Since square canopies are ram-air inflated and have no rigid members, there is a physical limit of about 3.5:1 to the aspect ratio. If the span is too wide, the canopy will experience deployment problems, and

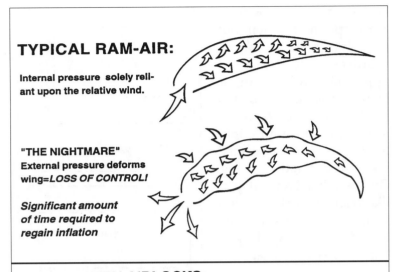

TYPICAL RAM-AIR:

Internal pressure solely reliant upon the relative wind.

"THE NIGHTMARE"
External pressure deforms wing=*LOSS OF CONTROL!*

Significant amount of time required to regain inflation

RAM-AIR WITH AIRLOCKS:

NORMAL FLIGHT:
Airlock is open. Internal pressure maintained by relative wind.

DYNAMIC FLIGHT:
During turns, braking, and turbulence airlock is closed. Internal pressure is maintained by valve.

Some canopies have airlocks to combat deflation
(Performance Designs drawing)

one tip will come around to kiss the other tip when the canopy folds in a fast turn. Since most of the *parasitic drag* in a canopy comes from the suspension lines, there is also a performance trade-off as the span is increased.

A high aspect ratio canopy will have a flatter glide angle, which you may or may not want. Generally, higher AR canopies will keep you in the air longer and will bring you back to the drop zone from a bad spot more often. But the flatter glide angle requires a flatter final approach and a longer landing area. If you love to nail the target, or you make a lot of demo jumps into tight areas, you may want a lower aspect ratio canopy. On the other hand, if you like relative work and you jump where trees are few and far between, buy a higher aspect ratio canopy.

Number of cells. Most ram-air canopies have seven or nine double cells. For a given cell size, an increase in cells will provide an increase in aspect ratio. If the cells are smaller, the increased number will result in a smoother airfoil. But increasing the cells also increases the weight and volume of the canopy due to added ribs and added lines. Suspension lines are combined, or *cascaded*, to reduce their number.

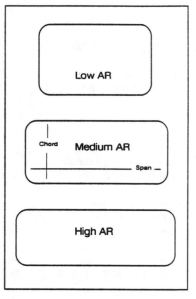

Aspect ratio compares the chord with the span (Precision Aerodynamics drawing)

When square canopies took over from rounds, most were five cells. Actually, they had ten half-cells. The five cell ram-airs were lowest in weight and volume, while being eas-

See how the wings striking against the air hold up the heavy eagle in the thin upper air, near to the elements of fire. And likewise see how the air moving over the sea strikes against the bellying sails, making the loaded heavy ship run; so that by these demonstrative and definite reasons you may know that man with his great contrived wings, battling the resistant air and conquering it, can subject it and rise above it.

—*Leonardo daVinci*

ier to build. Next, the seven cell models became popular and the manufacturers figured ways to keep their weight and volume down, even though these models had more fabric, lines and seams. The next step was the nine cell canopy, which offered increased performance through a better airfoil shape maintenance.

Construction. Ram-air canopies may be constructed spanwise or chordwise. The traditional chordwise method ran a single width of fabric (often 36" wide) from the leading edge to the trailing edge. By running the fabric spanwise from tip-to-tip, the cells can be wider than the width of the fabric. Wider cells mean fewer ribs and lines, and that means a reduction in weight and volume, while fewer lines means less parasitic drag. Swift canopies from Para-Flite were the first to use spanwise construction.

Fabric. Most ram-air canopies are made of very low permeability, ripstop nylon fabric. Weights of fabric are expressed in *ounces, per square yard* and common canopy fabrics weigh in at 1.1 oz. (maximum). Generally, heavier fabrics will retain their low permeability longer. Canopy fabric is

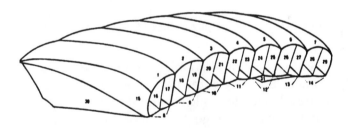

Chordwise construction

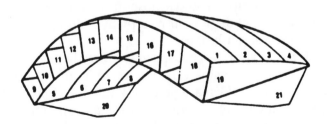

Spanwise construction

coated with urethane or silicone polymers to make it retain its non-permeability.

The *full glide speed* is the speed measured at a descending angle. It is not the horizontal speed. A 3:1 glide ratio is 72 degrees up from the vertical.

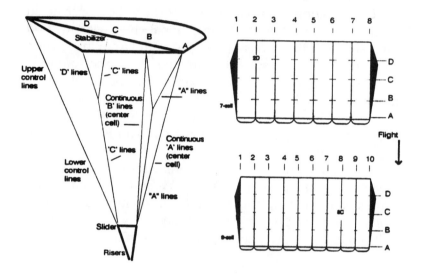

Line attachment nomenclature (Precision Aerodynamics drawings)

De-tuning. Ram-air canopies are de-tuned so they will not automatically glide at the flattest possible angle. The line lengths are adjusted to angle the chord of the canopy to mid-range. If the leading edge were set higher for maximum glide, the canopy would be too easy to stall when you pulled the toggles down into deep brakes—a dangerous condition. The rule is nose-up for glide, nose-down for stability. You can improve the glide of your canopy by pulling the toggles down to one-quarter brakes.

Sink rate is your descent speed expressed in feet per second. The lower your sink rate, the longer you will stay up. The easiest way to decrease your sink rate is to buy a larger canopy. If you want to experience a dramatic difference, borrow a large tandem canopy (built for two) and jump it solo. The larger canopy descends so slowly, you can even land it downwind softly, though this is not recommended. So what is the trade-off? The sink rate is reduced but the glide angle remains the same, and this means the forward speed is also reduced. You may find yourself landing softly, but you may also back up over the drop zone.

Canopy Name	Number of cells	Aspect Ratio	Fabric Porosity	Suspension Lines	Canopy Geometry	[M]ain or [R]eserve [E]mergency	Size Range sq ft
Xaos-27	27	2.73:1	0	HMA	X-Brace	M	58-118
Xaos-21	21	2.73:1	0	HMA	X-Brace	M	69-135
Nitron	9	2.56:1	0	HMA	I Beam	M	78-170
Fusion	9	2.61:1	0	HMA	I Beam	M	98-230
Falcon	9	3.00:1	0-3	Dacron	I Beam	MR	120-300
Synergy	7	2.22:1	0	HMA	I Beam	M	98-230
r-Max	7	2.21:1	0-3	Spectra	I Beam	R	108-288
Raven	7	2.25:1	0-3	Dacron	I Beam	MRE	120-288
Dash-M	7	2.25:1	0-3	Spectra	I Beam	R	109-288
TR-375/400	9	3.00:1	0-3	Vectran	I Beam	R	375-400
P-124	7	2.25:1	0-3	Spectra	I Beam	RE	179-280
Batwing	9	3.00:1	0	Spectra	I Beam	M	98-171
Monarch	9	3.00:1	0	Spectra	I Beam	M	120-215
Interceptor	7	2.5:1	0-3	Dacron	I Beam	M	180-250

Canopy specifications courtesy of Precision Aerodynamics

Wing loading compares your weight (you and your equipment's) with the area of the canopy, and is expressed in *pounds per square foot*. Manufacturers design their canopies for a certain weight range of jumpers. If your canopy is too small, it will be too zippy, both forward and down, and your landings will be hard. The canopy will stall at a higher speed and landings will have to be more precisely timed. Remember that the glide angle for a given aspect ratio is always the same, regardless of canopy size or your weight. If your canopy is too large, you won't have much forward speed and will be at the mercy of the wind. Of course, a larger canopy also means more weight and volume when packed up. Most jumpers want lighter and smaller rigs, and tend to choose a canopy that is too small. Choose a canopy

	RATE OF DESCENT				GLIDE
	Full Glide fps	50% Brake fps	100% Brake fps	Proper Flared Land. fps	Approx. Ratio max. L/D
CRUISLITE XL	15-17	11-14	8-12	1-10	3. to 1
CRUISLITE	16-19	11-14	16-18	0-5	3. to 1
NIMBUS	15-17	11-14	8-12	0-10	3.2 to 1
NIMBUS BETA	15-17	11-14	8-12	0-10	3.2 to 1
STRATO CLOUD DELTA	12-16	10-14	10-14	0-10	3 to 1
XL CLOUD	15-17	10-14	8-12	0-10	3.2 to 1
DC-5	14-18	10-14	8-12	0-10	2.8 to 1
PURSUIT 230	15-17	9-11	8-10	1-5	3 to 1
SWIFT RESERVE	15-17	12-14	16-18	5-10	3 to 1
CIRRUS RESERVE	13-15	11-13	11-13	0-5	3 to 1
ORION RESERVE*	13-14	7-9	8-9	0-5	2.6 to 1

	SPEED RANGE				360° TURN RATE	
	Full Glide mph	50% Brake mph	100% Brake mph	Proper Flared Land. mph	Full Glide sec.	50% Brake sec.
CRUISLITE XL	25-30	12-15	3-6	0-5	3-5	3-5
CRUISLITE	25-30	13-16	4-7	0-4	3-4	3-4
NIMBUS	25-30	12-15	3-6	0-5	3-4	3-4
NIMBUS BETA	25-30	12-15	3-6	0-5	3-4	3-4
STRATO CLOUD DELTA	25-30	10-15	3-6	0-5	3-5	3-5
XL CLOUD	25-30	10-15	3-6	0-5	4-6	3-5
DC-5	25-30	10-15	2-4	0-5	4-6	3-5
PURSUIT 230	28-32	14-16	4-6	0-5	3.4	4
SWIFT RESERVE	20-30	13-18	0	0-5	5-6	5-8
CIRRUS RESERVE	24-27	10-15	2-5	0-5	4	6
ORION RESERVE*	20-22	14-16	8-10	0-5	3-5	3-5

Canopy performance. These figures are for a range of Para-Flite canopies. They enable you to compare various specifications with performance.

size that provides you with the most margin on either side. If you have to compromise, go larger. If you are jumping at higher elevations and/or if the weather is usually hot or humid where you jump, go larger.

Remember that you must compute your *exit weight*, the total weight of you and all your equipment.

Using the given wing loading limits chart, an ideal loading is 0.77. If you weigh 150 lbs. and have 30 lbs. of equipment for a total of 180 lbs., you would divide 180 by 0.77. This equation tells you your ideal canopy would be about 234 sq. ft. in area for that type of canopy.

Use a range of .50 to .65 for an Accuracy canopy. Zero-P canopies require higher wing loading, perhaps 1.2, for maximum performance.

Wing Loading in Lbs/Sq Ft vs. Experience Level
Courtesy of Precision Aerodynamics

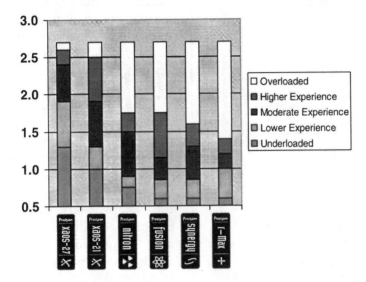

Suspension line. Your suspension lines may be made of Dacron®, Kevlar®, Vectran®, Spectra® or other man-made fibers. After a number of jumps, you will probably find your (loaded) suspension lines have stretched and your (relaxed) steering lines have shrunk. Compare opposite lines with each other and check your owner's manual for line lengths.

Opening force reduction. Opening forces are snatch force (when you accelerate the pilot chute and bagged canopy to your speed) and opening shock. The goal is to separate them as much as possible. Suspension line elasticity will absorb some of the shock but Microline™ (Spectra™) stretches less than Dacron®. Opening forces are also affected by canopy folding, slider position, bagging the canopy, line stow method, type of pilot chute, body position (do not pull head down; sitting up position is the best position), etc.

Sometimes the opening forces are so hard, you do not look forward to pull time. Here are some suggestions from Para-Flite and others for reducing opening shock on a Pursuit canopy:

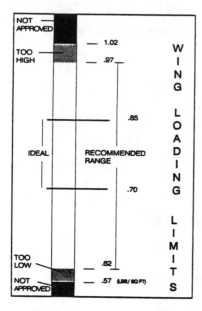

Wing loading limits for a medium performance canopy (Precision Aerodynamics drawing)

1. Ask your rigger to change the deployment brake setting from 15" above the A-line attachments to 8". Just finger-trap new loops into the brake lines 7" above the current loops.

2. Stow the slider in a rubber band on one of the center cell "B" lines (number 4 or 5). Put the rubber band through the loop where the line attaches to the canopy. Mark the rubber-banded line with red ink, so you will be able to locate it when the rubber band breaks. During packing, make sure you do not stow the slider over other lines. Check that the line with the rubber band is clear to its slider grommet. Stuff the entire slider (not including grommets) through the rubber band.

3. For a nine cell canopy, roll the nose of the canopy on itself. Roll the leading edges of cells 1, 2, 3 and 4 together and stuff them inside the center cell, and similarly roll 9, 8, 7, and 6, together and stuff them inside cell 5.

4. If these suggestions fail to reduce the opening shock enough, contact the manufacturer of your canopy, for alternative packing instructions (addresses in the Appendix).

Control line adjustment. See the owner's manuals for both your canopy and harness/container system, regarding control line adjustment. The harness/container manufacturer, not the canopy manufacturer, provides risers. The canopy

---

Most jumpers are buying canopies 15 to 30 square feet too small for their weight and experience. *—Bill Dause*

manufacturer has no way of knowing what kind of riser release hardware you want, or what color your harness/container system is. The canopy manufacturer will mark the control lines to indicate the proper toggle attachment point for most standard-length risers. Your rig could have been assembled incorrectly. Start with the attachment marks, jump the canopy and check the trailing edge of the canopy and the steering lines. The trailing edge of the canopy should line up with the lower surface, and the control lines should be barely taut when the canopy is in full glide.

For more technical details on ram-air canopies, see the design section of *The Parachute Manual* by Dan Poynter.

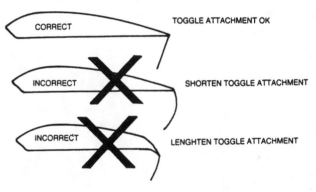

Canopy side view, in flight, with toggles released

Reserve canopies. Both the law and common sense require the sport jumper to carry a second, or *reserve*, parachute. While you may be packing your own main, this reserve must be periodically inspected and repacked by a licensed parachute rigger. The reserve must not have a descent rate exceeding 25 feet per second, according to FAA regulations, but shop for one that will land you at less than 18 fps.

The square reserve operates just like a square main except that the pilot chute, bridle and deployment bag are not tied on. The *free bag* on a ram-air is designed to allow the canopy to deploy even in a malfunctioned horseshoe condition.

A few rigs still have round reserve canopies that are less reliable and land very hard. Square reserve canopies not only offer quicker openings, faster forward speed, greater maneuverability and gentler landings than rounds, they also eliminate the need to learn the different handling characteristics of the older canopy. Over 95% of the new gear purchased today include square reserves.

The harness is an arrangement of nylon straps designed to conform to the shape of the body. Its purpose is to attach the body to the canopy and to provide for the distribution of the opening forces across itself and the body as comfortably as possible. The harness is designed around a sling that takes the greatest part of the opening load. The other straps are added only to keep the jumper from falling out of the basic sling. In fact, the diagonal back straps, for example, take only about 15% of the opening force. Sport saddles may be solid or split, and all are very well padded.

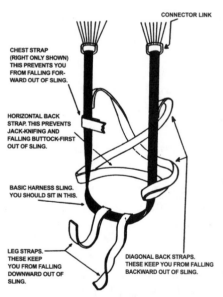
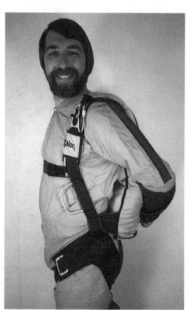

CONNECTOR LINK

CHEST STRAP (RIGHT ONLY SHOWN) THIS PREVENTS YOU FROM FALLING FORWARD OUT OF SLING.

HORIZONTAL BACK STRAP. THIS PREVENTS JACK-KNIFING AND FALLING BUTTOCK-FIRST OUT OF SLING.

BASIC HARNESS SLING. YOU SHOULD SIT IN THIS.

LEG STRAPS. THESE KEEP YOU FROM FALLING DOWNWARD OUT OF SLING.

DIAGONAL BACK STRAPS. THESE KEEP YOU FROM FALLING BACKWARD OUT OF SLING.

Basic harness sling with supporting straps added

The container, or *pack*, encloses the canopy and the deployment device and is locked closed by ripcord pins or cables through one or more loops through grommets.

Containers are employed for both main and reserves canopies and are usually mounted together on the back with the reserve container on top and the main container on the bottom.

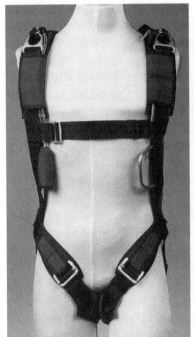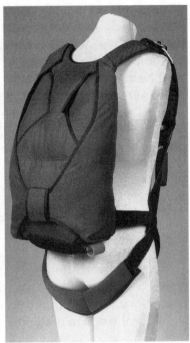

The Genera piggyback system with BOC throw-out pilot chute

The *packtray* is the line stow panel in the base of the container. When a deployment device is being used, the lines are usually stowed on the device rather than in the packtray. The container is often cut on the bias, 45 degrees to the weave of the fabric, to permit a bit of stretch during closing. Containers are not normally structural members of the parachute assembly; they simply attach to the harness and hold the canopy.

Container design is simply a question of packaging; where to put so many cubic inches of canopy. All the inside forces pushing out make the container want to assume a spherical shape, so some outside forces are needed to push the container back in, to compress the canopy. Tailoring, frames, bows, pack-opening bands and other devices are sometimes used. Reserves often use locking loops through the center of the pack. Many main canopies are pre-compressed inside a deployment bag and their throw-out pilot chute is stowed outside the container; the result is a smaller, thinner pack. Pull-out pilot chutes are stowed on top of the bag, but they do not take up nearly the space of spring-loaded pilot chutes.

The ripcord is a locking device that secures the closed parachute container; it does not open the pack, it simply releases it. The ripcord assembly may consist of a tubular metal handle (there are many shapes and materials to choose from), a cable of 3/32" diameter, 920 lb. stainless steel, the applicable number of properly spaced pins and a device to attach the cable to the handle, such as a swaged (pressed on) terminal ball. Or the grip may be a soft foam-stuffed handle or a plastic tube connected to a PVC or Teflon® coated cable. One ripcord assembly will activate the main parachute (except for rigs with throw-out or pull-out pilot chutes) and another will activate the reserve. On hand-deployed pilot chute rigs, the ripcord function is performed by either a curved or a straight pin that is pulled out of the locking loop by either the action of the pilot chute or the skydiver's hand.

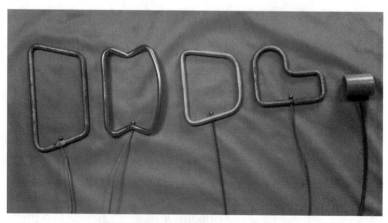

Ripcords come in many sizes and shapes

The force required to pull the ripcord will vary quite a bit, not only between rigs, but between pack jobs on the same rig; you can expect it to be between five and twenty-two pounds. Pull-out and throw-out activation devices on main parachutes are usually much easier to pull.

The ripcord pocket is designed to hold the ripcord in an accessible position. It may be made of fabric, elastic webbing, Velcro® closure or a steel clip and, if of fabric, it may receive its gripping quality from Velcro tape, an internal elastic cord or coil steel spring. Certain pockets are made to be compatible with certain ripcord handles; parts are not interchangeable.

The static line is a way of attaching the *ripcord* to the aircraft so that the parachute will be automatically activated as the jumper falls away. It consists of a special locking snap fastener, heavy webbing and a cable, sometimes with pins or a plastic-coated ripcord cable known as a *pigtail*. Pin type static lines must be routed through a guide ring on the container.

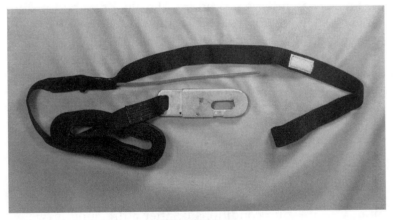

The static line

Be Safe
Have fun
Everything else is way down the list. —*Gary Peek*

With the direct bag system the arrangement is somewhat different. The deployment bag is attached to the static line and stays with the aircraft.

On static line jumps, the main ripcord is replaced with a dummy ripcord handle, so that the student may make Practice RipCord Pulls (PRCP). A dummy handle looks like the real one, but is fitted with a brightly colored *flag* so that the instructor can see when it has been pulled. The handle is also fitted with a strip of Velcro® to provide resistance similar to that felt in pulling the pin or cable from the locking loop. You must pull the handle from its pocket, and then continue pulling to separate the Velcro.

Hardware. Most of the metal fittings on the parachute are made of forged steel, and plated with cadmium to resist rusting. Newer sport hardware is stainless steel.

Canopy releases were originally designed for the jettisoning of the canopy so that the jumper could avoid being dragged in high winds, but sport jumpers adapted them for the breakaway reserve procedure. The older two-button and cable models made for the military by the Capewell Manufacturing Co. in Hartford, Connecticut, were later modified or replaced, because they had a tendency to hang up and occasionally caught a deploying pilot chute from a chest-mounted reserve. Now the Capewell release has been replaced by specially designed sport hardware, mostly 3-Ring releases.

Inspecting the 3-Ring release. Riser releases should be inspected prior to every jump. They should be disassembled and cleaned at the beginning of every jump day, but at least once a month. It should be done more often in humid, muddy or freezing conditions or after a dragging or water landing. Any mud or dirt must be removed. Use soap and water and then dry thoroughly. Any rusted parts must be replaced.

To test the 3-Ring release, secure the risers to the packed rig with their cover flaps or two strips of tape. Freezer tape works well because it won't leave adhesive on the nylon. Taping the risers insures they won't twist during your inspection. Position yourself behind the rig, reach around and grasp the breakaway handle. Pull the handle slowly to arm's length. Some cable may remain in the housing but both risers should release almost simultaneously. If one side releases before the other, the breakaway handle assembly may have been built for another harness or it may have been designed for use with an *RSL* (reserve static line). If both risers do not release when they are supposed to, tell your

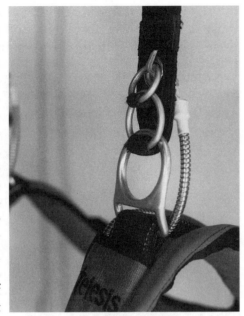

The 3-Ring canopy release in use

rigger. He or she will recheck the cables and may be able to correctly adjust the lengths by cutting and searing the longer one. Make sure the cable tips are smooth and tapered or they will catch on and fray the release loops when pulled through.

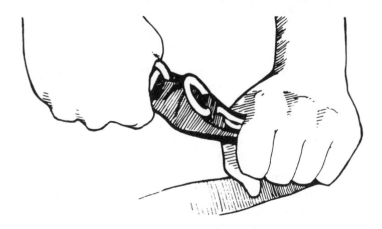

Twist each riser

The white locking loop that holds the smaller top ring must be flexible. Flex the loop to soften it and inspect it for wear. If it is stiff or dirty, use soap and water to clean and soften it.

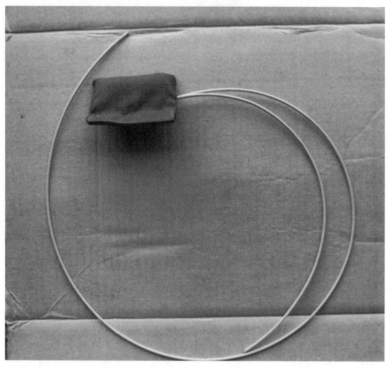

3-Ring release handle and cables

Grasp each riser to twist and flex the webbing near where it passes through each ring to remove any *set* or deformation in the webbing.

Check the Velcro on the release handle and main lift web. Make sure it is clean and holding well. Now, inspect the stitching that holds the large ring to the harness. If the large ring is stamped RW-1-82 or RW-1-83, contact your rigger or the manufacturer. Some of these rings were part of a bad batch: Not properly heat-treated, they are subject to deformation under high loads. A deformed ring will probably hang up. These rings must be tested and may have to be replaced. A previously tested ring should be marked, often with a lead seal on one side. The packing data card should also be correctly endorsed.

Pull downward on the release system cable housings. They should not move down more than ½″ but should be free to move upwards one to two inches. *The Racer* is an exception, so check your owner's manual. Check the terminal fittings at the ends of the housings. Make sure they are secure. Run the cables back and forth through the housings. Check for dents and obstructions.

Lightly lubricate the cables with a Silicone or Teflon® containing non-petroleum based fluid. Too much fluid will attract dirt and grit or may become tacky in cold weather. Just run the cables through a paper towel or cloth to wipe off old accumulations of dirt, and then apply some fluid to a clean paper towel and run the cables through it. Cables with any surface deformation should be replaced. See your rigger.

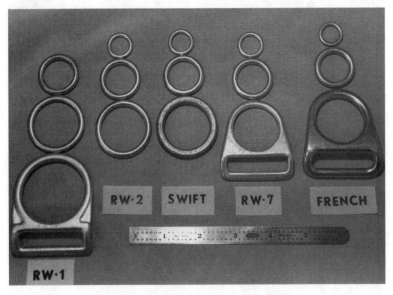

Rings come in different configurations and sizes

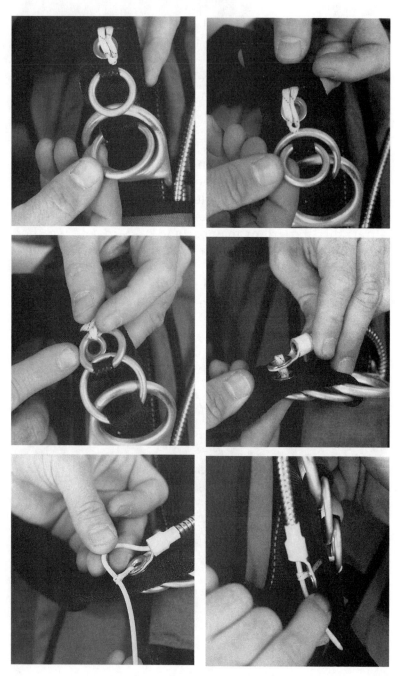

Assembling the 3-Ring release

Now reassemble the system, making sure the risers are not reversed. Put the middle ring under the base ring and flip it through. Place the small ring under the middle ring and flip it through. Put the loop over the small ring only, then thread it through the grommet in the riser to the back side. Thread the loop through the terminal end of the cable housing. Now pull the cable through the loop and stow it in the channel on the back of the riser. Check your work. On the top: The loop goes over the top, smallest ring only. The middle ring must not be caught on the loop at all. On the back: The loop must not be twisted. The cable must run out of the cable housing, through the loop and into the riser channel.

Some systems are assembled differently. Sometimes with narrower risers, the locking loop does not go through a grommet hole in the riser's webbing. Consult your rigger and your owner's manual.

Remove the tape holding the risers in place. If you find any wear or other problems, consult your rigger or the manufacturer.

Rapide links®. The most common connector link in use on sport equipment is the Rapide link or *French Connector*. The Rapide link is favored over the older military *L-bar*, separable and speed links because they are smaller, lighter, easier to use, less expensive and do not rotate in the riser. Unscrewed, the Rapide link will fail under a very light load. They must be checked regularly to make sure the barrel is screwed on completely. Conversely, they must not be over-tightened as this may split the barrel or strip the threads. Check the barrel regularly for tiny cracks. Install the Rapide link, twist the barrel on until hand-tight and then add 1/4 turn with a wrench (for five inch pounds of torque). Though the end of the link is peened to retard over-tightening, sometimes it is possible to screw the barrel off the ends of the threads. Make sure the threads are totally engaged. After ten jumps or so, recheck the links and retighten, if necessary.

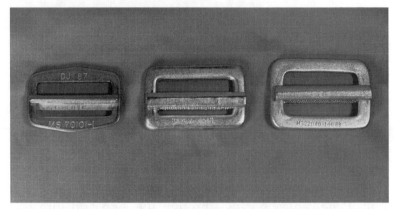

Friction adapters: L-R: 500# light, 2500# shallow, 2500# deep

Connector links: L-R: Rapide link, 3000# Army separable link,
3000# Navy speed link

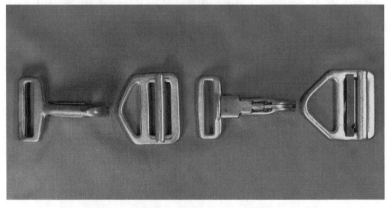

Snaps and rings: L-R: 2500# Air Force snap, shallow adjustable "V" ring,
Navy quick ejector snap, deep adjustable "V" ring

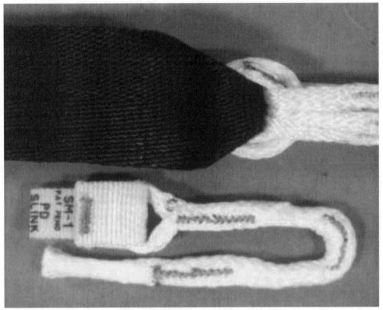

Slinks are non-metallic

Instruments. There are four ways to determine when you have reached pull altitude; stopwatch, altimeter (visual or audible), counting the seconds, and eyeballing the ground. *Eyeballing* is a good backup, but it isn't accurate when you are trying to locate a 3,000-foot mark in the sky. Depth perception is greatly reduced over water and at night, and eyeballing is rarely accurate at an unfamiliar drop zone. *Counting* works well on fives and tens, but it is difficult to be accurate in timing freefalls of more than ten seconds in this manner. USPA recommends the use of a *visual altimeter* on all jumps. Students should not use *audible altimeters* until they have demonstrated a satisfactory level of *altitude awareness* and they should be used by experienced jumpers only as reminders to check the visual altimeter or the ground.

The altimeter has an evacuated chamber called an *aneroid*, which is very sensitive to changes in air pressure. As you descend, the air pressure increases since the air gets thicker, and the aneroid bends inward. This aneroid movement is relayed and amplified through a series of gears, and a needle on the face of the instrument indicates the result.

The sport altimeters are much smaller and lighter than the standard aircraft equipment. All mechanical devices are subject to failure, so you should always check your altimeter against another one. Compare them when you are climbing for altitude; check yours against a friend's or the one in the instrument panel of the jump ship. But be careful; your altimeter is set for *ground level* and the aircraft's altimeter may be set for *sea level*.

You will not be able to see much movement in your altimeter until you graduate to 20-second freefalls. However, you will use the altimeter while flying your canopy on all jumps.

The altimeter is *zeroed* on the ground to calibrate it. If you are planning a demo jump off the DZ, you will have to find the elevation of the landing area and compensate for it by adjusting the altimeter.

Chest mount   Wrist mount

The instruments may be mounted on your chest or other harness strap, or on your wrist. Some jumpers prefer a fixed mount over the wrist mount, reasoning that you can't fly as well if you are constantly pulling in a flying surface (wrist) to see what your altitude is. Another argument for the fixed mount is that jumpers sometimes have had their wrist-mounted altimeters ripped off in relative work. On the other hand, a chest-mounted altimeter may be unreliable when falling on your back (SDB) as it is in the burble area of reduced pressure. Additionally, some students lose their arch when looking down at a chest altimeter.

Wrist mounted altimeters should be worn on the left wrist so they won't catch on hand-deployed pilot chutes.

Newer digital altimeters are available on the market, which give a digital (numerical) rather than an analog (dial) readout of the jumper's altitude. These are not geared devices. They are based upon a different type of pressure sensing system.

The parts of the altimeter.
A. Aneroid, an evacuated diaphram
B. Rocking shaft assembly
C. Sector gear
D. Calibration arm
E. Diaphram connecting link
F. Handstaff
G. Hairspring
H. Needle
I. Temperature compensator
J. Counterweight
K. Diaphram stop pin
L. Case
M. Opening in case.

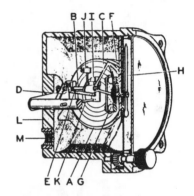

The dial-readout altimeter operates on an aneroid which is sensitive to changes in air pressure

The Digitude

The Dytter audio altimeter

The Skytronic

Just looking at the individual fatalities that occurred this year, 11 of the 28 might have lived had they been equipped with a functioning automatic activation device. —*Paul Sitter*

Audible altimeters, sometimes called *beepers* or *dirt alerts*, go beep, beep, beep in your ear at pre-set altitudes above the drop zone. The unit is designed to be mounted on the helmet near the ear. Some of the audible altimeters are the Dytter, Skytronic, and Time-Out!! See your dealer.

Never put your trust in just one method of altitude assessment and remember, *when in doubt, whip it out.*

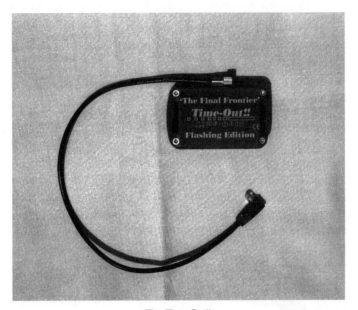

The Time-Out!!

The automatic activation device (AAD) is a parachute container release which combines a barometric device (similar to an altimeter) with a means of pulling the rip-cord of the main or the reserve, or cutting the locking loop. Additionally, some have a sensing mechanism that switches the opener on and off, so that it fires only if the wearer is descending through 1,000 feet at a high rate of speed; there is no need to turn the release on and off. This sensing mechanism saves wear and tear on the release system (or the expensive replacement of cutters), that would otherwise fire if you forgot to turn it off after opening. Microprocessor-based AADs operate at different parameters (descent speed and altitude) depending upon the purpose they were designed for (student, experienced, or tandem usage).

The USPA requires AADs to be mounted on the main or reserve of all students, since statistics show that the devices might cut the fatality rate as much as 50%. Experienced jumpers can make their own decision. But everyone, particularly students, must realize that the AAD is only a back-up system; mechanical devices can fail and should not be relied upon.

—**The Sentinel Mk2000**, a mechanical, electric, and gas-operated device, uses an aneroid, micro-switch and battery to fire a squib in a tube that pushes a piston to withdraw the locking (ripcord) pins. The Sentinel has both an altitude sensor and a rate of descent sensor; it operates when the user passes through 1,000 feet while still in freefall. Sentinels must be serviced periodically by Paratronics, Tel: (817) 460-2266; Fax: (817) 460-2266; jkca930@aol.com. The manufacturer is SSE, Tel: (609) 663-2234; info@sse-inc.com; http://www.sse-inc.com

The FXC Model 12000

—The FXC Model 12000 is barometric (altitude sensor), has a rate of descent sensor, and pulls the ripcord pins with a spring-loaded cable. The activation altitude is pre-set on the ground and the AAD will only fire if the jumper passes through that altitude at a rate faster than 40-60 feet per second, about one-third of terminal. Since good canopies descend at less than 20 feet per second, the AAD won't fire unless there is a problem. The Model 12000 may be mounted on either the main or the reserve.

—**KAP-3.** Czech and Russian models of the KAP-3 are used in Eastern Europe. They are similar in concept to the Model 12000 but do not have a rate sensor.

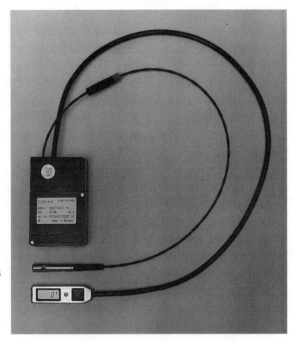

The Cypres

—**The Cypres** is digital with an altitude sensor, rate of descent sensor and battery which operate a (reefing line) cutter that severs the locking loop in the parachute container. The Cypres is completely automatic once you calibrate it to ground level by pushing the button per the instructor. There are four models: Expert, Student, Military and Tandem. Each is factory set to fire under different conditions. For example, the Expert model activates at 750 feet when it detects a rate of descent greater than 78 mph (35m/sec).

By the end of 1997, over 40,000 Cypres units were in the field; about 33,000 were Expert units for experienced skydivers. Cypres units must be returned to Airtec or SSK, 1008 Monroe Road, Lebanon, Ohio 45036. Tel: (513) 934-3201; Fax (513) 934-3208; ssk@pia.com, every four years for a complete factory check. See the Cypres Support Web Site: http://www.sskinc.com. As of 2001, there were 239 saves.

Cypres equipped. —*Allen Roulston*

—**The Astra** is similar to the Cypres in concept. It is digital with an altitude sensor, rate of descent sensor and battery which operate a (reefing line) cutter that severs the locking loop in the parachute container. FXC Corp., 3410 S. Susan Street, Santa Ana, CA 92704. Tel: (714) 556-7400; Fax (714) 641-5093; fxc@pia.com; www.pia.com/fxc

Do not drop an AAD-equipped rig. The sensor may contain a delicate lever arm that could be damaged in rough handling. Protect the AAD from moisture and dirt. Both the sensor and power boxes contain sensitive valves and metering devices. Check the manuals regarding battery life and look for the *low-batt* warning light or code. If the unit does not calibrate properly, send it for servicing.

Personal equipment. Jumpsuit, helmet, goggles, a knife and gloves are some of the personal equipment you will purchase.

1920 & '30s. Barnstormer.
This one used two parachutes, most did not.

1940s and 1950s. Military jumper.
They used
football helmets at first.

1960s. Sport jumpers used
much borrowed military gear
and some designed for
the sport.

Early 1970s. The sport jumper's gear is all specially designed for flying and most suits were bigger.

1980s. The sport jumper opted for tighter suits to provide greater descent speed for more control.

1990s. Jumpsuits become fashion statements and the grippers are built in.

Jumpsuit. A parachutist's outer garment was called *coveralls* in the early sixties and that was what it was designed to do; provide warmth and protection and keep the clothes clean. Into the seventies, it became a *jumpsuit*, no longer store-bought; it was well tailored, fancy, custom-made, specialized equipment. In the mid-seventies, with the great interest in relative work, the garments became bigger and were dubbed *flying suits* and some flying suits were huge. They had a lot of extra fabric under the arms, and cords inside to hook over the thumb so that you could pull the suit out by extending your arms. They had great flared bells on the arms and legs, and there was enough room inside for the whole team. The reason for all this cloth was for *range*; the relative worker wanted to be able to go faster or slower and to accelerate and decelerate more rapidly. Some jumpers didn't notice their jumpsuits were too large until they reached two-grand and found their sleeve was covering their ripcord hand.

In the mid-eighties, relative work teams switched to skin-tight jumpsuits that provided a faster rate of fall. With all of them falling faster, the transitions became quicker. Then to equalize fall rates, the slower fallers added weight vests.

Sure-grips are rib-like handles added to the arms and legs of the jumpsuit so that team members can get a grip on you. Grippers have become more important now that jumpsuits are so tight.

Choose a suit to match the fall rate of the people with whom you are jumping. —*Pat Schraufnagel*

Traditionally, jumpsuits were made of heavy or light cotton. Newer jumpsuits are often made of synthetics or a poly/cotton blend. Some of the synthetics, such as the elastic Spandex, may melt if they come into contact with power lines. Some synthetics will not only melt, they will burn too.

Helmet. You will need a helmet to protect your head during rushed relative work exits, in freefall with colliding jumpers, during opening to save the ears from errant connector links, and while landing. Make sure the helmet is well-constructed, has a secure strap or durable snap, does not restrict your vision or hearing, and is cut high in the back so you can get your head back to look up in freefall. Some experienced jumpers prefer a soft, stylish leather helmet (frap hat) which may keep their hair

A full-coverage hard-shell helmet with visor

in place but does little to protect their heads from collision injuries (with each other or with the ground). Jumping without a helmet is the prerogative of the experienced jumper.

Earplugs. It was just stated that a helmet should not restrict hearing, yet continually and repeatedly subjecting oneself to the high noise environment of the aircraft and freefall environment can degrade one's hearing. Soft foam earplugs that are removable after the freefall is over can be a very worthwhile item to include in your equipment list. After all, once you start losing your hearing, you rarely get it back.

Some old timers remember the helmetless skydiver who survived a night landing onto a roof in Antioch, but died from head injuries suffered when she fell off the roof. —*Eric Roberts*

Goggles. The main reason for wearing goggles is to keep your eyes from watering up. But goggles will also ward off some of the small things flying around at altitude, which could injure an eye. You may not bother with goggles when on static line; someone else will be spotting and you won't be in the fast air very long. But you cannot perform safe, competent relative work unless you can see clearly. Some jumpers suffer more from eye tearing than others. You will have to test yourself to find out.

Be wary of large rubber or plastic soft-sided (chemical type) goggles with wide frames. They restrict the peripheral vision and make it difficult to locate the ripcord. Big goggles also have a tendency to blow off in freefall. If you wear glasses, there are goggles that will fit over them, or you may prefer to wear only the glasses secured with an eyeglass strap. Get goggles with clear lenses only, and steer away from the other "flavors." You will need all the light you can find when jumping late in the day. Most snap-on visors and face shields are out, they often blow off in freefall. But the full-coverage helmets such as *Factory Diver, Renegade, Head Hunter* and *Carbon Fire* are specifically designed for skydiving.

Gloves provide warmth and protection for your hands; they should be worn if the temperature at jump altitude is below 40 degrees Fahrenheit. As you climb, the temperature drops at a rate of about 3.5 degrees per thousand feet. That is 35 degrees less at 10,000 feet than at ground level—it adds up fast. Gloves should be as thin as the temperature will allow, and you should use them when practicing your ripcord pulls and emergency procedures.

Footwear. In the early days of sport parachuting, everyone wore army boots just like the airborne troops without realizing that their missions were quite different. The paratroops use the parachute for transportation, a means to an end. The sport jumper is interested only in the means, and has no intention of following the jump with a 40-mile *problem* (hike). Throughout the sixties, most jumpers wore the imported French Paraboot which has a thick pneumatic sole, good ankle support, and fit well if you had wide feet. Later, as square canopies took over, most jumpers switched to lighter footgear, usually running shoes. Boots with lacing hooks are absolutely out. They could catch a pilot chute, suspension line, or deploying canopy.

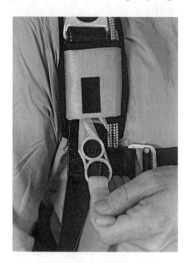

A hook knife is designed to cut suspension lines and static lines in an emergency

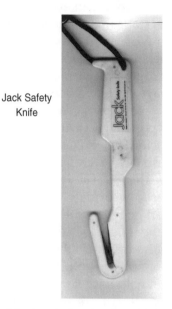

Jack Safety Knife

Hook knife. An open, accessible hook knife should be carried, preferably on the harness. A small pocket with a Velcro closure is a good place. The knife may be used to cut suspension lines and static lines in an emergency. Every skydiver should wear one and every jump ship should be equipped with one. Folding hook knives should be protected and carried in the open position.

Fitting the parachute assembly. Proper harness fit and adjustment are essential for comfort, as well as good flying. Few skydivers understand the fitting of the parachute, yet it is so very important. A poor fit can take all the fun out of the jump.

Loosen the front (main lift web) chest and leg straps. Don the harness by placing it over the shoulders. Thread the chest strap but do NOT tighten it yet. Bend over at the waist, reach under the pack and push it up high on the shoulders. If there is a full saddle, slide the saddle down over the buttocks, making sure the leg straps are not misrouted. Hook up the leg straps and tighten them. (If you have thread-through leg straps, you will probably step through them rather than unthread and rethread them.) Adjust the main lift webs (if adjustable) so that the canopy release hardware is located in and above the hollow of the shoulders. Grasp the diagonal back straps (if adjustable) and cinch them down. Pull them forward and down to the front, until the harness feels snug around the body. The harness should be snug, but not so tight you can't walk. Adjust

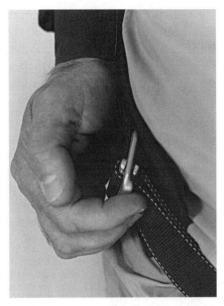

To loosen the web, pull on the back end of the hardware. To tighten the web, pull the free end.

the chest strap. Thread and tighten the bellyband if you have one. Stow all excess webbing in the strap channels or elastic keepers provided so that they do not flap in the wind.

Now your gear is on and you are ready for the pre-boarding equipment check.

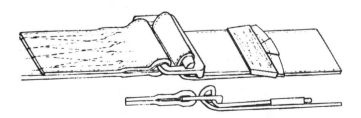

Correct threading of the friction adapter

Quickfit (adjustable) adapters, as found on chest and leg straps, may be easily loosened by pulling on the anvil of the hardware with the fingers, 90 degrees away from the sliding strap. This is easily accomplished even when the harness is on tightly, and the strap is under tension. Lifting the anvil orients the hardware so that it will not grip the webbing; the strap slips out due to its own tension.

Check all adjustable hardware for correct threading. Note that the anvil (ridge) on the underside of the frame forces a greater bend in the web. Improperly threaded hardware may slip. All webbing ends must be spread and sewn, or rolled and sewn, so that they cannot slip out of the hardware.

The equipment check is that all-over gear inspection, sometimes referred to as a *pin check* which you conduct on each other prior to boarding the jump aircraft. It is also called a *gear check*, as a lot of the newer equipment uses other methods to secure the closed containers. In any event, there is much more to check than pins. Initially, your instructor will check you. Later, another jumper will check you on your load, and you will check him or her. This final visual and physical pre-jump checkout is not to pass judgment on the design of the equipment; it is a double check to ensure it was put it on correctly. Over the years, numerous lives have been lost due to the lack of a proper gear check, including a freefall photographer who jumped with no gear on at all! A gear check is the cheapest skydiving *insurance* that you will ever find. Get one.

The following equipment check outline refers specifically to piggyback equipment with a back mounted reserve, but it is generally applicable to all parachuting gear. The check should be systematic to ensure that nothing is overlooked. It should start in the front, run from top to bottom, and then continue in the back from helmet to footwear. So let's get started.

The *helmet* should be snug so it can't slip down over the eyes, leaving the wearer *in the dark*. Grab the sides and try to rotate it. The strap must be secure. If it has a snap, the snap must be effective. Helmets lift off the head easily in terminal freefall, and this not only deprives the owner of its protection when he or she needs it, it presents a danger to spectators below.

Goggles or glasses must be secure and clean. Check for a retainer strap.

The *canopy releases* should be positioned down to the hollow of the shoulder, just below the collarbone. Put your hands on them and rotate them outwards so that you can check the mating and routing of the parts.

Ripcords and cutaway handle properly stowed and routed. Make sure the housings are routed under the riser and are tacked to the harness within 3" of their ends to avoid floating handles.

Reserve static line (Stevens system). Make sure it is hooked up and routed properly.

Now moving down, check the *chest strap* for routing and hardware threading. If the chest strap has a snap, click it to make sure there isn't any cloth caught in it. Quick ejector snaps demand closer inspection; make sure they are fully seated by pushing the wing closed. Inspect the routing of the chest strap to make sure it is not around the main lift web or threaded through a ripcord handle. Is the *hook knife* accessible?

—**AAD**. If the rig has a *front-mounted* AAD control, check to make sure that it is properly set and operational as required. If it requires ground-level calibration, perform that task per the manufacturer's directions. If there are any visibly-exposed components of the AAD, make sure that they are assembled properly.

—**Instruments**. Altimeter zeroed. Calibrate the automatic opener according to the owner's manual. Make sure the instruments do not block the view of the handles. Check the *radio* on students.

Make sure the canopy release *handle* is removable, but firmly in place. Periodically, the Velcro handle should be peeled away.

See that the friction adapters on the *main lift webs* (if

The pin check defined: A systematic inspection of another skydiver to ensure that all equipment is properly worn and routed. This inspection is not just for students, but for all jumpers on the load.

—*Don Towner*

applicable) are threaded correctly and that the web ends are rolled back and sewn.

Grasp the handle of the *throw-out pilot chute,* if there is one. Is it stowed properly in its pocket and is the bridle properly routed? Trace the bridle routing with your finger. Pay particular attention to where the bridle exits the pilot chute pouch. If the throw-out is on the belly-band, is the bellyband routed under anything, like the main lift web, or is it twisted? Is the belly-band securely fastened?

This throw-out pilot chute bridle is routed incorrectly—under the main lift web. If not routed correcting, emergency procedures will be necessary.

Occasionally, you may encounter a *chest reserve:* Ask if there is a pilot chute installed, feel for it or check for a *pilot chute removed* tag. The presence or absence of a pilot chute makes a difference in the selection of reserve procedure, and the wearer may have borrowed this chest pack. Kneel down and firmly grasp the reserve handle in the left hand twisting it gently in its pocket. This action will disclose a tight pocket and, of course, it will be impossible to grasp the handle if there is a pack-opening band over it. With the right hand, open the pin protector flap. Pull the handle gently to just barely slide the pins, then grasp the last pin and pull to reseat them. Check the position of the instrument panel if there is one. Sometimes it is pushed too far forward, overlapping the pilot chute which may prevent it from springing out. Make sure the side carrying handles are secured back under a pack-opening band so that one won't be grabbed in a hasty search for the ripcord handle. Is the bellyband routed properly and secured to the main container? Now lift the reserve by pushing up from the bottom. Try to rock it upward; it should be tight.

Move on to the *leg straps,* checking friction adapter hardware for threading, and snaps for trapped fabric. Quick ejector snaps need a comfort pad between them and the jumpsuit. Loose straps should be stowed in the leg strap channel or retained by harness keepers or rubber bands, as a loose one may flutter in freefall, and this is very painful. Or the loose strap may get in the way of a throw-out pilot chute. Jumpers have been known to tug on loose leg straps when they thought they were extracting their pilot chute. On the ground, the problem is not so obvious because the straps hang down, out of the way. Make sure leg straps are not twisted. A twisted leg strap with a throw-out pilot chute system will result in a pilot chute in tow and possibly a horseshoe malfunction, the most dangerous kind. Make sure you do not cross the leg straps. This may sound funny, but more than one student has found it very painful.

Stand away and make an overall visual inspection of the *front.* An unzipped leg pocket or cuff could put an inexperienced jumper into a turn. If there are lacing hooks on the boots, they must be taped over to prevent them from grabbing errant pilot chutes, suspension lines, or fabric.

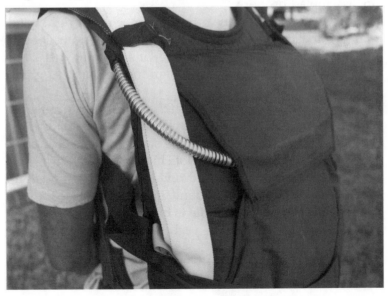

This main will probably activate the reserve when it deploys

Now, going around to the *back*, grab the housings and pull them sharply upwards. If they are not the expanding type, if the cable is long enough and if the housing is secure at both ends, the canopy won't dump out on the ground, or the canopy releases will not activate.

Make sure the main risers are routed over the reserve ripcord housing, are not twisted and the toggles are not showing.

Starting with the *reserve*: Open the ripcord pin protector flap. Make sure the pins or cables are properly seated. Check the grommets for excessive wear. Check the security of the seal to insure that no one has been inside except a rigger; and then look at the packing data card to make sure the reserve is in date. This is primarily to cover yourself in case the FAA shows up. Look at the hooks on the pack opening bands if the container has them, to make sure they haven't worn holes in the container to grab something inside.

—**AAD**. If the rig has a *rear-mounted* AAD control, check to make sure that it is properly set and operational as required. If it requires ground level calibration, perform that task per the manufacturer's directions. If there are any visibly exposed components of the AAD, make sure that they are assembled properly.

Now grasp the *cable* near the handle with the right hand, place your left hand on the cable near the locking loop to pull the cable back and forth in a sawing motion. This action will reveal kinks, as well as foreign matter, such as gravel inside the housing.

Look at the *friction adapters* on the back straps (if they are exposed) and make sure they are properly threaded; check for webbing twists. Make sure the strap ends are stowed so they won't trail and snare a pilot chute.

Check the routing of the throw-out pilot chute *bridle*, or pull-out pilot chute handle, and the threading of the pin. Make sure the pull-out handle is firmly seated.

If there is a *static line*, inspect its assembly to the rig, the

---

There's more to check than pins. — *J. Scott Hamilton*

snap and the webbing. Make sure the webbing is properly routed.

Now, a pat on the backpack will signify to the jumper that the check is complete. The whole operation probably took less than a minute.

Once everyone has been checked, equipment should not be removed or altered without a new check. Always perform a *pre-exit check* on your own gear just prior to jump run.

You will want to begin making equipment checks as early as possible in your jumping career, to help you learn about your own gear.

Parachute Packing. The carrying, untangling, inspection, packing, and minor maintenance of a sport parachute consumes a large percentage of a jumper's time. Initially, it will take 1/2 hour or more to properly pack a main parachute under supervision, but as you become more familiar with the packing sequence, this time will be cut to a few minutes.

This section is designed to introduce you to parachute packing in order to help you better understand the operation of your own equipment. The parachute is a straightforward mechanical device. Yet many people picture it as very mysterious, as though it were guaranteed to fail if not packed absolutely perfectly.

The main parachute may be packed by an FAA certificated parachute rigger or the user, while the reserve may only be packed by a rigger. The rigger gives the reserve a thorough inspection, applies a lead seal to some safety tie thread, and then fills in and signs the packing data card. The FAA says you may not use a parachute that has not been packed within the last 120 days. You will pack your main parachute under supervision until you are signed off to do so without supervision. Prerequisites for the signature are the capability to inspect and assess damage, being able to pack, being able to untangle the parachute, and the ability to conduct the pre-jump equipment inspection. All this will

No one ever died because of a pin check. —*Paul Sitter*

require a considerable knowledge of the parachute, and you will probably start learning to pack just after your first jump.

Pull-up cord. About the only tool required for packing the sport main is a pull-up cord. The cord is used to pull a locking loop up through the grommets in the pack flaps, so that the locking pin can be inserted. Route the cord *under* the pin and pull the cord out slowly so you won't wear out the closure loop.

The parachute rigger seals the reserve after packing

The packing procedure. Pack on a packing mat or dry lawn, out of the wind and out of the sun. Avoid asphalt and concrete as they will cause extra wear to the assembly. Inspect the parachute prior to packing. Carefully check the bridle attachment point, the canopy, the slider stops, the connector links, the slider bumpers on the Rapide links, the slider, the lines, the control line locking loops, the harness and containers.

The ram-air main canopy may be *stack packed* or *pro packed* (sometimes referred to as a *stand-up pack job*). These instructions from Precision Aerodynamics outline the pro packing method. Now, start by stowing your deployment brakes and then:

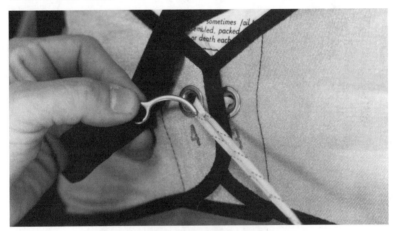

Using the pull-up cord

The Pro-pack

Main Canopy Folding Instructions

The Line Check

1. Crouch next to the risers and face you canopy. Slip the fingers of your left hand between each left-hand riser and between the left-hand steering line and the risers. Do the same with your right hand. The idea is to have each line group and each steering line occupying its own slot between two of your fingers.

2. Stand between the right- and left-hand riser groups and start moving up the lines, allowing them to slide between you fingers. Push the slider ahead, until you reach the bottom of the canopy.

At this point, it's possible to determine whether or not your canopy and lines are straight. If you have twists in the lines as shown, your rig has done a "loop" through your risers at some point. To fix this, drop the lines, stretch the canopy and lines out again and straighten out the entanglement. Get help from a rigger if you have any questions. Repeat the line check after cleaning to confirm you have done it correctly.

3. If you have something that looks like this, it's likely a control line is passed around everything else.
A control line which passes around everything else will result in a malfunction that will almost surely require a breakaway.

To fix this, lay the canopy down on the ground. Starting at the canopy, find the second and third lines on one end cell (these are called the B and C lines). Carefully follow these two lines down through the slider to the links on the risers. You should be able to see where you will need to pass your rig through the lines to correct the steering line routing. Again, seek capable assistance if you have any questions.

Flaking the Leading Edge

4. When you reach your canopy, pull both hands apart as far as the slider will allow. Shake the canopy a couple times to settle everything.

5. Now step to one side, outside the lines and transfer the lines in one hand to the other. . .

6. . . . so you are holding all the lines in one hand—preferably with your stronger arm.

7. Locate the leading edge of the canopy, it should be facing your rig. (If it is facing "up" or away form your rig, it might mean your canopy has been attached backward.)

8. Starting with the end cell nearest your legs, flake the entire leading edge with one hand as shown.

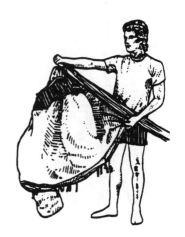

9. Pull each cell all the way out and keep it in your hand. Then move to the next cell, taking care not to miss any, until all of them are in your hand.

10. When you've got the entire leading edge flaked . . .

11. . . . tuck it between your knees and hold it there.

Clearing the Stabilizers

12. Since the liens are bunched up in the middle, pull out each stabilizer panel one by one until they form an irregular shape resembling the petals of a flower viewed from the top.

13. Find the group of A lines on the one side of the canopy. With the canopy held in front of you as you have it now, the A lines are the front part of the line group that go through the front slider grommets, the ones that should be closest to you.

(Each load-bearing cell rib has four lines attached to it: the A line at the leading edge, followed by the B and then the C lines, ending with the D line closest to (but not on) the trailing edge. Some cells have control lines attached to them at the trailing edge. The A and B lines pass though the front grommets of the slider, while the C, D and control lines all pass through the rear grommets.)

14. Since there is a lot of fabric between the A and B line attachment points, it's easy to separate the two line groups; (See the drawing.)

Now you're going to S fold the rest of the canopy like the stabilizers. Put your hand in between the A and B lines on the side (near where they pass their own grommet) and pull them out to one side. This will give the cells on one side the correct type of flaking. Now repeat with the other A and B group, pulling the fold out the other side.

15. Now that you've pulled out the canopy between the A and B line groups, do the same thing between the two groups out to each side. When you look down between the stabilizer folds after you've done your "flaking," the folds should look nice and neat like this.

Flaking the Tailing Edge
16. Now find the D line group, the group of lines nearest the tail. (Not the control lines; they are attached at the trailing edge.)

17. Take the whole D line group on the side.

18. . . . pull it out gently; then fold it with one motion to put a real fold in the fabric between the C and D lines. Do the same thing on the other side.

19. Now grasp the control lines where they attach to the trailing edge, pull the entire trailing edge out and drop it straight down.

20. Flake the trailing edge neatly on each side as shown. The center portion of the trailing edge—the section between the left-hand and the right-hand control lines—can't be flaked and will hang down. You'll straighten this out next.

21. Reach down and pick up the very middle point of the trailing edge (the ID panel is sewn to the top of the center cell near the trailing edge.) Lift it up and put the very middle seam up with the slider grommets, holding it in place with your thumb or finger.

If your canopy is new, or if it tends to open uncomfortably fast, then follow the steps 22 through 25. Otherwise, skip to 26.

Optional (For Slower Openings)
22. Loosen your knees grip on the leading edge of the canopy. Find the very middle of it. (It's easy. Just run your hand down between the front two slider grommets; exactly half the lines will be on one side and half on the other.)

23. While leaving the very middle cell hanging, pick up all the others on one side and roll them in toward the middle.

24. Do the same on the other side. When you're done, this is how the leading edge should look.

25. This shows how steps 23 and 24 help slow down openings. As the canopy opens (remember, this illustration shows the canopy upside down), the center cell inflates and the side are slowed somewhat by the fact that they are rolled separately. The result is more controlled, symmetrical inflation.

If you want your canopy to open fast, just leave the leading edge hanging neatly flacked, don't roll it at all.

26. You have in your hand a neatly flaked canopy. The leading edge is brushing up against you legs and the middle of the trailing edge is still being held along with all the lines.

27. On one side, start at the middle of the trailing edge being held under your thumb and pull the excess material straight out. You're pulling out the trailing edge of the canopy that extends from the inside control line to the very center of the trailing edge.

28. Holding the lines firmly with the other hand, wrap that part of the trailing edge halfway around the canopy. Hold it in place with your knees. Fold the trailing edge on the other side of the canopy in the same way.

BE CAREFUL WHEN PULLING THE TRAILING EDGE AROUND THE BUNDLE, BE SURE TO LEAVE THE CONTROL LINES UNDISTRUBED. IF YOU WRAP THE CONTROL LINES AROUND THE BUNDLE ALONG WITH THE TRAILING EDGE, YOU MAY INDUCE A LINEOVER MALFUNCTION.

29. Take both trailing edge pieces in one hand and . . .

30. . . . roll them together in to the middle so they completely encase the rest of the canopy.

31. Place your free hand carefully under the bundle.

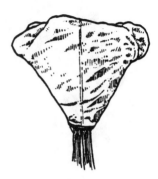

32. Swing it out slightly so that lines stay taut and gently lay it on the floor.

33. As it rests on the floor, the canopy should be triangular in shape as shown.

34. Tuck the side under starting at the slider and working up, making the canopy into a flattened cylinder shape.

35. Move to the side of the canopy and put one hand under the slider edge of the bundle. Place the other hand on too a little farther up.

36. Make a small S fold as shown.

37. Now put one hand under the top of the bundle and make an S fold in the opposite direction, as shown.

38. You should now have a neat, compact bundle. Try to make the folds so that the bundle ends up being just a little wider than the deployment bag.

39. Place your knee in the middle of the canopy to keep it together when you pull the bag over it.

40. With your knee still in place, pull the bag over the canopy one side at a time. Hold the corner of the canopy bundle up while you pull the bag over it, then roll the canopy into the corner of the bag. This helps get the canopy firmly into the corners, making it a neater pack job.

41. The whole canopy should be in the bag before you remove your knee.
Follow your harness/container manufacturer's instructions for closing the bag, stowing the lines, placing it in the pack tray and closing the container.

It takes practice to pack both quickly and neatly. Every jumper has their own "system" to make the job easier, and you'll quickly develop one of your own.

The above is not meant to be a complete do-it-yourself packing course. You will be closely supervised as you learn, and you should always ask about a procedure if you are not absolutely sure. These instructions will serve as an introduction to packing and will help you to better understand the operation of your gear.

Parachute care. Protect your parachute by avoiding abrasion (do not drag it on the ground), fluids (no water jumps) and sunlight (do not pack in the open). The ultra-violet rays of the sun will deteriorate your canopy very rapidly. If you take 15 minutes to pack outdoors, then after 280 jumps, your canopy has been in the sun the equivalent of a week of ten-hour days, and that is enough to lower the strength by 50%. Nylon never recovers; it just gets weaker and weaker. The above week in the sun does not even count the two to four minutes of exposure on each jump. So pick up your canopy after landing and carry it to a clean, shaded packing area. High heat is also bad for nylon, so do not leave your parachute in the trunk of your car on a hot day. Do not wash your canopy and do not jump in the rain. Any water will make the fabric more porous. For details on what affects nylon, see Chapter Nine of *The Parachute Manual* by Dan Poynter.

Parachute repairs and alterations. Inspect your gear frequently for damage and wear. Repairs to a *reserve* assembly must be performed by an FAA certificated parachute rigger. A rigger must do most repairs to a main parachute assembly, but there are a few you may perform if you have adequate knowledge and skill. You are certainly authorized to inspect your gear, and this chapter has described a number of things to look for. Major repairs and alterations to parachutes may only be performed by a master rigger, while minor repairs and maintenance may be performed by a senior or master rigger.

Try some silicone spray on your main canopy. Spraying the lines will help prevent slider hang-ups and abraded lines. Sprayed on rubber bands, the bands become soft, flexible and stretch better. Sprayed on risers that brush past Velcro hook, the webs avoid getting the *fuzzies*. Silicone or Teflon spray will slick-up the 3-Ring release cables for easy, wear-free pulls. The silicone spray sold in scuba shops is a food-service grade, pure silicone that does not contain petroleum distillates.

Frayed and broken rubber bands should be replaced.

Small tears and holes in the main canopy may be repaired with ripstop tape. Check with your rigger.

Buying a parachute used to be easier and a lot less expensive. Of course you got what you paid for, too. In the old days, up to the mid-seventies, most parts were pretty much interchangeable. Most canopies would fit

---

Buying used equipment piecemeal—a container from one person, reserve canopy from another and a main from a third source—often creates problems getting the parts to fit together properly, because of the melange of sizes and shapes out there. Even an experienced jumper who knows what is available, and is looking for used gear, would do well to buy complete rigs that were ordered originally as a matching unit.

—Bill Dause

most containers, and most harnesses could be adjusted to fit all. Today there are so many canopy and container sizes that both must be measured and stamped with their volume in cubic inches to insure compatibility. Since it is nearly impossible to purchase a used part here, and a used component there, to assemble the right rig for you, you might as well buy new ones. If you buy new equipment, you not only will get a harness that fits, but the canopies will be sized for your weight and will be designed for your kind of jumping, and you will get your choice of colors as well.

Just as there are many types of parachuting, there are many types of specialized main canopies. If you like competition accuracy, you will want a relatively large canopy that will sink well and remain stable in deep brakes. If you are planning to do primarily canopy relative work, you will want a canopy without cascaded (joined) front-center lines.

CRW jumpers wrap their legs around these lines and they can become caught in the confluence of cascaded lines. If your main interest is relative work, you will choose a low-weight, low-volume canopy with a good glide to make up for bad spots. Ask your instructor, ask skydivers who do the type of jumping you like, and check the wing loading discussion in this chapter to make sure the canopy you buy is not too large or too small.

Many skydiving centers have pro shops providing both gear and advice

Be very wary of F-111 main canopies with

more than 300 jumps on them and Zero Porosity canopies with more than 500. Always have a competent rigger inspect used gear before you buy it. The zero porosity fabric has a permeability of less than one-half cubic foot of air per minute (CFM) when it is first manufactured. After a few jumps, the thin fabric begins to open up, and it becomes more porous with each jump. When the permeability reaches eight CFM, some performance is lost. When it reaches thirteen CFM, the canopy will descend faster and may snivel on opening. Any canopy with 500 or more jumps may be fairly porous, may be slightly deteriorated due to its exposure to the ultraviolet rays from the sun, and may even have been used for a water jump. The life of a canopy may be 2,000 jumps but the effective life may be closer to 1,000 jumps. Manufacturers suggest relining canopies between 500 to 700 jumps due to line length changes and wear which does affect the performance of the canopy or upon any noticeable change in its flight characteristics.

Since the buying (skydiving) public wants their parachutes to be low-weight and low-volume, the manufacturers are using lighter materials. The trade-off is that the gear does not last as long as it used to. The service life of today's parachutes is not short, but it is shorter than it used to be. Now, manufacturers are even considering stamping their gear with a service life date. They explain their actions are not planned obsolescence, but a way to warn the owner to have the older gear checked by the factory or a rigger. Test jump a used canopy before buying it.

If you do decide to buy used equipment, have the gear checked out by a rigger. Get an estimate to replace worn Velcro and make all the other minor repairs.

Be very wary of a reserve canopy that has been deployed. Reserves must be at 100% factory strength. Even a single use may damage the canopy, and the damage may not be visible. Check the packing data card against the data panel on the canopy and make sure you have all the cards. Any deployment should be noted on the card. Always have a reserve canopy thoroughly checked by a rigger before purchase.

Do not buy a round canopy with mesh vents, unless a rigger has checked them. Some mesh has a high acid content that damages adjacent nylon panels over time.

Don't be tempted to save weight and bulk by buying a reserve which is too small for you. —*Gary Thompson*

Chapter Eight

Specialized Jumps

To most people, a parachute jump is a parachute jump, and it is pretty scary at that. To a seasoned skydiver, there are as many types of jumps as there are ignorant people. You can make low ones or high ones, on land or in the water, at noon or after dark, carrying smoke on a demo or a camera to record your friends, singly or with a team, out of a plane or a balloon, practicing for the Competition Style event or—the list is endless. And, while this book deals with the parachute principally as a means of recreation, no book would be complete without a mention of the many other uses. The military airborne troops and the fire-fighting smokejumpers use the parachute for quick vertical transportation; military aviators use the parachute as survival equipment and, of course, it is used to drop equipment, to slow racecars, etc. In the next few pages, we will examine some of these other uses of the parachute.

Night jumps are not only fun to make, they often turn an otherwise dull evening into a great skydiving social occasion. After jumping, it is time to party. Night jumps are more than just an extension of daylight jumping, because of the added preparation that is required. One must have lighted instruments, a flashlight to check the canopy after opening, a light visible for three miles (FARs) which may be a flashing red warning light, a strobe light, or something of equivalent visibility, lighted target, lighted wind drift indicator, additional ground crew, etc. So it is no wonder that night jumps are made

A hop n'
pop after dark

less than regularly. Since two night jumps (one solo and one RW) of at least 20 seconds duration are required for the USPA D License, most drop zones schedule them two or three times a year. You will not be eligible to make a night jump until you have your USPA B License, but you may attend the ground training any time. For further details on night jumping, consult USPA's *Skydiver's Information Manual,* "Section 6-4."

Water jumps are a great combination of aviation and water sports, something you will want to do at least once every summer. While unintentional water landings have taken a number of lives, pre-planned water jumps have a good record.

Both planned and unplanned, water jumps terminate in the water. But just like the survival score card for each of them, the approach to them is different. (Review the discussion in Chapter Four.)

When you plan to go into the water, you need less protective clothing, and want to avoid a soggy jumpsuit that will make swimming difficult. So chute up in a helmet, T-shirt, swim suit, running shoes (you might miss the lake) and a life vest. Freefall without your familiar jumpsuit will be interesting; there is very little air drag on the extremities and you will probably flail about trying to grab some air.

Do not subject your good ram-air main canopy to a water

Intentional water jumps are good practice for unplanned water landings

jump. The water will increase the permeability of the fabric. Water jumps are a good opportunity to try a round canopy.

After the jump, you will have some equipment to clean and dry. If you went into clean, fresh water, the main parachute may be suspended in the shade to drip and dry. The reserve should be taken to a parachute loft for repacking, and it is best to leave it in its protective container rather than risk snagging the canopy. If the water was salty, suspend the canopy and hose it off with fresh water. Neither fresh nor salt

Do not wear a jumpsuit for water jumps

water will injure nylon, but they will damage cotton, so dry out any cotton parts right away. Pay special attention to the hardware; dry it so it won't rust.

Dry training for unintentional water jumps is required for your USPA A License. Wet training (with all your gear in a pool) is required for your USPA B License. You must have at least a USPA A License to make an intentional water jump and you may attend wet training at any time, so ask your instructor for a schedule. Consult USPA's *Skydiver's Information Manual*, "Section 6-5," for more information.

High-altitude jumps. Most sport jumps are initiated from relatively low altitudes for a number of reasons. Except for the largest team maneuvers, virtually all types of jumping can be adequately performed on 45- to 60-second freefalls, so 9,500 feet and 12,500 feet have become common exit altitudes. The air becomes thinner as you climb higher, and airplanes don't run as efficiently, so they become more

Landing in snow is great fun, especially when it's soft and powdery

expensive to operate. In the thinner and thinner air, the body falls faster. So you reach a point where a little more altitude just isn't worth the extra effort or expense.

Most small jump airplanes can't get enough oxygen for their engines when hauling a full load of jumpers above 13,000 feet, and most jumpers begin to notice the effects of oxygen starvation on themselves at about this level. The lack of oxygen (*hypoxia*) affects each person in a different way, but it usually begins with a light-headed feeling. Without sufficient oxygen, the brain doesn't operate too well; spotting and other skydiving chores become less accurate.

It is possible to go much higher; skydivers do it all the time, but extra equipment is required. Commercial airliners regularly fly at 25,000 feet to 40,000 feet with pressurized cabins. If you go above 8,000 feet for more than 30 minutes, you should have supplemental oxygen aboard the aircraft. In fact, with oxygen, you can go all the way up to 40,000 feet before a pressure suit or pressurized cabin becomes necessary. With pressure suits, parachutists have ascended in gas balloons to more than 100,000 feet.

The temperature generally decreases at the rate of 3.5 degrees Fahrenheit per thousand feet with altitude; just keeping warm can be a big problem. The temperature could be 70 degrees on the ground and minus 35 degrees at 30,000 feet.

The chamber ride teaches each jumper to recognize his or her own symptoms of oxygen starvation

Physiological flight training is available at several Air Force bases around the U.S. by applying through the USPA, and many sport parachutists take advantage of the two-day course, even if they aren't planning to make a high one. The classroom session is followed by a *chamber ride*; the class enters a large room-size capsule and the air is pumped out to simulate altitude ascension. As they go *higher and higher*, each person has the opportunity to observe his or her own individual reactions to the ever decreasing level of oxygen. Then they learn that, when they put on their oxygen masks, it takes only a couple of deep breaths to clear the head and bring them back to normal.

For more information on high altitude jumps, consult USPA's *Skydiver's Information Manual*, "Section 6-7."

Motorized cameras are helmet-mounted; the photographer flies in the middle of all the action.

Camera jumps. The reason that the aerial photographs in this book are so clear is that they were taken by jumping photographers, air-to-air; the photographers were up close to the action. Whuffos, with no understanding of freefall parachuting, often think the photographs were taken from an aircraft (*in a 120-mph dive?*).

If you would like to get into air-to-air videography, you must be good at both parts: photography and relative work. The first choice you will face will be between still or motion picture cameras. Freefall photographers use motor-driven 35-mm cameras, with about a 35 mm angle lens and a 1/250-

second, or faster, shutter speed. Those shooting movies often use a 16-mm, N-9 gun camera with a wide-angle lens. Both are electrically operated, usually with a hand switch.

Most freefall photographers shoot video. Video provides instant feedback on your technique and it is less expensive than film. Video photographers usually use small camcorders with a wide-angle lens.

The best photos are taken on bright days, or when there are just a few white cumulus clouds in the background, either early or late in the day when the sun is low.

It is difficult to monitor the altitude when shooting pictures, so you must be sure to choose reliable subjects who will give you a clear signal at pull time. As a back up, wear an audible altimeter. Also, be careful not to deploy your pilot chute into your helmet-mounted camera.

Most DZs have photo units to record first jumps. They are a great source of photo equipment and technique information.

For more information on camera flying, consult the *USPA's Skydiver's Information Manual*, "Section 6-8." There are also many good resources available commercially on this subject matter. Ask around and find out from the camera flyers at your DZ where they learned their trade and for help learning it yourself.

A sure way to win friends in parachuting is to buy a camera; the sky above is full of camera hogs.

Demonstration jumps are made away from an established drop zone, and are for the benefit/instruction of the spectators. They are fun to make and fun to watch. The challenge of a good performance into a tight DZ is one that most parachutists will eagerly seek. Of course, one must be careful to do an especially good job; it's bad press to miss the target.

A good demonstration jump requires a great deal of prior planning, from lining up the aircraft with proper radios and pilot, to clearing the jump with the FAA, state and local officials. It is a lot of work to make all the arrangements and get all the required paperwork.

For more information, consult the *USPA's Skydiver's Information Manual*, "Section 7" which gives extensive background on all of the requirements of an Exhibition (Demonstration) Jump and the Professional Exhibition Rating.

Demo jumps are great crowd pleasers

Boot-mounted smoke generators accent the fall and
aid the spectator in locating the jumpers

Wing suit jumps use a very specialized suit with extra fabric between the legs and they have much more material from the waist to the arms than normal skydiving suits do. These suits owe their origin to "batwings" (the rigid winged suits, not the modern day parachutes) from back in the early days of parachuting, but are less hazardous due to their not using rigid materials in those fabric areas. Using these suits, freefall skydiving takes on a whole new aspect of extended horizontal drives and much slower fall rates. There is an extensive discussion on these suits in the Skydiver's Information Manual, "Section 6-9."

Wing Suit

Pre-planned breakaway jumps are not currently listed in the Skydiver's Information Manual as a requirement for licensing, however they are mentioned in the Exhibition Jump Recommendations in the SIM, Section 7-1 paragraph I.2.c. If you ever intend to go on to become a Tandem Instructor, you will need to have one of these breakaway jumps logged for that rating. Intentional pre-planned breakaway jumps involve the carrying of a third parachute: either a second reserve (usually an attachable chest type) or a special configuration of two main parachutes with mated riser assemblies going to the 3-Ring release mechanism of which one could be detached from the other. Several demonstration films of emergency procedures utilized either of these configurations. These types of jumps are very impressive, but there is a need for a parachute-recovery person so that the released parachute doesn't permanently disappear.

BASE jumping is conducted from fixed objects rather than aircraft (BASE stands for Building, Antenna, Span, Earth). For more information, contact the U.S. BASE

Owen Quinn dives off what used to be the World Trade Center

If it weren't for aircraft, we would all be BASE jumpers.
—*John Miller*

Tim Domenico dives off El Capitan in Yosemite

An airborne jump

Association, Jean Boenish, 12619 Manor Drive, Suite 454, Hawthorne, CA 90250. Tel: (310) 676-1935.

Military jumping. After basic training in the Army, there are a number of parachuting enlistment options: the Airborne, Special Forces, Rangers, HALO and the Golden Knights. Airborne training takes three weeks at Fort Benning, Georgia. It takes five static line jumps to earn your wings. See your Army recruiter.

HALO (High Altitude, Low Opening) troops are trained to infiltrate hostile territory by flying in very high, out of earshot, and freefalling down to silently open and glide in for a grouped landing behind enemy lines.

HAHO (High Altitude, High Opening) troops are similarly trained, but they deploy their canopies high above the ground and use the long distance traveling capability of their canopies to exit their aircraft far away from the intended landing point and to get to it virtually undetected.

The Army Parachute Team, *Golden Knights,* consists of two demonstration jump teams and a competition team.

The Golden Knights have demonstration teams and competition teams

They make hundreds of demo jumps each year as part of the army's recruiting program, while the competition team has produced numerous national and world champions. The home of the USAPT is Fort Bragg, North Carolina.

At the Air Force Academy in Colorado, students not only receive a free education, they may learn parachuting for credits.

The Smoke Jumpers, the parachuting firefighters, have become an effective weapon in the constant battle against forest fires.

The parachute was first used to fight fires in 1925, when equipment and supplies were dropped to firefighters on the

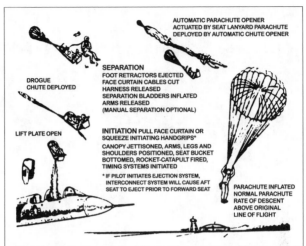

Ejection seat sequence

AUTOMATIC PARACHUTE OPENER ACTUATED BY SEAT LANYARD PARACHUTE DEPLOYED BY AUTOMATIC CHUTE OPENER

DROGUE CHUTE DEPLOYED

SEPARATION
FOOT RETRACTORS EJECTED
FACE CURTAIN CABLES CUT
HARNESS RELEASED
SEPARATION BLADDERS INFLATED
ARMS RELEASED
(MANUAL SEPARATION OPTIONAL)

LIFT PLATE OPEN

INITIATION PULL FACE CURTAIN OR SQUEEZE INITIATING HANDGRIPS*
CANOPY JETTISONED, ARMS, LEGS AND SHOULDERS POSITIONED, SEAT BUCKET BOTTOMED, ROCKET-CATAPULT FIRED, TIMING SYSTEMS INITIATED
* IF PILOT INITIATES EJECTION SYSTEM, INTERCONNECT SYSTEM WILL CAUSE AFT SEAT TO EJECT PRIOR TO FORWARD SEAT

PARACHUTE INFLATED
NORMAL PARACHUTE
RATE OF DESCENT
ABOVE ORIGINAL
LINE OF FLIGHT

ground. Time is of the essence when a fire begins, and it was later realized that the fastest means of transportation to otherwise inaccessible areas would be via aircraft and parachutes. The time saved in reaching a fire would be measured in days; the amount it cost to fight the fire, reduced by thousands of dollars; and the amount of land and timber saved, in the millions of dollars.

The Forest Service operates a school in Missoula, Montana, to serve the 12 smoke jumper bases in Alaska and the lower 48. Some 400 applications are received each year for perhaps 20 openings, and training is so tough that about half the students wash out. Would-be applicants should be aware that the Forest Service is more interested in candidates with prior fire fighting experience than in seasoned parachutists. In fact, smoke jumping is so different, a sport parachutist finds that many freefall habits have to be broken during training. The SmokeJumpers, like the Airborne, use the parachute only as quick, efficient vertical transportation. There are about 385 SmokeJumpers in the U.S., who average 13 to 25 jumps each fire season into rough terrain. For more information, write SmokeJumpers, U.S. Department of Agriculture, Forest Service, Missoula, MT 59801. Or, US Department of Agriculture, Forest Service, Auditor's Bldg., 201 14th Street SW @ Independence SW, Washington, DC 20250.

Wind tunnels provide skydiving without parachute packing

Vertical wind tunnels permit skydiving without constant repacking. Extended flight times allow you to learn a lot about freefall in a very short time but tunnel work is very tiring.

For more information, see:

http://www.skyventures.com
http://www.verticalwind.com
http://www.freeflightskydiving.com/windtun.html
http://www.bodyflight.net/
http://www.flyawayindoorskydiving.com/

We can't let you put this book down without giving you some idea of the additional fun that you can have beyond what this book has described.

There are a multitude of fun disciplines beyond belly to earth relative work.

Freestyle is an aerobatic discipline that has several instructional tapes available to introduce you to that aspect of skydiving.

Other than belly flying, people can fly head up, head down, on their backs, and in a sitting position. **(A word of caution**...make sure that if you pursue these other disciplines that your gear is suitable for the higher speeds that are achieved in the head up and head down realms.)

Skysurfing is another option where small footboards (like snowboards) are worn to allow the skydiver to "surf" the air in a variety of positions. This can also be part of a freestyle competition.

Relative work in three dimensions is also a reality now that vertical (non-belly to earth) fliers are building formations both vertically and horizontally, sometimes mixing those formations with head-up, belly, sit, and head-down fliers. Opportunities for new formations are endless.

There is even a dive called **a "Mr. Bill" dive** where two jumpers (one very strong and one preferably very light) exit the aircraft holding onto each other and only one of them deploys shortly after exit while they each try to hold onto each other. The person who doesn't deploy their system immediately gets to climb up on top of the other jumper and at an agreed upon altitude, depart that jumper into a very low airspeed start of a freefall.

Balloon jumps: Like any aircraft, a balloon is capable of carrying skydivers aloft and allowing them to exit. This exit is into almost "dead" air so the jumper is using momentum and body position for the first few seconds to maintain stability (like going off a very high diving board). After a few seconds of freefall, the air resistance builds up enough to allow the jumper to use body position and wind resistance to control his flight.

Helicopter jumps: Yes, skydivers exit helicopters too. The rotor downwash on exit also gives the skydiver a unique "less than optimal control" feeling for several seconds until the relative wind picks up.

Jet jumps: Have you ever heard of D. B. Cooper? Well, occasionally at "The World Freefall Convention," a Boeing 727 is specially configured to allow the tail ramp to be lowered in flight and jumpers can exit that aircraft at a high rate of speed. This is one time that they have to slow down to relative work speed after exiting an aircraft!

Bomber jumps: Yes, there are special organizations that do take charitable donations and allow you to jump from such unusual aircraft as a B-17 and B-25. No, I don't think the B-52s and the B-1s or B-2s will be available to the jumping public for a considerable period of time.

Above all else, no matter what discipline you pursue, remember to do it safely and always remember why we skydive: **TO HAVE FUN!!!!!!**

Skydiving: It is not just a matter of life and death . . . it is much more important than that.

Chapter Nine

Advancement in Skydiving

Now that you have made your first jump and admit to being hooked, it is time to plan where you are going. Many roads to sport parachuting advancement are open to you. You may qualify for awards for a number of jumps, time in freefall and various types of jumps. You may enter competition as a contestant or judge, become an instructor or run for office. There are many avenues and you may decide to pursue one, many or all of them. Some roads do not even require jumping participation, but all demand dedication to a great sport.

This chapter explains each of the roads to advancement. For more information, see the references listed in the Appendix such as *The Skydiver's Information Manual* (SIM).

Licenses. The USPA issues four classes of parachuting licenses recognized by all member nations of the Fédération Aéronautique Internationale. With a license, you may travel and jump almost anywhere in the world. See the *Skydiver's Information Manual*. The requirements for each class of license follow.

Section 3-1: USPA Licenses

A. Background

1. License requirements are intended to encourage the development of the knowledge and skills which should be acquired by each skydiver as experience is gained.

2. USPA licenses, recognized in all FAI member countries,

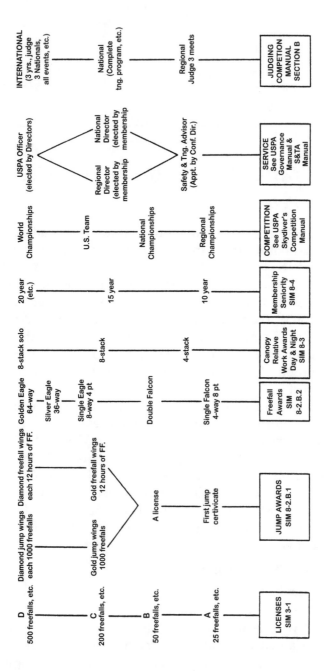

Many roads to advancement are open to the skydiver; you may elect to pursue one or all.

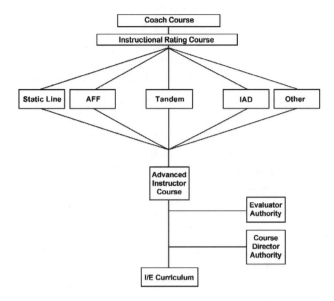

serve as official documentation that the stated experience and skills have been attained.

3. Licenses are a valuable instructional tool in that they serve both as goals to be accomplished and as a guideline to acquire the skills and knowledge necessary to provide a reasonable level of safety and enjoyment.

4. USPA license authority

   a. The United States Parachute Association is authorized by the National Aeronautic Association and the Federation Aeronautique Internationale to issue internationally recognized sporting licenses.

   b. Licenses are issued based upon demonstration of skill, knowledge, and experience and are ranked according to the level of accomplishment.

B. General conditions for licenses

   1. USPA licenses are valid only while the holder is a current regular USPA member; there is no other renewal requirement.

   2. USPA licenses are valid in all FAI member countries and, while valid, entitle the holder to participate in open skydiving events organized in FAI member countries.

3. USPA issues licenses only to USPA members who meet the conditions set forth for that license.

4. License qualifications made during military training jumps may be properly recorded on the application for that USPA license and verified by the appropriate USPA official.

5. Total freefall time is defined to include both freefall and droguefall time.

6. USPA licenses may be refused, suspended, or revoked only when authorized by the USPA Board of Directors or in compliance with existing USPA Board directives.

C. **Logging jumps for licenses and ratings**

1. Skydives offered as evidence of qualification must have been:

   a. made in accordance with the USPA requirements in effect at the time of the jump

   b. legibly recorded in chronological order in an appropriate log that contains the following information:

      (1) jump number

      (2) date

      (3) location

      (4) exit altitude

      (5) freefall length (time)

      (6) type of jump (formation skydiving, freeflying, canopy formation, style, etc.)

      (7) landing distance from the target

      (8) equipment used

      (9) verifying signature

2. Jumps for license and rating qualifications must be signed by another licensed skydiver, a pilot, or a USPA National or FAI Judge who witnessed the jump.

3. Jumps to meet skill requirements must be signed by a USPA Instructor, Instructor Examiner, Safety & Training Advisor, or a member of the USPA Board of Directors.

D. **Verification of Application**

1. Experience verification: The certifying official should verify that the number of jumps and total freefall time

are correct and meet the listed requirements for the license sought.

2. Skill verification: Jump numbers, scores, or date of completion require the initials of a current USPA Instructor, S&TA, I/E, or USPA Board member.

3. Knowledge verification: For the B, C, and D license, the certifying official should make sure that the exam answer sheet(s) is forwarded along with the application.

4. Signature Verification: Applications for all licenses must be signed by an appropriate official before the application is forwarded to USPA Headquarters.

   a. USPA Instructors may verify A, B, and C licenses.

   b. S&TAs, I/Es, and USPA Board members may verify any license application.

E. **License privileges and requirements**
   A License

1. Persons holding a USPA A license may pack their own main parachute, engage in basic group jumps, perform water jumps, and must have

   a. completed 25 jumps

   b. completed all requirements listed on the USPA A License Proficiency Card or USPA A License Progression Card (ISP)

   c. received the signature and official stamp on the USPA A License Proficiency Card or USPA A License Progression Card (ISP)

   Note: For USPA A-license registration purposes only, USPA Headquarters will accept either completed card signed by a USPA Instructor (signature on file at USPA Headquarters) without the official stamp. The registration fee must be included.

   B License

2. Persons holding a USPA B license are able to exercise all privileges of an A-license holder, perform night jumps, and must have

   a. obtained a USPA A license

   b. completed 50 jumps including:

(1) accumulated at least ten minutes of controlled freefall time

(2) landed within ten meters of target center on ten jumps

c. demonstrated the ability to perform individual maneuvers (a figure 8, backloop, figure 8, backloop) in freefall in 18 seconds or less

d. documentation of live water landing training with full equipment in accordance with the procedures in the Skydiver's Information Manual

e. passed a written exam conducted by a current USPA I, I/E, S&TA, or USPA Board member.

C License

3. Persons holding a USPA C license are able to exercise all privileges of a B licensed jumper, are eligible for the USPA Coach ratings, may ride as passenger on USPA Tandem Instructor training and rating renewal jumps, and must have-

a. met all current requirements for or hold a USPA B license

b. completed 200 jumps including accumulating at least 20 minutes of controlled freefall time

c. landed within five meters of target center on 20 jumps

d. completed at least four points on a 4-way or larger random skydive or perform individual maneuvers (a figure 8, backloop, figure 8, backloop) in freefall in 15 seconds or less

e. Passed a written exam conducted by a current USPA AFF, IAD, or Static-Line Instructor, I/E, S&TA, or USPA Board member.

D License

4. Persons holding a USPA D license are able to exercise all privileges of a C license holder, participate in certain demonstration jumps, are eligible for all USPA ratings, and must have-

a. met all current requirements for or hold a USPA C license

    b. completed 500 jumps including accumulating at least one hour of controlled freefall time

    c. landed within two meters of target center on 25 jumps

    d. demonstrated the ability to perform individual maneuvers (either of the following):

        (1) during freefall, perform in sequence within 18 seconds-a backloop, front loop, left 360-degree turn, right 360-degree turn, right barrel roll and left barrel roll

        (2) completed at least two points on an 8-way or larger random skydive

    e. made two night jumps (one solo and one in a group) with a freefall of at least 20 seconds

        (1) with verification of prior night jump training from a USPA Instructor

        (2) with the advice of an S&TA, in accordance with USPA BSRs

    f. passed a written exam conducted by a current USPA I/E, S&TA, or a USPA Board member.

F. Restricted USPA licenses

    1. Under extreme circumstances, such as physical handicaps, a USPA Restricted license may be issued to applicants who are unable to meet all of the specific license requirements.

    2. A person may be qualified for a Restricted license if the rating holder has (all of the following):

        a. submitted a petition to the Safety & Training Committee, containing:

            (1) type of license requested

            (2) specific license requirement(s) which cannot be met

            (3) circumstances which prevent compliance with license requirements

            (4) license application completed, except for the restricted activities

        b. met all requirements for the license desired except for those listed in the petition

3. Each application will be considered individually on its own merit, totally without precedent.
4. Restricted license numbers will be followed by the letter "R" (e.g., C-11376R).

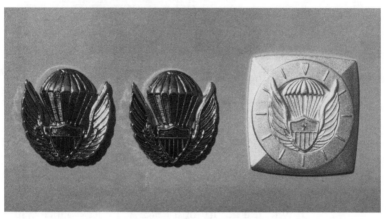

Jump number awards

Awards. A number of achievements in sport parachuting are recognized by the USPA through a system of awards. See the *Skydiver's Information Manual*, secton 10.

—**First Jump Certificate**—Authorized by USPA to be presented by instructors and instructor/examiners to those persons making their first sport parachute jump under the provisions of the *Basic Safety Requirements*.

—**Membership Seniority Certificates** are issued in five-year increments to those with ten or more years of accumulated USPA membership.

—**Parachutist Wings**—Created by the USPA in 1962, a design symbolic of a national aero sport with the wings of flight, the U.S. national shield, and the open parachute. Issued to all license holders.

—**Gold Expert Wings**—Awarded to those USPA members holding the USPA D License who have made 1,000 freefall parachute jumps, under the provisions of the *Basic Safety Requirements*. Gold Wings with diamonds are awarded to those accumulating up to 10,000 jumps, and Gold Wings with rubies are awarded to those making up to 20,000 jumps. The jumps must be verified by a Regional Director or

National Director, or by USPA Headquarters.

—**Gold Freefall Badges**—Awarded to those USPA members holding the USPA D License who have recorded 12 hours of freefall time, all jumps being made under the provisions of the Basic Safety Regulations. Badges have diamonds for each additional 12 hours through 120 hours and then rubies are added. The time must be verified by a Regional or National Director, or by USPA Headquarters.

—**Sequential Relative Work Awards.** *Falcon Awards* are available to individual relative workers who have performed eight or more sequential formations on a 4-way or larger relative work jump. *Eagle Awards* are available to those who have performed four or more sequential formations on an 8-way or larger relative work jump.

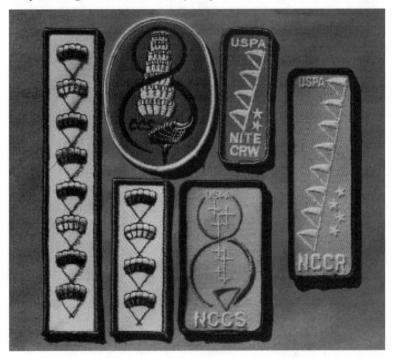

CRW awards

—**Canopy Relative Work Awards.** The *Four Stack Award* is available to those who have successfully participated in canopy formations of four or larger. The *CCR* is awarded to a Canopy Crest Recipient for participating in canopy formations of eight or larger. The *CCS* is awarded to those who have entered eighth or later, on a formation of eight or larger. Night versions of the CRW awards are also available.

Competition is an important part of sport parachuting. In fact, some say that you must have competition to just call it a *sport*. While there are those who enjoy non-evaluated jumping, most skydivers get into competition sooner or later, at least at the local level. Many clubs run student events, with slightly modified rules, so you will probably be making competitive jumps very soon. See USPA Part 50.

The *classical* or original events are accuracy and style. Newer team events are 4-way, 8-way, 10-way, and 20-way relative work, canopy relative work events and others.

The 5 cm. disc is often part of an electronic scoring pad

—**Accuracy** is the earliest and simplest of the parachuting events. You exit the aircraft at 750 meters (2500 feet), open, and steer to land as close as possible to a 5 cm. (less than two inches) disc. In national competition, most landings are so close, the judges don't even bother to measure beyond five meters. In student competition, accuracy is sometimes modified into a *hit and run* event, where the competitor lands as close as possible and then is timed until he or she steps on the target. See USPA Part 51.

Turning good Style requires a tight body position

—**The Style** competitor exits the aircraft at 2000 meters (6600 feet), falls in a tight position for about 15 seconds to build up speed, and then whips into a series of maneuvers for time. All three groups are: *turn, turn, backloop, turn, turn, backloop* but there are three combinations. One is right turn, left turn, backloop, right turn, left turn, backloop. Years ago, a time of 15 seconds was good, but now you aren't competitive unless you are under eight seconds. And the turns and loops must be good; the judges dock points for undershoots, overshoots and other types of sloppiness. See USPA Part 51.

—**The Para-Ski Championships** combine accuracy jumping and giant slalom skiing. These events are popular in both the U.S. and Europe. See USPA Part 52.

The Four-Way event

—Team Freefall Events.

The *Four-Way event* begins at 2900 meters (9500 feet) and consists of a series of pre-selected random freefall formations. If the team completes the sequence within the 35 seconds working time, it begins to repeat the maneuvers.

Eight-Way sequential requires the team to exit at 3600 meters (12,000 feet) and perform a series of maneuvers, one after the other. Since some of the formations are drawn at random, it is impossible to practice for specific competition. Instead, the teams must do a lot of hot diving and flying to learn to work together and fly well. See USPA Part 55.

The Ten-Way speed star was the earliest form of team competition and it drew so much interest that it changed the sport and the competition. In Ten-Way, the team exits the aircraft at 2300 meters (7500 feet) and puts a 10-way star together as fast as possible. In the early days, it was an accomplishment to form a trickily balanced star. Now they are being formed regularly in just a few seconds.

—Freestyle competition involves an individual skydiver with a cameraperson teammate. Judging is done on video monitors on the ground.

—Skysurfing competition is like freestyle but is done with a board.

—Canopy Formation events are *Four-Way Rotation, Four-Way Sequential* and *Eight-Way Speed.* See USPA Part 53.

> One nice thing about our sport of parachuting is that the competitors make the rules. —*Eilif Ness, President of the FAI*

—**Airblade Running** is done by flying down a slope passing to the (correct) side of planted airblades. (Tensioned, vertical flags that are unique to skydiving.)

Competition Levels

—**The Regional Skydiving Championship** recognizes regional champions. The U.S. is divided into 14 regional areas. See USPA Part 54.

—**The National Skydiving Championship** chooses the National Champions and selects the U.S. Skydiving Team. Men and women compete in separate divisions in the individual events, but the team events are mixed.

—**The National Collegiate Parachuting Championship** is for full-time undergraduates. Three classes—novice, intermediate and master—compete in style, accuracy, relative work and CRW. See NCPC Part 50.

—**The World Parachuting Championship** takes place each year, with most events scheduled for every other year. Another important international event is the CISM Meet for military sport parachutists.

Service. These positions are appointive or elective. For complete details, see USPA SOPs 5 and 10.

The Safety & Training Advisor

—**Safety & Training Advisor.** The S&TA is an advisor, administrator and representative, appointed by the Regional

Director to be his or her direct representative at the drop zone to which the S&TA is assigned. The S&TA may certify all USPA licenses and advises on night, water and exhibition jumps. He or she may verify annual renewal requirements for all instructor ratings. There are over 350 S&TA's across North America.

—**Director.** A member of the USPA Board of Directors elected by the USPA membership to serve as a Regional Director or National Director. Directors meet at least twice annually, serve two-year terms, and may be re-elected. See *SIM,* "Sec. 1-1."

—**Regional Director.** Elected by members of the 14 conference areas. Has equal representation with National Directors on the USPA Board of Directors.

—**National Director.** Elected by all the general membership. Represents all the members in the USPA (*Ministers without Portfolio*). Usually elected for their ability to make particular contributions to the sport. The Board has eight National Directors.

—**Officer.** Elected by the Board of Directors from among members of the Board. Elected every two years with the seating of each new Board. There are four USPA Officers: President, Vice-President, Secretary and Treasurer. They sit on an Executive Committee along with the Chairman of the Board, an at-large member.

Instruction. Competence in the instruction and supervision of students and (when required) other parachutists is addressed by a system of instruction ratings starting with a Coach rating, progressing to an Instructor rating, and finally, an Instructor Examiner rating. Separate discipline ratings are issued to instructors specifically for the S/L, IAD, AFF, and Tandem programs. There are also Coach Course Directors, Instructional Ratings Course Directors, and AFF Certification Course Directors (the AFF CCDs are appointed by USPA's Board of Directors as the need arises). Tandem equipment manufacturers certify Tandem Examiners on the manufacturers specific equipment and the USPA Tandem Instructor Program is the means by which those examiners train and qualify others to use manufacturer specific equipment to perform Tandem jumps.

—**Coaches:** Jump with/coach students once the students are cleared off of direct supervision in Category E of the USPA's ISP.

Instructors and Examiners supervise student training

—**Instructors** (I) teach skydiving. They instruct students in the theoretical and practical skydiving skills required to obtain a USPA A License.

—**Instructor/Examiners** (I/E) have passed extensive written and practical tests. I/E's may verify applications for all USPA licenses and USPA ratings, as well as provide guidance for night, water and exhibition jumps.

—**AFF Course Directors.** The AFF program is overseen by several specially appointed course directors. They travel to skydiving centers to conduct AFF Training Camps and to rate qualified candidates.

—**Coach Course Directors** teach the basic fundamentals of instruction, jump safety, jump performance evaluation, and the structure of the ISP to people wishing to become involved in working with students.

Happiness is successfully cutting away from a malfunction onto a steerable reserve, at a meet, and coming in for a dead center, standing up; and refusing the rejump. —*Captain Bob*

Judging. Where there is competition, there must be judges; competitive events, by their very nature, require evaluation. While judges used to stand in the sun with high power spotting scopes, now they sit in air-conditioned rooms, staring at video monitors.

There are three levels in judging: regional, national and international, and judges are rated before they may judge each type of event. Before a judge is selected to judge a national championship, he or she must complete a judge-training program at a previous nationals. After several years of exceptional work, he or she may be nominated for the FAI International Judges' List. Judges maintain log books to record the competitions they work, and there is a judging committee that constantly monitors their progress.

Others have developed a high level of proficiency in scoring, recording and other support positions

Other ratings and awards in the fields of parachutes and skydiving are issued by the federal government and private groups. These are in addition to the USPA recognition mentioned earlier.

Parachute riggers are certified by the federal government through the Federal Aviation Administration. One may become a *Senior Rigger* after considerable schooling and a battery of tests, written, oral and practical. After working for three years in the field and packing at least 200 parachutes, he or she is eligible to take other tests to qualify as a *Master Parachute Rigger*. For more information, see Federal Aviation Regulations, Part 65, *Parachute Rigging Course* and *Parachute Rigger Study Guide*, listed in the Appendix.

The Star Crest

The Bob Buquor Memorial Star Crest is a series of awards for achievement in relative work, established and conducted by Bill Newell in memory of Bob Buquor, the parachuting photographer who was primarily responsible for the development of large star relative work. The basic SCR is issued to anyone who takes part in an eight or larger star for a minimum of five seconds. Very difficult to learn in the early days, over 14,400 Star Crests have been issued to date. More than 2,300 skydivers have qualified for their NSCR by making an 8-way at night.

The SCS (Star Crest Solo) is for those who have entered the star eighth or later, as this is a bit harder than going out and playing base for a bunch of good flyers. Over 8,100 Star Crest Solos have been issued so far.

The SCSA (Star Crest Skydiver Award) is for those who have participated in a "hoop dive" (where two people hold a weighted Hula Hoop® and at least eight others go through the hoop to form an 8-way or larger on the other side of the hoop.) The letter "N" preceding the award initials indicates that the skydive was performed at night. For information, contact Bill Newell at the Bob Buquor Memorial Star Crest, 3418-A Mona Way, Bakersfield, CA 93309; Tel: (661) 831-7771; Web site: http://www.scr-awards.com

INTERNATIONAL SPORT AVIATION
competition and records

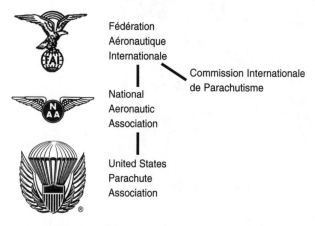

Fédération Aéronautique Internationale

Commission Internationale de Parachutisme

National Aeronautic Association

United States Parachute Association

The relationship of associations

International sport aviation. The official national organization of sport parachutists in the United States is the United States Parachute Association (USPA), a non-profit division of the National Aeronautic Association. The USPA is the official representative of the Fédération Aéronautique Internationale (FAI) for parachuting in the United States, and it is the national representative body for skydivers. It is the only organization sanctioning sport parachuting competition and records in the United States.

Join the USPA and become part of the great worldwide fraternity of parachuting; get *Parachutist* magazine and find out what's happening. For more information and an application blank, see the Appendix and www.uspa.org.

For information on the Canadian Sport Parachuting Association, see the Appendix.

The Parachute Industry Association is an international collection of nearly 200 parachute manufacturers, dealers and others offering products and services to the sport, industry and military. For information on the PIA, see the Appendix and www.pia.com.

I've found my thing—I'm hooked.

Appendix

For More Information

A good jump-off place on the web is the Para Publishing site at http://www.ParaPublishing.com. It will lead you to most of the drop zones, associations, manufacturers, dealers and so on.

Skydiving Centers

Drop zones are located all over the world. To locate the one nearest you, look under "Parachutes" and/or "Skydiving instruction" in the Yellow Pages of your telephone directory. Also see http://www.uspa.org/dz/index.htm

Association & Clubs

There are national parachute associations or aero clubs in many countries. For the latest list, see the Fédération Aéronautique Internationale (FAI) web site at http://www. fai.org/fai_members/

Parachute Industry Association
3833 West Oakton Street
Skokie, IL 60076
847-674-9742
Hq@pia.com
http://www.pia.com/

United States Parachute Association
1440-P Duke Street
Alexandria, VA 22314
Tel: (703) 836-3495
Fax: (703) 836-2843
uspa@uspa.org
http://www.uspa.org

Canadian Sport Parachuting Association
300 Forced Road
Russell ON   K4R 1A1
613-445-1881
office@cspa.ca
http://www.cspa.ca/

Parachute Equipment Companies
Most of the parachute manufacturers and dealers have extensive web sites. For a list, see http://www.pia.com/links.html

Books
Contact the sources for latest price and delivery information, see your local parachute dealer or visit http://skydivingmagazine.com/booksvcb.htm.

Blackmon, Deborah. *The Rigger's Sourcebook*. 1997. Bravo Bravo Aviation, DeborahBlackmon@earthlink.net. Compilation of packing instructions.

Buchanan, Tom. *JUMP! Skydiving Made Fun & Easy*. McGraw-Hill, 2003.

Butler, Manley. *How to Get an FAA TSO for Parachutes*. 1984. Butler Parachutes, http://www.butlerparachutes.com/

Derosalia, John. *Mental Training for Skydiving & Life*. SkyMind Publishers, 1991.

Dormire, Byron T. *Demo Details*. Dormire Publishing Co. How to make a demo jump.

Emerson, Kim & **Antebi**, Marcus. *Skydiver's Survival Guide*. Pier Media, 2001.

Germain, Brian S. *Vertical Journey*. http://www.BigAirSportz.com

Ippoliti, Rita. *Falling into Place*. Kryos Publishing, 2003.

Jenkins, Starr. *Smokejumpers, 49 Brothers in the Sky*. 1995. Merritt Starr Books, PO Box 1165, San Luis Obispo, CA 93406. Story of the Smokejumpers.

Johnson, Erik. *Understanding the Skydive*. Lamplighter Press, 2002.

Kent, Norman. *Norman Kent Photos*. Norman Kent Productions, http://www.normankent.com/. Gorgeous coffee-table book.

Klein, Didier. *Emotions Bleues*. ParaMag, http://www.para-mag.com/

Koyn, Tamara. *Freestyle Notes* 1989 and *More Freestyle Notes* 1993. http://www.koyn.com/CloudDancer/

Knacke, Theo. *Parachute Recovery Systems Design Manual.* http://ParaPublishing.com. A technical design manual for recovery systems.

Meyer, Jan. *Parachuting Manual with Log for Accelerated Freefall.* http://ParaPublishing.com. A brief, basic text for the novice.

Milam, Melody J. *Powerdive; Mental Muscle for Skydivers.* Saraca Publications, PO Box 122823, Fort Worth, TX 76121. Mental training for the sport.

Poynter, Dan. *Parachuting Manual with Log.* http://ParaPublishing.com. A brief, basic round canopy/conventional gear, text for the novice.

Poynter, Dan. *Parachuting Manual with Log For Square/Piggyback Equipment.* http://ParaPublishing.com. A brief, basic square canopy and piggyback container, text for the novice.

Poynter, Dan. *Parachute Rigging Course.* http://ParaPublishing.com. A course of study for the FAA senior rigger certificate.

Poynter, Dan & **Blackmon**, Deborah. *Parachute Rigger Study Guide.* http://ParaPublishing.com. Answers and explanations for the FAA test questions.

Poynter, Dan & **Turoff**, Mike. *Parachuting Instructor/Examiner Course.* http://ParaPublishing.com. A home study course for the USPA I/E rating.

Poynter, Dan. *The Parachute Manual. Volume One.* http://ParaPublishing.com. A technical treatise on the parachute; of special interest to parachute riggers.

Poynter, Dan. *The Parachute Manual. Volume Two.* http://ParaPublishing.com. A technical treatise on the parachute; of special interest to parachute riggers.

Poynter, Dan & **Turoff**, Mike. *Parachuting, The Skydiver's Handbook.* http://ParaPublishing.com. The most detailed and accurate basic-to-intermediate text on the sport.

Poynter, Dan. *Paracaidismo.* http://ParaPublishing.com. *Parachuting, The Skydiver's Handbook* in Spanish.

Poynter, Dan. *Manual Basico de Paracaidismo.* http://ParaPublishing.com. *Parachuting Manual With Log* in Spanish.

Stuart, Dale. *Aerial Freestyle Guide Book.* http://www.winddance.com/. A world champion teaches freestyle skydiving.

Weldon, Patrick. *Flying the Camera.* Classic Publishing, 1999.

Works, Pat and Jan. 1988. *The Art of Freefall Relative Work.* http://www.works-words.com.

Owner's Manuals and Packing Instructions. The manufacturers of sport and emergency parachutes also publish manuals that describe the use, packing and maintenance of each particular assembly. The owner or rigger of the parachute should always read these manuals, and they are also excellent sources of accurate and detailed information for the parachute instructor. Most manuals may be obtained for a small fee by contacting the manufacturer. Also see the listing of manuals in the Para-Gear catalog.

Parachute Magazines and Newsletters
Write for a sample copy and a subscription blank.

Parachutist Magazine
http://www.uspa.org

Skydiving Magazine
http://skydivingmagazine.com/

PIA ParaNewsbriefs
http://www.pia.com/

Tandem News
http://www.StrongParachutes.com

AirBornAgain
http://members.aol.com/christskyd/

Can Para Magazine, Canada.
http://www.cspa.ca

BC Sport Parachute Council Newsletter, Canada.
http://www.bcspc.bc.ca/
Air Press, Brasil.
http://www.airpress.com.br/

Frittfall, Norway.
http://www.frittfall.no/

Blue Sky, Germany.
Bluesky@t-online.de

Pink News, Austria
http://www.pink.at

Skydive the Mag, Great Britain.
http://www.skydivemag.com/

Sportparachutist Magazin, The Netherlands.
chudiak@freeler.nl

USPA Publications
The U.S. Parachute Association publishes the *Skydiver's Information Manual* and other useful documents. See
http://www.uspa.org/publications/manuals.htm

Federal Aviation Administration Publications
FAA regulations may be obtained from local FAA offices, most parachute equipment dealers and the Superintendent of Documents. See
http://www2.faa.gov/avr/arm/index.cfm

FAR Part 21 prescribes certification procedures for obtaining a TSO for parachutes.

Part 65—*Certification of Airmen Other Than Flight Crewmembers.* This details the requirements and procedures for becoming an FAA Parachute Rigger.

Part 91—*General Operating and Flight Rules.* This Part establishes federal regulations for general flight operations in the U.S.

Part 105—*Parachute Jumping.* This regulation covers skydiving operations, instruction and equipment.

Parachute Rigger Certification Guide (Advisory Circular 65-5A). This booklet gives detailed information on how to apply for an FAA Rigger Certificate. Included are sample questions from the written exam and other useful information.

Use of Oxygen (Advisory Circular 91-8A). This publication gives recommended and required procedures for the use of supplemental oxygen during flight.

Sport Parachute Jumping (Advisory Circular 105-2-C). Also lists aircraft approved for flight with one door removed.

Airman's Information Manual, Part 1, Basic Flight Manual and ATC Procedures. Published primarily for pilots, this book contains current information on all aspects of using U.S. airspace and airports. It is useful to the sport parachuting instructor who wants to know the latest word on all details of navigation aids, ATC procedures, airspace structure, pilot-controller terminology. Issued four times per year.

Parachuting Video Tapes
Training, packing and just plain fun, there are videos on every aspect of parachutes and skydiving. Write for descriptive brochure and current prices.

Para-Gear Equipment Co.
http://www.ParaGear.com

Pier Video
http://www.pierltd.com

Norman Kent Productions
http://www.NormanKent.com

Precision Aerodynamics
http://precision.aerodynamics.com/

Skydiving Compact Discs (CD)

Para Publishing
http://ParaPublishing.com

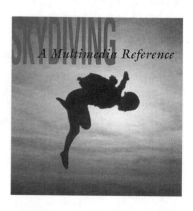

Glossary

Study these essential terms until you can not only define them, but explain them.

AAD: Automatic Activation Device.

"A" License: Issued by the USPA to skydivers with 25 or more jumps, who are off student status.

AC: Advisory Circular. An FAA publication used to explain the FARs.

A/C: Aircraft.

AD: Airworthiness Directive. Published by the FAA.

Advancement: see *Chapter 9*

Accelerated FreeFall (AFF): A special course of instruction which does not make use of a static line.

AFF: Accelerated FreeFall.

AFF I/E: Accelerated FreeFall Instructor/Examiner.

AGL: Above Ground Level. As opposed to ASL, Above Sea Level.

Aircraft: A device that is used, or intended to be used, for flight in the air.
Includes airplanes, helicopters, gliders, balloons and dirigibles.

Alteration: Changes to the original configuration, such as removal of a gore, installation of D rings, addition of a sleeve, dyeing of the canopy, or any other major change to any portion of the parachute from its original manufacturer's specifications.

Approved: An item which, in its present form, has received official certification from the FAA. This approval may be indicated by a TSO stamped on the article or carry a military designation such as NAF, AAF, or AN. Any surplus military parachute has been *approved* at time of manufacture. If the parachute is altered, such as removing a gore from the canopy, installing D-rings on the harness, adding a sleeve, etc., it is no longer an *approved* parachute.

APT: Army Parachute Team, The Golden Knights.

AS-8015A: Aerospace Standard 8015A, published by the Society of Automotive Engineers, sets forth the tests and minimum safety and performance standards which a parachute must meet to receive approval under TSO C-23c.

Aspect ratio: The ratio between the span and the chord of a wing. For rectangular canopies, it is the span divided by the chord.

Automatic Activation Device (AAD): A self-contained device attached to the ripcord assembly, other than a static line, which automatically initiates parachute pack opening at a preset altitude, time, percentage of terminal velocity, or combination thereof.

Auxiliary parachute: FAA: Reserve parachute. British: Pilot chute.

"B" License: USPA's second level license.

Back sliding: Moving backward in freefall, usually with the head high and the feet low. See *Chapter 5*

BASE jumping: (Building, Antenna, Span, Earth). Fixed object jumping, rather than from aircraft.

Basic parachutist course: The course of instruction in sport parachuting beginning with the first jump training and progressing through all the novice skills and knowledge needed to qualify for the A License. After successfully completing the Basic Parachutist Course, the parachutist is fully capable of safe and competent parachuting without a jumpmaster's supervision. See *Chapters 1, 2 and 5*

Basic safety requirements: Minimum requirements which are essential for safe sport parachuting activities. Formulated by the USPA.

Batwings: Large rigid or semi-rigid surfaces which are attached to the arms and body to decrease rate of descent and increase glide. See *jumpsuit* (Also the name of the canopy!)

Board of directors: Those officials elected by the general membership of the USPA every two years as set forth in the USPA by-laws; authorized by the by-laws to have general charge and control of the affairs, funds and property of the organization; shall carry out the objectives of the organization and its by-laws; elects officers from among current Board members. The USPA Board of Directors shall consist of:

  a) National Directors—those Directors elected at large by the general membership; and

  b) Regional Directors—those Directors of a specifie geographical area, elected by and responsible for, representing the interests of the parachutists of his or her area.

Break Off: Separation after a formation in RW or CRW.

Breakaway: A jettisoning of the malfunctioned main parachute by activating riser releases and deploying the reserve. See *Cutaway*.

BSR: Basic Safety Requirements

Buffeting: Rocking up and down in freefall. This occurs when the skydiver is too stiff, or not relaxed.

"C" License: USPA's third level license.

Canadian Sport Parachuting Association: The organization which governs sport parachuting activities in Canada.

Canopy: The sheet of fabric and lines of a parachute assembly that provides necessary deceleration for a survivable landing. See *Chapter 6*

Canopy relative work (CRW): The intentional maneuvering of two or more open canopies in close proximity or contact with each other during descent.

Canopy releases: Devices which allow immediate release of the main parachute canopy. They disconnect the harness main lift webs from the risers.

One type is manufactured by Capewell and is sometimes called the *Capewell Release*. Another example is the 3-Ring release.

Canopy transfer: Deploying the reserve canopy prior to jettisoning the main canopy. Subscribed to by some, when the main is damaged or tangled at a low altitude, usually on a CRW jump.

Capewell: A hardware manufacturer in Hartford, Connecticut.

Caterpillar Club: Established by Leslie Irvin for those who have saved their lives with a parachute.

CCR: Canopy Crest Recipient.

CCS: Canopy Crest Soloist.

Certificated: Describes a personnel parachute that has been awarded an FAA TSO Certificate. Also used to refer to other FAA-approved parachutes such as government surplus personnel models that were manufactured under military contract. FAA also uses the term to describe persons it has approved for various functions such as pilot, rigger, etc.

Chord: The distance from the leading edge to the trailing edge of a ram-air canopy.

CIP: Commission Internationale de Parachutism. An FAI Commission.

Closing speed: The speed at which two bodies approach each other. This can refer to RW or CRW.

Cloth extensions: Small triangular pieces of cloth normally sewn into the armpits, between the thighs, etc., of the jumpsuit to slow the rate of descent during freefall and to increase the glide ratio. These are not *batwings*.

Coach: A USPA-, or similar association-, rated skydiver who is authorized to train students under the direct supervision of a USPA Instructor in the ISP or jump with students after the student is signed off for Category E of the ISP.

Coach Course: The first course of the USPA's instructional rating system which provides candidates with the introduction to basic instructional and learning techniques including the process of evaluating a student's learning. This course also tests the candidate's ability to perform relative work with freefall students to include observing and critiquing a student's performance.

Compatible: Two parts of a parachute, such as a harness/container system and a canopy, which have been tested and been found to work together.

Container: That portion of the parachute assembly that holds the canopy in place after being folded. This is not to be confused with the term *pack*.

Crabbing: Directing the canopy across the line of wind direction.

Cross connector straps: Straps running from riser to riser. On student rigs, they run side to side to prevent canopy collapse if one canopy release fails to separate. On CRW rigs, they run from front to rear to prevent sliding back up the risers during "planes."

Cross pull: The position of the ripcord handle on the left-hand inboard side of the harness. An inboard pull or cross-chest pull.

Crossports: Vents cut in ribs of ram-air canopies to ensure even pressurization.

CRW: Canopy Relative Work.

CSPA: Canadian Sport Parachuting Association.

Cutaway: The cutting of risers or suspension lines with a knife or the handle which is pulled to mechanically release the deployed canopy while the parachutist is still in the air. Also used interchangeably with *Breakaway*.

"D" License: USPA's highest license.

Danger: see *Chapter 4*

Delayed drop: A live parachute descent where the activation of the parachute is delayed longer than is necessary to clear the aircraft. Skydiving makes the term obsolete.

Delayed opening: The normal deployment of a parachute, delayed by an automatic device. See *Freefall*.

Delta position: A modified stable freefall position made by a jumper drawing the arms back near the sides, which results in a head-low attitude and increases his or her rate of descent and horizontal movement.

Demonstration jump: A jump made away from an established drop zone for the benefit of spectators. Also called an *exhibition jump* or *display jump*.

Deployment: That portion of a parachute's operation occurring from the moment of pack opening, or pilot chute release, to the instant the suspension lines are fully stretched, but prior to the inflation of the canopy.

Deployment bag: An envelope, usually fabric, and usually enclosed in a parachute pack, containing a parachute canopy. A means may, or may not, be provided for stowage of suspension lines. A pilot parachute lifts a deployment bag away from a parachute pack, causing the suspension lines to be extended before the canopy emerges from the deployment bag.

Deployment device: A sleeve, bag, diaper or other device used to provide orderly lines-first deployment and to reduce opening shock.

Diaper: A deployment device consisting of a panel of fabric attached to the lower part of a canopy that prevents canopy inflation until line stretch. Reduces opening shock and malfunctions.

Direct supervision: A person physically present during instruction in skydiving or rigging. The supervisor is responsible for the actions of those supervised.

Doctrine: Principles, policies and concepts applicable to a subject, which are derived from experience or theory, compiled and taught for guidance. It represents the best available thought that can be defended by reason. Doctrine on each phase of parachuting is published by the USPA.

Door exit: Leaving an aircraft without touching any part of the aircraft outside of the door; made without positioning or bracing to achieve a stable fall position.

Downplane: Where two (or more) CRW jumpers grip (usually at the legs) to face the leading edges of their canopies toward the ground. The result is dramatic, high-speed flying—straight down.

Drogue: A smaller canopy deployed to slow and stabilize the load, usually prior to main canopy deployment. A drogue chute is used on tandem jumps.

Drop altitude: Actual altitude of an aircraft above the ground at the time of release of equipment or personnel.

Drop zone: A specified area into which personnel or equipment are dropped by parachute.

Dual assembly: A two-canopy parachute system.

Dummy Ripcord Pull (DRCP): see *Practice RipCord Pull.*

DZ: Drop zone. Skydiving center.

Emergency Parachute: A certificated parachute that is intended for emergency use. A reserve.

Equipment: see *Chapter 7*

Equipment check (*pin check*): A visual and physical check made by an instructor, a coach or a jump leader on all parachutists, prior to boarding and prior to exiting the aircraft.

European Parachuting League: An affiliate of the USPA, which looks after the members' interests in Europe.

Exhibition jump: A demonstration jump made away from a recognized drop zone for the benefit and instruction of spectators, the sole purpose of which is not a record attempt. The preferred term is *demonstration jump.*

Exit point: The place where a jumper exits the aircraft.

Exit weight: The weight of a jumper, including all equipment.

FAR: Federal Aviation Regulation.

Federal Aviation Administration (FAA): The FAA's primary function and responsibility involves control and monitoring of the nation's air space; the certification of all civil aircraft and engines; licensing of all civil pilots, mechanics; administration of the Federal Aid to Airports Program, and operation of the two federally owned civil airports serving Washington, D.C.

Fédération Aéronautique Internationale (FAI): A multinational organization that governs all aviation sports, establishes all official aviation records and sanctions official international competitions. Operates through a nonprofit National Aero Club in each country.

Field packing: The temporary stowing of the canopy, etc., in the container after a jump, so that it may be more easily transported to the packing area.

FJC: First jump course. See *Chapter 2*

Flare: A temporary reduction in the vertical and horizontal speeds of a ramair canopy, performed during landing by pushing both steering toggles down. Also a device used to attach suspension lines to the bottom skin of a Ram Air canopy.

Flying the canopy: See *Chapter 6*

FPS: Feet per second.

Freefall: A skydive in which the parachute is activated manually by the jumper at his or her discretion. The portion of the jump between exit and canopy deployment. See *Chapter 5*

Frog position: A modified stable freefall position made by the parachutist without an arch, with the legs slightly bent and the arms in a U position.

FSDO: Flight Standards District Office

GADO: General Aviation District Office.

Go toggles: A non-locking front riser pulley system for mechanical advantage used during CRW.

Glide: The horizontal and vertical flight of a descending canopy.

GMM: General Membership Meeting of the USPA or CSPA, which are held once each year.

Global Positioning System: (GPS)

GW: Gold wings.

HAHO: High Altitude, High Opening. A type of military jump.

HALO: High Altitude, Low Opening. A type of freefall military jump.

Hand deploy pilot chute: The springless pilot chute used in hand deploy parachute systems. See *Throw-out Pilot Chute* and *Pull-out pilot chute.*

Harness: An arrangement of cotton, linen or nylon webbing, which is designed to conform to the shape of the load to be carried. It secures the load properly, so that the opening shock and the weight of the load are evenly distributed during the descent.

Hazards, parachuting: Ditches, telephone and power lines, poles, towers, houses, buildings, hangars, automobiles, highways, airplanes, trees over 10 feet in height, water and any other obstacles or object which would cause death or severe injury to the jumper.

Hesitation: When the pilot chute momentarily flutters in the low-pressure area behind the jumper, rather than catching air.

Holding: Facing the canopy into the wind to minimize ground speed.

Hop and pop: See *Jump and pull*

Hook knife: A knife with a razor sharp blade or blades designed to cut suspension lines.

Housing clamp stiffener: A metal plate sewn to the top flap of a back-type parachute container, and used to hold the ripcord cable housing in place and to give rigidity to the housing.

ICC: Instructor Certification Course, an Instructional Rating Course. Soon to be called the Advanced Instructor Course.

I/E: Instructor/Examiner.

Instructor: The holder of this rating possesses all of the privileges of a USPA Coach and is rated as capable of safely and competently instructing student and novice parachutists in all areas of the USPA's Integrated Student Program specific to the training discipline in which he or she is rated.

Instructor Assisted Deployment (IAD): When the instructor holds the pilot chute in the airstream while the student exits; the static line is eliminated.

Instructor Certification Course: A course registered with, and approved by, the USPA conducted to train, qualify and rate USPA instructors. Soon to be called the Advanced Instructor Course.

Instructor/Examiner: Possesses all privileges of a USPA instructor. An I/E is capable of instruction in all areas of parachuting, including accuracy, style, RW, night, water and high altitude jumps. The I/E is capable of briefing news media and the general public, as well as state and local government agencies, concerning parachuting.

Instructor seminar: A gathering of five or more USPA instructors and/or Instructor/Examiners to exchange, discuss, and introduce new ideas to develop, improve, or assure the quality of techniques of instruction of sport parachuting.

International parachuting license: An FAI training, competitive, or exhibition parachuting license, issued by the USPA to qualified applicants who meet the minimum requirements as set forth by the USPA, and verified by a USPA, S&TA, USPA instructor, or other designated official.

Judge: An official who evaluates competitive parachuting performance.

Jump and pull (*hop 'n pop*): Pulling the ripcord immediately upon clearing the aircraft (within three seconds).

Jump run: The level predetermined flight of the aircraft, at reduced airspeed, prior to exit.

Lift-to-drag ratio: L/D The lift generated by the canopy divided by the drag produced, expressed as a ratio.

Line dock: An advanced CRW technique where one canopy is above the head of the person receiving the dock.

Main parachute: The primary parachute of a dual (two canopy) assembly.

Maintenance: Inspection, overhaul, repair, preservation and replacement of parts, but excludes preventive maintenance.

Major alteration: An alteration not listed in the aircraft, engine, or propeller specifications: 1) that might appreciably affect weight, balance, structural strength, performance, powerplant operation, flight characteristics, or other qualities affecting airworthiness; or 2) that is not done according to accepted practices or cannot be done by elementary operations.

Major repair: A repair that: 1) if improperly done, might appreciably affect weight, balance, structure strength, performance, powerplant operation, flight characteristics or other qualities affecting airworthiness; or 2) is not according to accepted practices or cannot be done by elementary operations. The term *major repair* includes replacement of canopy panels, reinforcing tapes, lateral bands, suspension lines, horizontal back straps and diagonal backstraps.

Malfunction: The complete or partial failure of the parachute canopy to effect proper opening and descent. Some malfunctions are: canopy damage, twisted suspension lines, bag lock, streamer, an inversion or partial inversion of the canopy.

Military specification (Mil Spec): A procurement specification promulgated by the military agencies, and used for the procurement of military supplies and equipment. The parachute specs were taken over by the PIA in 1997.

Minor repair: A repair other than a major repair. Minor repairs includes such operations as: replacing canopies, containers, pack opening bands, cable housings, dual mounting plates, automatic ripcord releases, harness assemblies, repairs to containers; repair of stitching; replacement of harness hardware, where major stitching is not required; replacement of ripcord pockets; patching holes in canopies, etc.

Modification: 1) A change. 2) Often refers to the removal of the canopy area of a round canopy to achieve steerability and forward glide.

MSL: Mean Sea Level.

National Aeronautic Association: NAA. The Aero Club representing the FAI in the U.S. The USPA is a division of the NAA.

National Collegiate Parachuting Committee (NCPC): An affiliate of the United States Parachute Association. Supports and encourages parachuting as a collegiate sport; assists collegiate parachutists in gaining recognition and support of their school; conducts an annual National Collegiate Parachuting Championship.

National Director (ND): Those directors elected at large by the general membership.

Night jump: A parachute jump made from one hour after official sunset to one hour before official sunrise.

NOTAM: NOTice to AirMen. An air traffic advisory or notice, filed by an airspace user with an ATC facility.

Novice: A parachutist trainee who has progressed to the aerial phase of training, but who has not qualified for a USPA A License.

Open body of water: Any body of water in which a parachutist might drown upon landing.

Opening point: The ground point of reference over which the parachutist should open his parachute to enable him to fly to the center of the target area.

Opening shock: The deceleration force felt by the jumper when the canopy opens. It is affected by velocity, atmospheric conditions, body position, type of canopy, method of deployment, etc.

Oscillation: 1. The swinging of the suspended load under the canopy. 2. In CRW, the swaying or swinging of a CRW formation caused by poor docking, bad air, or too much movement of the people in the formation.

Outboard: Facing to the outside, such as a ripcord facing to the side of the jumper, rather than toward the breast bone.

Overloaded Canopy: When the canopy is too small for your weight, loaded beyond the manufacturer's recommendations.

Pack: Such as backpack or chestpack; and FAA term for the parachute assembly, less the harness. That is, it means the container, canopy, suspension lines, pilot chute, risers and connector links. The term *pack* and *container* are not synonymous. Also the process of folding a parachute and placing it in its container for use (pack job).

Pack tray: The portion of the container or deployment device in which the lines are stowed.

Parachute: A fabric device designed to slow the descent of a falling load. The word *parachute* is formed from the French words, *para*, shield or guard against, and *chute*, fall. Thus, *parachute* literally means *to defend from a fall*.

Parachute, free type: A parachute that is not attached to an aircraft but is operated by the jumper at his discretion.

Parachute, static-line operated: A parachute operated by a length of webbing after a jumper has fallen the length of the static line.

Parachute Industry Association (PIA): An association of manufacturers, dealers and suppliers of parachutes and skydiving accessories, based in the U.S.

Parachute landing fall (PLF): The method of falling down on landing by which the jumper resists, absorbs and distributes the landing forces over various muscular parts of the body, rather than on just the legs.

Parachutist: A person engaging in intentional parachuting, such as a sport parachutist, member of a military airborne unit, or smokejumper.

Partial inversion: A type of round canopy deployment malfunction. It occurs when one or more gore sections near the skirt become inverted during deployment and form a small pocket that inflates, causing a partial inversion of the canopy. The condition may or may not work out, or may become a complete inversion; i.e., the canopy turns completely inside out. It is the skirt, not the line, which is over; not to be confused with a *line-over*. Also called a *Mae West*.

PC: Para-Commander canopy.

Permeability: see *porosity*

Pilot chute: A small parachute used to accelerate deployment; constructed in much the same manner as a round canopy and from similar material. Some types of pilot chutes are equipped with a spring-operated, quick opening device. The frame is compressed so as to open immediately when released from the pack.

Pilot chute assist system: A temporary connection of breakcord, Velcro, etc., between the static line and the pilot chute of a sport parachute, which pulls the pilot chute out of the pack and into the airstream before it separates.

Plane: A vertical CRW formation, where the grip consists of the feet of one jumper in the risers of another.

Planing: A CRW transition from a stack to a plane.

Poised exit: A departure from an aircraft in which the jumper uses any external structure to brace himself and to assist in gaining a stable position immediately as he leaves the aircraft.

Porosity: Usually refers to what is technically known as *permeability*. The ratio of void or interstitial area to total area of a cloth. Expressed in percent. Term is used for ringslot, ribbon, ringsail, rotofoil and sport-modified round canopies.

Practice Pilot Chute Toss/Throw: The act of simulating or actually tossing a flag of material or crepe paper from the pilot chute pouch or touching the actual pilot chute, demonstrating the coordinated arm movement necessary to perform this task in a timely and stable manner.

Practice RipCord Pull (PRCP): A static line training jump, wherein the jumper pulls a ripcord handle from the pocket in order to demonstrate his ability to do so. Also called a *Dummy RipCord Pull*.

Premature opening: Opening of a parachute before the user is clear of the aircraft; any accidental opening of a parachute.

Progressive Freefall: The name for Accelerated FreeFall training in Canada.

Pud: The handle on a pullout pilot chute.

Pull-out pilot chute: A hand deployed system with a springless pilot chute. Pulling the handle extracts the container-locking pin and then pulls the pilot chute out into the airstream.

Regional Director (RD): A USPA director elected to represent jumpers in a specific geographical area.

Relative wind: The wind or air approaching a freefalling skydiver or flying parachute.

Relative work (RW): Aerial maneuvers by two or more freefalling parachutists in order to form a star, or other formation.

Reserve parachute: The second or *auxiliary* parachute worn by a person making an intentional jump to be used if the main parachute malfunctions.

Reserve static line: Line attached to a main parachute riser and to the reserve ripcord handle, cable or housing to effect automatic opening of the reserve following a breakaway. Stevens lanyard.

Rigger, Parachute: A person certificated by the FAA to pack, alter and/or maintain parachutes. Senior and Master.

Riser dock: A CRW maneuver, involving a momentum dock that delivers the risers into the hands of the receiver.

RSL: Reserve Static Line

Running: Directing the canopy downwind to maximize ground speed.

Safety & Training Advisor (S&TA): A local person appointed by the Regional Director as his or her representative, who is available to provide advice and administrative assistance as the USPA representative at an individual drop zone.

SCR: Star Crest Recipient.

SCS: Star Crest Soloist.

Single Operation System (SOS): Any system that combines a single point riser release and a reserve ripcord, so that pulling one handle will both release the risers and pull the reserve.

Skydiving: The freefall portion of a parachute jump.

S/L: Static line.

Slider: A piece of fabric attached to the suspension lines of a ram-air canopy, which controls inflation by progressively sliding down the suspension lines during deployment. A reefing device.

SOP: Standard Operating Procedure.

Span: The distance from wing tip to wing tip of a ram-air canopy.

Split saddle: The lower part of a harness which has independent leg straps, no saddle cross strap.

Sport parachutist: One who engages in parachuting as an avocation rather than as a vocation or duty. A skydiver.

Spot: The exit point.

Spotting: Selecting the course to fly, directing the pilot, and selecting the correct ground reference point over which to leave the aircraft, so that the jumper will have the best opportunity to land in the target area.

Stable fall position: A position attained by the freefalling parachutist in which he makes only controlled, preplanned movements. Usually face-to earth.

Stability: That property of a body which causes it, when its equilibrium is disturbed, to develop forces or movements tending to restore the original condition. In skydiving, having control of body position during freefall (not "Z" or unstable).

Stack: A vertical CRW formation with the jumpers gripping the canopy or lines at the canopy attachment.

Static line (S/L): A line attached to the aircraft and to the parachute, which initiates deployment of the parachute as the load falls away from the aircraft.

Static line jump: A parachute jump during which deployment of the parachute is initiated by means of a static line attached to the aircraft, used primarily in student training and by military rapid deployment forces.

STC: Supplemental Type Certificate. An STC is usually required to remove an aircraft door for jumping.

Stevens lanyard: Part of the Single Operation System **(SOS)** which activates the reserve when the main canopy is jettisoned. Named for the inventor, Perry Stevens.

Student: A parachutist trainee who has not qualified for a USPA Class A License.

Suspension lines: Cords, usually nylon, Kevlar or Dacron, which connect the large cloth surface canopy to the risers.

"T" Type parachute: U.S. Army description for troop or training parachutes.

Tandem jump: A parachute jump with two people under the same canopy.

Target (disc, pea gravel, *peas*): The prepared landing area. In competition, a five cm. disc.

Technical Standard Order: U.S. Government regulations applying to standards of materials and products. Parachutes are covered by TSO-C23c (b, c, or d).

Terminal velocity: The equilibrium speed at which a body falls through the air (14.7 psi) when resistance to the air (your size) equals the pull of gravity (your weight) to establish the approximate figure of 120 mph (in the flat stable position); reached after the 10th second of freefall.

3-Ring release: A riser release system consisting of three interlocking rings.

Throw-out pilot chute: A hand-deployed pilot chute system in which the skydiver grasps a springless pilot chute and vigorously throws it into the airstream.

Tracking: A position assumed by the freefalling parachutist in order to attain maximum horizontal movement.

Training: see *Chapter 1*

Training Pilot Chute Toss: A practice simulated pilot chute throw with the Instructor Assisted Deployment system used for student training.

Trim tabs: A locking front riser pulley system for adjusting a canopy's angle of attack or flight attitude.

TSO: Technical Standard Order. The FAA regulation that requires certain minimum performance standards and specifications for the certification of a parachute design.

USPA Judge: A parachuting official appointed by USPA for a specific term. Judges may act as contest directors at competitions and may monitor record attempts for USPA and FAI.

United States Parachute Association (USPA): A voluntary membership association of skydivers, which is a non-profit division of the NAA, governing sport parachuting activities in the United States.

Waivers: Permission granted by a competent authority to deviate from the BSRs. Authority to grant waivers is vested in the Board of Directors, the Executive Committee, and in a few cases, the Safety & Training Advisor and/or Instructor Examiner.

Water jump: A parachute jump that ends with an intentional landing in an open body of water.

Wind drift indicator (WDI): A device used to predict wind drift, so constructed as to descend at a rate comparable to a parachutist of average weight descending under a fully deployed main canopy of average specifications. Usually a weighted strip of crepe paper 10 inches wide and 20 feet long.

Windsock: A pole-mounted cloth tube of varying diameter, which shifts with the wind changes, indicating ground wind velocity and direction.

Wing loading: The payload weight divided by the planform area of a canopy. It represents the average force per area that is exerted on the canopy; e.g., a 200 sq. ft. canopy supporting an exit weight of 175 lbs., yields a wing loading of .875.

WHUFFO: A non-jumping spectator. Often heard to say: *Whuffo they jump out of airplanes?* A "ground hog."

WPC: World Parachuting Championship.

Index

Bill Ottley drops out of a biplane

A no-frills flight on a Twin Beech

The pilot survived this ejection

Some of the publications available from Para Publishing

QUICK ORDER FORM

Satisfaction guaranteed

- Fax orders: (805) 968-1379. Send this form.
- **Telephone orders:** Call 1(800) PARAPUB toll free, (727-2782). Have your credit card ready.
- **email orders:** orders@ParaPublishing.com.
- **Postal orders:** Para Publishing, Dan Poynter, PO Box 8206-985, Santa Barbara, CA 93118-8206. USA. Telephone: (805) 968-7277

Please send the following Books, Discs or Courses. I understand that I may return any of them for a full refund—for any reason, no questions asked.

- ❑ Parachuting, The Skydiver's Handbook @ $19.95
- ❑ Parachuting, The Skydiver's Handbook on CD @ $29.95
- ❑ Parachuting Manual for the Static Line and Tandem Course. @ $2.95
- ❑ Parachuting Manual for the AFF Course. @ $3.95
- ❑ Parachute Rigging Course @ $19.95
- ❑ Parachute Rigger Study Guide @ $19.95
- ❑ Parachute Rigger Study Guide on Disk (PC-Windows® version) @ $29.95
- ❑ Parachuting I/E Course @ $14.95
- ❑ The Parachute Manual Vol. I @ $49.95
- ❑ The Parachute Manual Vol. II @ $49.95

Please send more FREE information on:

❑ Other books,   ❑ Speaking/Seminars,   ❑ Mailing lists,   ❑ Consulting

Name: _____

Address: _____

City: _____ State: _____ Zip: _____ - _____

Tel: _____ Email: _____

Sales tax: Please add 7.75% for products shipped to California addresses.

Shipping by air:

US: $4 for the first book or disk and $2.00 for each additional product.

International: $9 for 1st book or disk; $5 for each additional product (estimate).

Payment: ❑ Cheque,   ❑ Credit card:

❑ Visa,   ❑ MasterCard,   ❑ Optima,   ❑ AMEX,   ❑ Discover

Card number: _____

Name on card: _____ Exp. date: _____/_____

QUICK ORDER FORM

Satisfaction guaranteed

Fax orders: (805) 968-1379. Send this form.

Telephone orders: Call 1(800) PARAPUB toll free, (727-2782).
Have your credit card ready.

email orders: orders@ParaPublishing.com.

Postal orders: Para Publishing, Dan Poynter, PO Box 8206-985,
Santa Barbara, CA 93118-8206. USA. Telephone: (805) 968-7277

Please send the following Books, Discs or Courses. I understand that I may
return any of them for a full refund—for any reason, no questions asked.

❑ Parachuting, The Skydiver's Handbook @ $19.95

❑ Parachuting, The Skydiver's Handbook on CD @ $29.95

❑ Parachuting Manual for the Static Line and Tandem Course. @ $2.95

❑ Parachuting Manual for the AFF Course. @ $3.95

❑ Parachute Rigging Course @ $19.95

❑ Parachute Rigger Study Guide @ $19.95

❑ Parachute Rigger Study Guide on Disk (PC-Windows® version) @ $29.95

❑ Parachuting I/E Course @ $14.95

❑ The Parachute Manual Vol. I @ $49.95

❑ The Parachute Manual Vol. II @ $49.95

Please send more FREE information on:

❑ Other books, ❑ Speaking/Seminars, ❑ Mailing lists, ❑ Consulting

Name: _____

Address: _____

City: _____ State: _____ Zip: _____-_____

Tel: _____ Email: _____

Sales tax: Please add 7.75% for products shipped to California addresses.

Shipping by air:

US: $4 for the first book or disk and $2.00 for each additional product.

International: $9 for 1st book or disk; $5 for each additional product
(estimate).

Payment: ❑ Cheque, ❑ Credit card:

❑ Visa, ❑ MasterCard, ❑ Optima, ❑ AMEX, ❑ Discover

Card number: _____

Name on card: _____ Exp. date: _____/_____

QUICK ORDER FORM

Satisfaction guaranteed

▯ Fax orders: (805) 968-1379. Send this form.

☎ **Telephone orders:** Call 1(800) PARAPUB toll free, (727-2782).
Have your credit card ready.

▭ **email orders:** orders@ParaPublishing.com.

✉ **Postal orders:** Para Publishing, Dan Poynter, PO Box 8206-985,
Santa Barbara, CA 93118-8206. USA. Telephone: (805) 968-7277

Please send the following Books, Discs or Courses. I understand that I may
return any of them for a full refund—for any reason, no questions asked.

❑ Parachuting, The Skydiver's Handbook @ $19.95
❑ Parachuting, The Skydiver's Handbook on CD @ $29.95
❑ Parachuting Manual for the Static Line and Tandem Course. @ $2.95
❑ Parachuting Manual for the AFF Course. @ $3.95
❑ Parachute Rigging Course @ $19.95
❑ Parachute Rigger Study Guide @ $19.95
❑ Parachute Rigger Study Guide on Disk (PC-Windows® version) @ $29.95
❑ Parachuting I/E Course @ $14.95
❑ The Parachute Manual Vol. I @ $49.95
❑ The Parachute Manual Vol. II @ $49.95

Please send more FREE information on:
❑ Other books, ❑ Speaking/Seminars, ❑ Mailing lists, ❑ Consulting

Name: _____

Address: _____

City: _____ State: _____ Zip: _____ - _____

Tel: _____ Email: _____
Sales tax: Please add 7.75% for products shipped to California addresses.
Shipping by air:
US: $4 for the first book or disk and $2.00 for each additional product.
International: $9 for 1st book or disk; $5 for each additional product
(estimate).
Payment: ❑ Cheque, ❑ Credit card:
❑ Visa, ❑ MasterCard, ❑ Optima, ❑ AMEX, ❑ Discover

Card number: _____

Name on card: _____ Exp. date: _____/_____